MW01679963

NCE Exam Prep 2022-2023

Study Guide + 600 Test Questions and Detailed Answer Explanations for the National Counselor Exam (Includes 3 Full-Length Practice Tests)

Table of Contents

Chapter 1: Introduction....6

Chapter 2: Conducting Counseling-Based Research....7

Chapter 3: Beginning the Therapeutic Process....11

Chapter 4: Ethical and Legal Issues in Counseling....15

Chapter 5: Taking Care of Specially-Abled Clients....20

Chapter 6: Conducting Interviews....23

Chapter 7: Determining the Level of Care Needed....30

Chapter 8: Choosing the Appropriate Kind of Care....37

Chapter 9: Geriatrics....43

Chapter 10: Parenting and Its Effect on a Child's Development....49

Chapter 11: Relationships of a Romantic Nature....55

Chapter 12: Mental Stress and Its Manifestations....62

Chapter 13: Adjustment Disorders....70

Chapter 14: Physical Illnesses....75

Chapter 15: Communicating with Patients About Their Course of Treatment....83

Chapter 16: Guiding the Treatment Plan....88

Chapter 17: Aligning Treatment According to Patient Profile....93

Chapter 18: Counseling Interventions....102

Chapter 19: Ensuring the Health, Safety and Comfort of Patients....106

Chapter 20: Managing Emotions....113

Chapter 21: Group Therapy....119

Chapter 22: Positive Attributes of Every Effective Counselor....128

Chapter 23: Channeling Empathy into a Counseling Session 133

Test 1 138

Test 1 Answers 203

Test 2 244

Test 2 Answers 307

Test 3 349

Test 3 Answers 413

Chapter 1: Introduction

The National Counselor Examination (NCE) assesses the candidate's understanding and awareness of theory-based and skill-centric questions required to practice as an entry-level counselor securely and professionally. The exam was created based on a nationwide performance appraisal of more than 16,000 credentialed counselors that identified empirically supported work behaviors that were ascertained to be most pertinent for qualified professional responsibilities.

The NCE represents each of the original eight CACREP (Council for Accreditation of Counseling and Related Educational Programs) subject areas, with a questionnaire design derived from the five job characteristics identified by the National Board for Certified Counselors' (NBCC) national workforce planning.

Formal Examination

The NCE exam consists of 200 multiple-choice questions (MCQs), 160 of which are scored and 40 of which are not. These 40 MCQs provide statistical data for items that will be used in future exams. Scored and unscored questions cannot be distinguished from each other by exam takers. The test is 3 hours and 45 minutes long. The highest score possible is 160.

Administration of Examination

The exam is given in pencil and paper format at more than 75 nationwide locations and 350 campuses across the United States. The NBCC is working alongside Pearson VUE to facilitate the digital deployment of the assessments, which are typically administered by Pearson VUE test centers or in colleges used as test centers.

The exam is given twice a year, in April and in October, usually on the third Saturday of each month.

Deferred Examinations

If you notify the NBCC more than 30 days before the exam date, you may postpone your exam date without fines. If you submit your application less than 30 days before the exam, or if you do not take your exam on the designated date, you will be charged a $150 reregistration fee next time you apply to take the exam. If a crisis (injury, family emergency, etc.) precludes you from taking the exam, depending on the specific situation, you may be qualified for a waiver of the license renewal fee.

Chapter 2: Conducting Counseling-Based Research

When people seek counseling, they usually fill out intake forms, answer questions in interviews, verbally express their issues and needs, display nonverbal cues and fill in assessment questionnaires. Some of the information is numerical, such as age and test scores. Other information can be counted, such as the number of times a student experiences test anxiety in a given day. This information allows the counselor to better understand an individual and the scope of his or her concerns.

Counselors and counselor educators may choose to specialize in counseling research as a career path. When they collect data using an empirical approach, they adhere to a set of rules.

Choose a Problem or a Topic

Researchers start with a problem to solve. They frequently pose the problem as a question.

Devise a Hypothesis

Researchers present their hypotheses after formulating broad questions. Most research includes many propositions, which are predictions based on prior studies or a theory.

Create a Research Design

Research designs are methods for structuring a study so that researchers can be confident that the data they gather will actually answer the questions they posed. A study's design specifies who will participate, where it will be conducted, how researchers collect data and any other procedures required to ensure reliable information is gathered.

Collect Information

Once all of the procedures are in place, the research team can begin collecting data. People can participate in online surveys or respond to questions at the conclusion of a counseling session or program. Some people may take standardized tests.

Analyze the Information

After the information has been gathered, it is usually organized into a database. The researchers then use software to calculate a wide range of facts and figures to describe the study's participants and address questions posed at the beginning.

Analyze the Results

The outcomes of statistical computations can be interpreted in a variety of ways. It can be hard to decipher sophisticated calculations. Researchers may become fixated on one finding and overlook other analyses that refute their initial conclusion.

Disseminate the Results

Dissemination is the final step in the research process. Researchers report their findings in a research paper or give a presentation at a conference. Because this allows someone else the opportunity to ask questions about the research methods and how the results were analyzed, public dissemination is critical to a rational counseling method. Science is self-correcting in this way.

What is Done with the Assessment Data

Counselors use the information they collect about their clients in a variety of ways. Some counselors are primarily interested in behavioral patterns. Others use it to develop appropriate counseling methods. For example, if a client complains about not being able to socialize, the counselor may examine the client's behavior in interpersonal relationships and employ behavioral strategies that support social-cognitive development and personal strategies that deal with social interactions.

During counseling, assessment is a continuous process. The assessment informs the counselor about the severity of the issues and how the client is dealing with them.

Counselors who do not evaluate their clients' issues are more likely to draw incorrect conclusions and use ineffective or irrelevant counseling techniques and methods. As a result, not only is more time spent on sporadic counseling, but clients may also leave with the same problems they brought to the first session.

Confidentiality, Privacy and Privileged Communication in Counseling

Privacy

The right of clients to choose who has access to data about them is referred to as privacy (Thompson & Rudolph, 1996). In most cases, parents of minors end up making all privacy-related decisions on their behalf, such as signing consent, releasing information and gaining access to medical and cognitive therapy records. In counseling, decisions about safeguarding children's anonymity and safety must be considered from both a legal and ethical standpoint.

Privilege

Client privilege is a legal right that protects the client's private therapy information from being revealed in judicial proceedings. Legislation in each state establishes privilege. Client privilege is not granted to all clients; it is determined by the type of psychiatric discipline covered by state law. In some states, adolescents under the age of 16 are granted privileges for specific problems (Reid, 1999). Although attorneys frequently subpoena councilors or their records in the course of legal discovery (e.g., in child custody cases), the legal right to advantaged interaction can only be forfeited by the client.

Counseling: Working with Children

One of the most perplexing ethical issues that counselors face when working with children is deciding what and how much detail they should share with the parents. Many people believe that minors should be afforded the same level of confidentiality as adults. In some cases, even if minors are legally able to access therapy for mental health care, they may not have the legal authority to authorize the release of information to third parties. In some states, providers can limit what information is provided if its disclosure would prove detrimental to a child.

Counselors are frequently required by law to act as agents of social control, which necessitates breaching confidentiality. Confidential information must be disclosed when there are threats of harm to oneself or someone else or when it is discovered that a child or an elder is being abused.

Any children or adolescents who appear to be depressed should be questioned to see if they have suicidal thoughts, a plan to harm themselves and/or the means to carry out that plan. Parents must be informed of a child's suicidal ideation or intent, and the counselor must work with them to act appropriately.

The right to privacy, consent forms, the use of touch, counselor proficiency, culturally diverse issues and divorce are all common concerns when it comes to counseling children.

When working with children, teenagers and their families, clinicians must consider a variety of legal and ethical issues. However, most ethics courses in graduate training courses do not place a strong emphasis on these issues.

There has been little support in the psychiatric literature on ethical issues that may arise when counseling minors outside the school setting. With the exception of breaking confidentiality to report child rape, ethics textbooks only describe issues related to handling minors (Lawrence and Kurpius, 2000). However, when it comes to treating children in families, there are innumerable legal and ethical issues to consider.

Conclusion

When a counselor is working with a group, he or she should make it clear to the team members that they must respect each other's confidentiality and adhere to the group's ground rules. First and foremost, counselors should choose group members who have similar needs and goals. They must also ensure that reasonable safeguards are in place to protect clients from physical or psychological harm caused by other group members.

Chapter 3: Beginning the Therapeutic Process

Psychotherapy is a treatment option for people suffering from a variety of psychiatric issues and emotional problems. It can help with problems such as coping with daily life, the effects of trauma, psychiatric problems, the loss of a loved one and particular mental disorders such as depression or anxiety. There are several types of psychotherapy treatments, and some of them may be more effective for specific issues. Psychotherapy can be used in conjunction with other treatments, such as medication.

Beginning Therapy Sessions as a Counselor

Both children and young people can benefit from therapy, which can be done in an individual, parent-assisted, couples or professional context. Sessions are usually held once a week for 30–50 minutes. In psychotherapy, both the patient and the counselor must be engaged deeply. Working together efficiently and benefiting from psychotherapy requires a person to build a relationship of trust with a therapist.

Psychotherapy can be brief (a few sessions) for urgent concerns or long term (months or years) for long-standing and complex problems. The patient and the therapist work together to set treatment goals and schedules for how often and how long they will meet.

Seligman's Influence on Humane Counseling Practices

According to Martin Seligman (1996), assessment should strive to recognize the client's significance and uniqueness. In a way, it's as if you're saying to the person, "You're unique, and I'd like to learn more about you and why you are the way you are."

The following are some of Seligman's reasons for assessing a client:

- It allows counselors to make a precise diagnosis.
- It assesses a person's appropriateness for a specific treatment plan.
- It ensures that counselors have the tools they need to create a treatment plan.
- It makes goal-setting and goal achievement more manageable.
- It allows for the assessment of the climate or context.

The Steps of the Counseling Process

1. Encourage the patient to express his or her feelings.

2. Affirm the feeling with reflective listening.

3. Allow the client to speak.

4. Fill in any gaps in the client's knowledge.

5. Discuss the client's perspectives and goals.

6. Communicate what it will take to get to the required point

7. Watch for signs of trouble and be prepared for possible threats and violence.

8. Encourage the client to focus good energy on finding a solution.

9. Plan follow-up meetings and provide feedback regularly.

10. Concur on the steps the client needs to take to adapt to a changing environment.

These steps can be broken down into five stages.

Stage One: Initial Disclosure and Relationship Building

The first step entails establishing a relationship with clients and involving them in discussions about issues that directly affect them. The first interview is crucial because the client reads the counselor's verbal and nonverbal communication and makes inferences about the counselor and the counseling scenario. A relationship can refer to the ties that bind two people in love, the bond between family members, good friends or coworkers or even the bond between an individual and his or her pet.

The counselor builds a relationship with a client based on trust, respect and a shared goal. A significant positive environment is created when there is a good rapport between both the client and the counselor.

Carl Rogers emphasizes the importance of the development of the counselor-client relationship. Empathy, genuineness and unconditional caring are three key conditions for establishing an effective counselor-client relationship. These qualities are communicated to the client through the counselor's verbal and nonverbal messages.

Stage Two: Problem Assessment and In-Depth Exploration

While the counselor and the client are forming a relationship, a second process, issue evaluation, is underway. This step entails gathering and categorizing data about the client's living situation and reasons for getting treatment. Anything a counselor does to gather data and draw conclusions about a client's concerns is referred to as assessment. The first step in the counseling process is to conduct an assessment. However, some forms of assessment occur throughout the therapeutic relationship with the goal of locating missing puzzle pieces.

Stage Three: Goal-Setting – Action Commitment

Goal-setting is critical to the success of counseling. It entails committing to a set of circumstances, a path or a result. Goals are the desired results or consequences for the client at the conclusion of counseling. Goals assist both the counselor and the client in determining what can and cannot be achieved through counseling. With the assistance of a counselor, clients determine various ways in which they may want to solve their problems and what course of treatment should be taken to remedy those problems.

Both the counselor and client have a deeper understanding of what needs to be done when the goals are clear.

Stage Four: Intervention In Counseling

Depending on the theoretical positions to which a counselor adheres, there are various points of view of what a counselor should do with his or her clients. The person-centered approach, for example, implies that the counselor focuses on the counselor-client relationship. The behavioral approach tries to get clients to participate in activities that will help them change their behavior.

When a counseling intervention is finished, clients should:

- Follow through on plans
- Be able to manage and deal with daily functions
- Acknowledge the existence of a support network and know how to use it
- Find it easier to identify strategies for long-term healing.

Stage Five: Evaluation, Termination or Referral

Terminating the counseling process requires tact and sensitivity, as the client will be aware that the session must come to an end. Even if the client and the staff move on to the next step, each stage continues. For example, after establishing a relationship, the counselor moves on to stage two, which entails analyzing the client's problem. Meanwhile, the counselor continues to build on the relationship that has already been established. In other words, stage one, or the formation of a relationship, does not end; rather, it continues until stage five, when the client is terminated or referred for further action.

Conclusion

The main goal of counseling is to strengthen the therapeutic relationship and get the client to participate in therapy. It must provide enough safety for clients to let down their defenses. In the early stages of therapy, further interconnected processes merge: ensuring safety, paying attention, detecting and thinking clearly, enabling change and being open to interpersonal interactions.

Chapter 4: Ethical and Legal Issues in Counseling

Professional counseling groups have established ethical standards for practitioners. The basic rule is that an individual must always be treated with respect and courtesy, which can only be accomplished by therapists who act with honesty, truthfulness and impartiality when conducting their sessions.

When a therapist initially interacts with a client in a manner that creates one set of standards and then acts in a way that contradicts those expectations, unethical behavior is likely to occur. Such behavior can be seen when, for example, in the first session, the counselor verbally or nonverbally directs the session in a manner that indicates mutual understanding, consideration and confidentiality. Then, in the second session, the counselor acts in a way that contradicts these expectations.

Unethical Conduct

Unethical behavior can take a variety of forms, including:

- A breach of confidentiality
- Trying to impose one's values on a client
- Instilling in a client a sense of dependency
- Unscrupulous financial arrangements, such as charging exorbitant fees
- Inaccurate advertising of one's abilities or credentials
- Practicing beyond the scope of one's education and experience
- Potential conflicts of interest, i.e., having a business or sexual relationship with the patient.

Informed Consent is a Client's Right

Informed consent begins with a client interview and continues throughout the relationship. It involves clients' privilege to be notified about the nature of their client-counselor relationship and to make their own decisions. From the beginning of the relationship, clients should be informed about confidentiality.

Counselors must act in the best interests of those who cannot consent voluntarily, including clients who are minors or disabled.

Client Records

Counselors should:

a) Provide clients with access to records upon request

b) Ensure transparency of transfer

c) Obtain authorization to record

d) Maintain confidentiality in research

e) Guarantee in consultations.

Confidentiality Is Governed by Key Principles

The information revealed in counseling is referred to as an "entrusted secret" by Schneider (1963). He outlined seven general guidelines for maintaining confidentiality and communicating with others. These guidelines are:

1. Confidentiality is a relative rather than an unmitigated obligation because conditions can change it.

2. The content of the evidence determines confidentiality, i.e., harmless material does not connect the counselor to nondisclosure, but material required for a counselor/agency to operate efficiently is frequently released from confidentiality bonds.

3. The counselee has an intrinsic right to honesty and prestige. Confidentiality is always constrained by the counselee's innate right to credibility and reputation, to total secrecy and to resist aggression.

4. Even if it is against the law, the counselor can safeguard such rights.

5. Confidentiality is also restricted by a counselor's rights to protect his or her own public image and honesty, resist damage or aggressive behavior and maintain privileged interaction.

6. Confidentiality is restricted by the rights of a third person or community.

<u>Confidentiality Limitations</u>

a. Presumed child sexual abuse must be reported.

b. Threats to injure others must be reported immediately.

Obligations to Protect and Warn

It is the counselor's responsibility to notify related people/family members in the event of unusual circumstances, such as:

1. Child abuse and incest
2. A child client's runaway plan
3. Confidentiality violations
4. Severe risk to others, such as in the case of an HIV-positive client. The ACA Code of Ethics added this as a new benchmark in 1995. Tarasoff v. Board of Regents of the University of California (1969), wherein California courts ruled that the university and its workers were negligent when they failed to notify an alleged target of a threat, resulting in the victim's murder, is a well-known example.
5. Self-inflicted harm:
    a. Most suicides can be avoided if we learn to recognize, assess and effectively intervene in crises (Fujimura et al., 1985).
    b. Wubbolding (1996) proposes a few questions to help identify danger; for example, suicidal people usually appear hopeless. This understanding can be used to spot such cases.

Client Rights: Honoring the Autonomy and Diversity of the Client

If a client's right to privacy is violated, the following issues may arise:

1. The client may become dependent.
2. Counselors may have difficulty terminating cases.
3. Difficult clients may have to do for themselves what they are unable to do.
4. The helping process may become a mystery.
5. Prejudice may arise.

Multiple Clients: Couples and Family Counseling

When counselors are seeing numerous relatives in a family, they should make it clear how they feel about each person. They should also know how to handle a family member's disclosure. For example, if a husband has AIDS, then the wife must be aware of the situation. If she isn't, then she must be made aware through the actions of the counselor.

Similarly, if an adolescent son is abusing drugs and confides in his counselor, the counselor must inform the parents of the adolescent's drug use due to the potential for severe implications. Some counselors believe that keeping secrets within a family is counterproductive, while others believe that it is necessary to keep data confidential. However, the final decision is based on the seriousness of the situation and the potential consequences of maintaining confidentiality.

Collaborative Work

When a counselor is working with a group, he or she should make it clear to the group members that they must respect each other's secrecy and adhere to the group's ground rules. First and foremost, counselors should choose group members who have similar needs and goals. They must also ensure that reasonable safeguards are in place to protect clients from physical or psychological harm caused by other group members.

Knowledge of Standards

Counselors who work in the field should be familiar with ethical standards. They must operate within their areas of expertise, including education, expertise, skills, specialty areas, etc. Additionally, they should stay consistently current in the field and request peer monitoring to assess their effectiveness.

Testifying in a Court of Law

A therapist may be called upon to provide expert evidence in a court case in some circumstances. Therapists must provide an accurate and detailed testimony about what they have discovered in these situations, reporting only the facts. It's critical to stay focused on specific clinical data and assessments. A counselor should never have a financial stake in the outcome of this kind of testimony.

Billing Procedures

Therapists must ensure that they bill only for the services offered and precisely account for the time spent on a visit, whether invoicing a client or a health insurer.

Conclusion

Mental health counselors are not exempt from having personal problems. There is a moral consideration for mental health counselors to seek consultation if they are undergoing emotional problems due to a recent breakup, a chemical use relapse or major anxiety. If personal problems affect counselors' steadiness, impartiality, conviction or focus, they may need to take a break from therapy.

Similarly, psychiatric therapists may face ethical dilemmas about whether their personal experience or relationship to a particular client is a conflict and requires a referral to another counselor. When working in a small town with few therapists, such quandaries may be prevalent.

Chapter 5: Taking Care of Specially-Abled Clients

All people with intellectual or other disabilities are protected under the Americans with Disabilities Act. This law prohibits employers from discriminating against specially-abled people and requires public buildings to be accessible to all people. Employers are required to make accommodations for such individuals.

Private buildings, rehab centers and workshops that help specially-abled people find jobs and homes and connect with other community members are all services that can prove beneficial for people with developmental disabilities.

Understanding the Political and Historical Perceptions of Disabilities and Their Influence on Counseling Practices

Counselors who work with people with disabilities and/or their families should be aware of how historical and political perceptions of disabilities influence social and cultural beliefs (Rubin and Roessler, 2008). They also have a professional responsibility to be aware of their own word choices and terminology when referring to people with disabilities. More explicitly, they must consider whether they regard the special person as someone with the same rights, demands and desires as everyone else, or as barely capable, less than, pitiful, severely disabled or physically/mentally challenged.

Counselors can improve their insight and awareness of issues that affect children and families by learning about the various economic and community barriers they frequently face. Counselors should work with their clients to:

1. Identify the most significant barriers
2. Investigate how the identified hurdles inhibit clients' ability to function or prevent them from trying to cope more favorably
3. Ascertain which hurdles are within clients' control to modify
4. Help clients develop coping strategies to overcome those hurdles.

This process is not always simple or linear, and it may take some time and effort.

Consent From Specially-Abled Clients

Certain principles govern the ability to accept or refuse treatment. Patients should be able to comprehend and modify information they receive, must understand the situation and its possible ramifications and express a choice. The diagnosis, the suggested treatment with its risks and benefits, potential therapies and the conclusion without treatment are all part of fact-based awareness. Low IQ, developmental dysfunctions, dementia, attention deficit disorders or cognitive impairment can all impair factual comprehension. When denial, delusions, suicidality or confusion are present in the client's manner, the therapeutic approach must change.

Adjusting to People with Disabilities

Individuals with disabilities, as well as the counseling relationship, must adjust to their disabilities. Counselors must explore the meaning of adaptation, factors that may influence its growth and incidence, and conceptual perspectives of disability modification to put the experience of coping with disability into context. Learning such information and effectively integrating it takes time and effort on the part of the counselor, especially since most counseling and psychology initiatives do not provide proper training in such matters.

When clients lack the capacity to give informed consent, advocates should protect their clients' interests by obtaining permission from a legally recognized third party (e.g., a guardian, caregiver or individuals involved) and inform the clients of the choices they have by using methods that suit their level of understanding. Advocates should ensure that the third party acts in accordance with the needs of the clients and preferences in such cases. Advocates should also take appropriate steps to improve the ability of such clients to give informed consent.

System of Discussion with Senior Counselors

Through discussion with senior advocacy employees, a counselor should strive to deal with complicated behaviors in a consistent manner while safeguarding clients from abuse. If advocates determine there is a case of abuse or neglect, they should explain it with the help of a supervisor and/or advocacy coordinator. Advocacy coordinators consider and implement policy, key concepts and pertinent regulatory matters to the specific case at hand while meticulously documenting the process.

The techniques and methods that counselors can use in the therapeutic relationship go beyond the many individual and social issues, as well as the coping and adjustment to the disability process.

The techniques described in this section are not necessarily associated with different counseling strategies or theories; however, many of them are aimed at altering people's thoughts, feelings and behavior patterns in relation to themselves, others or God. Some strategies have been thoroughly examined and are known to reduce fears (e.g., forgiveness, self-compassion) or are widely discussed as critical skills for living well with an impairment.

Conclusion

People who have long-term disabilities find communities of like-minded people and come to accept their disabilities as a part of their identity, but adults who are unexpectedly disabled may hold ableist viewpoints that make the situation tougher. They might not know anyone who is disabled and may believe that because they have a disability, their choices and options are limited.

Suddenly losing physical or emotional abilities can feel like death. It has the potential to be traumatic, resulting in relationship stress, suicidal thoughts, panic attacks and fear. This is why such events have to be managed by counselors with utmost empathy and regard.

Chapter 6: Conducting Interviews

The Biopsychosocial Evaluation

The biopsychosocial (BPS) structure is a cognitive evolution and functioning method that highlights the importance of an individual's institutional view and the assimilation of genetic, physiological and cultural forces into a person's perspective. The BPS interview, which mental health professionals and counselors usually do at the start of therapy, looks for biological, cognitive and socioeconomic aspects that may be contributing to a client's problem(s). It's referred to as a comprehensive approach because it considers a client at all stages.

The BPS interview is used because problems rarely exist in isolation. Each problem can compound or have a different effect on another. To discern the reason behind a problem, a counselor must also consider the surroundings. Just looking at a person is not enough.

Biological

Questions about medical or genetic concerns, age, cognitive skills or physical characteristics are part of the BPS biological ("bio") component. The following are examples of questions that target the bio aspect of the BPS assessment:

1. Do you consume alcoholic beverages or illegal substances? How often?
2. Do you or anyone in your family have a background in alcohol and drug abuse?
3. Is there a history of suicidal or homicidal thoughts and actions (creation of ideas and concepts) in your family?
4. Do you have any medical issues that are interfering with your life?
5. Do you take any prescription drugs? If that's the case, what are they?

Psychological

The BPS psychological ("psycho") component includes questions about a person's health, thoughts, habits, feelings, emotions and trauma or abuse history, such as:

1. What adjectives would you use to describe yourself? (Assessing self-esteem.)
2. What do you think your strengths are? What are your flaws?
3. Have you ever visited a therapist or received counseling?

4. Have you ever entertained suicidal or homicidal ideas, plans or intentions?

Social

The BPS assessment's social component examines the client's social and cultural influences. This includes questions about the client's previous and current familial relationships, friendships and psychological benefits, job strain, marriage, community engagement, church, religious beliefs, faith and finances.

1. What kinds of community organizations are you a part of?
2. What kind of help can you expect from your family?
3. Are your friends qualified and available to provide social support as part of your treatment?
4. How much of your stress is caused by your job and working environment?

What to Keep in Mind When Writing a Biopsychosocial Assessment

Subjective Impressions vs. Objective Facts

Objective Facts

These include:

1. What the client, other people attached to the client (e.g., family members) and/or coworkers involved with the case say. This can include how the client perceives his or her own situation.
2. Collaborating with colleagues to share relevant data about a client for case organizing and consultation purposes.
3. Establishing a written account of "where the client is at" during service delivery at a specific point in time; the psychosocial evaluation account provides benchmark information about a client when he or she enters the agency for service.
4. Reflecting on, fine-tuning the thought process and raising concerns about the client and his or her situation. This also allows the counselor-case supervisor to assess data and perceptions about the client.

Subjective Impressions

These include:

1. The counselor-case manager's insight and perspective, beliefs, intuitions, guesses, observations and assumptions about the client and his or her circumstances (e.g., presenting problem) are based on empirical information presented by (or about) the client.

2. Statements made by the counselor-case manager about the underpinning or latent interpretations or intentions of the client's statements, actions, behavioral patterns, perceptions, interactions and feelings.

Diagnostic Interview

The clinical interview is a basic assessment and involvement methodology that all behavioral and mental health experts should learn and use throughout their careers. Nondirective hearing, inquiring, disagreement, interpretation, urgency and psychoeducation are among the interviewing skills used by psychotherapists of all backgrounds (psychological theories), professional disciplines and treatment settings.

The clinical interview serves as an assessment (e.g., neurocognitive or investigative examination) or as a signal for the start of therapy or counseling as a process. The clinical interview process entails formal or informal evaluation in either case.

The Universal Model for Clinical Interviewing

A popular method is followed by all clinical interviewers. Shea (1998) proposed a five-stage model:

1. Introduction
2. Opening
3. Body
4. Closing
5. Termination.

Each stage has its own set of relational and technical responsibilities.

Introduction

The first contact is the start of the introduction stage. An introduction can take place over the phone, online or when potential clients read about a therapist (e.g., online descriptions, informed consent, etc.). Customers' expectations, role insertion, first observations and the initial building of rapport are all important activities.

Mental health professionals who interact with clients in a courteous and culturally responsive manner are more likely to foster trust and collaboration, culminating in more credible and accurate assessment data (Ganzini et al., 2013). Accurate opening remarks that welcome collaboration are part of technical methodologies.

Opening

The beginning establishes a focal point. At the start of a clinical assessment, most mental health practitioners will ask, "What issues bring you to therapy today?" This question encourages clients to describe their current problem (also known as the "presenting complaint" by psychiatrists). Clinicians should be aware that asking more social questions (e.g., "How are you today?" or "How was your week?") can inadvertently prompt clients to engage in a less concentrated and more ranting-style opening stage. Similarly, asking direct questions before building rapport and trust can lead to dismissiveness and deception (Shea, 1998).

Many modern therapists prefer positive-sounding opening statements or questions. Instead of asking about clients' troubles, therapists might ask, "What are your goals for today's meeting?" Cultural modifications may be required to ensure client comfort and ensure that opening queries are socially useful and applicable.

The initial statement may be preplanned or aimed toward acquiring an overview of prospective psychotic illnesses (e.g., "Does anyone in your family have a history of mental health problems?") when concentrating on a clinical diagnosis and using an organized or semi-structured interview guide.

Body

What occurs during the body phase is determined by the interview's purpose. If the goal is to gather data for a clinical diagnosis, the body will include diagnostic-focused questions. If the goal is to start psychotherapy, on the other hand, the focus may quickly shift to the problem's history and what individual characteristics, individuals and perceptions (including previous therapy) clients have found useful. The interview aims to assess clients, and the body stage aims to gather details about them. Clinicians ask clients about their serious illnesses, such as their intensity, length, severity and quality.

Various question procedures are followed during structured interviews. These protocols are intended to assist clinicians in remaining focused while collecting credible and accurate assessment information.

Closing

It is the clinician's obligation to organize and close the session in such a way that the principal interview objectives are met. These objectives and tasks can be:

1. Providing support and encouragement to clients
2. Reverting to role initiation and client perceptions
3. Summarizing key aspects of the topic
4. Providing an early case synthesis or mental illness diagnosis
5. Providing hope
6. Concentrating on homework, future meetings and scheduling.

Termination

Termination refers to the end of a session and the parting of ways. The termination stage necessitates the ability to work under pressure and show deliberate responsiveness and receptiveness to how clients may react to endings in general, especially having to leave the therapy office.

Termination can be a difficult situation to deal with. Clinicians frequently do not have enough information to make a prognosis at the end of an initial meeting. When there is diagnostic instability, clinicians may need to schedule a second or third session to gather more evidence about a client's symptoms. Collateral informants may be essential in triangulating diagnostic information.

What Exactly Is Culture?

Culture refers to learned and passed-down systems of awareness, concepts, rules and processes from one generation to the next. Language, religion and spirituality are all part of a culture, as are social structures, stages of life, ceremonial rituals, norms and ethical and practical systems. Cultures are open, evolving, highly dynamic concepts. Most people today are exposed to numerous cultures, which they use to shape their own identities and to interpret situations.

The CFI's Components

The Cultural Formation Interview (CFI) is made up of three parts. The first component is a 16-question core interview with prompts to help clinicians understand the cultural context of each question. Each component focuses on the following:

- Cultural preconceptions of the problem's source, interpretation and support (including national culture)
- Cultural factors influencing self-coping and previous help-seeking methodologies

- Cultural factors influencing current assistance-seeking behaviors.

A second participant component of the CFI evokes the perspectives of people nearest to the patient, such as family members, acquaintances and care providers, to help obtain collateral details. This is especially useful when the patient's ability to make observations/statements has deteriorated, and it can also provide supplementary information when patients prefer to enlist the help of loved ones to explain their objectives and improve their care.

The third component consists of 12 supplementary modules that broaden the dimensions of the core and informant CFIs and can result in a more complex project assessment.

As these examples show, the CFI's ultimate goal is to assist clinicians in better understanding human suffering. Our world is becoming more complicated with each passing day. We're finding it more difficult to communicate with one another across multiple languages, heritages, practices and customs. These concerns are magnified in health care and illness—the times when we are most vulnerable and in desperate need of being heard and understood. The CFI is a potent and evidence-based tool for ensuring that diagnostic encounters stay human as we strive for individualized and patient-centered health care.

Conducting an Initial Interview

The initial interview puts the counselor's skills, understanding and abilities to the test. The advanced modeling of the initial interview will significantly impact the subsequent breakthroughs and outcomes of a counseling process. Informed consent gives clients enough information about counseling and its risks to allow them to make an informed, consensual and rational decision about whether or not to participate.

Errors committed during the first session are usually much more damaging than those committed after an excellent working relationship is formed.

The framework of the interview can vary, but it usually follows three stages.

1. First and foremost, counselors should build trust and foster a cooperative environment.
2. Second, counselors must regularly examine clients' crises or problems.
3. Finally, counselors should delve deeper into clients' emotions.

When counselors feel they have developed a supportive or professional relationship with clients at the end of the initial interview, they have accomplished a major therapy objective.

Effective counseling skills start with a thorough self-evaluation, which includes looking at the counselor's own feelings and communication abilities. Based on this assessment, counselors must be pragmatic about their own counseling abilities and refrain from trying to solve every problem that arises.

Directive vs. Nondirective Approach

Counselors must decide to use a prescriptive or participative strategy based on an analysis of their own skill-sets as well as the needs of clients. The directive approach is best when the counselor needs to control the interview situation, while the nondirective framework is best when the interviewee prefers to manage the situation.

The counselor should take a client-centered approach and respond in one of two ways: strongly directive or extremely nondirective. The interviewee is encouraged to continue analyzing and communicating ideas with highly nondirective answers. The interviewee receives directives and ultimatums from highly directive responses. These types of responses are at opposite ends of a spectrum and can be considered extremes.

Therapists should carefully consider interviews after they have been successfully closed so that they can improve their skills.

Conclusion

The purpose of these interviews is to gain an empathic understanding of how the patient feels. This comprehension is essential for establishing rapport. When the therapist listens carefully and expresses appreciation for the patient's problems and fears, the patient feels understood. This sense of understanding serves as the foundation for all subsequent treatment, allowing the clinician to start a relationship in which a partnership for treatment can be formed.

Chapter 7: Determining the Level of Care Needed

Mental Status Examination (MSE)

An MSE is an important tool for doctors when making mental health prognoses. Physicians can better evaluate and differentiate psychiatric disorders if they are acquainted with the elements of the examination. The MSE includes the patient's previous medical history and data collected by the physician throughout the clinical visit.

Incorporating key components of the neurological examination into a regularly scheduled initial consultation and assessing when a more thorough analysis or referral is required are significant issues. An MSE may be advantageous when a physician suspects that something isn't quite right with a patient.

What an MSE Assesses

Relevant concerns and techniques to evaluate the patient's appearance and overall demeanor, motor function, speech, emotions and affect, thought process, thought product, sensory disruptions, sensorium and brain function, insight and judgment are used to identify symptoms of various psychological disorders in such circumstances. The MSE can aid in the differentiation of mood disorders, thought disorders and cognitive impairment, and it can guide diagnosis and treatment and consultation to a mental health professional or other psychologists.

The MSE can help doctors distinguish between various systemic diseases, neurocognitive and psychiatric disorders like delirium and dementia, borderline personality disorders and schizophrenia. The examination may consist of a few quick observations made during a routine patient visit, or it could be a more detailed analysis by the doctor.

How an MSE Must Be Conducted

An effective therapist must establish a style in which much of the MSE is conducted through informal observations during routine history and physical examinations. The way a patient describes the current illness's history will reveal a lot about the patient's general appearance and personality, vigilance, speech, interaction, affect and attitude. Imposing some structure on these findings and elevating them from subconscious sensations to clinically relevant explanations of behavior is thus a key tool in mental status testing.

Treatment Modalities

When someone seeks treatment, whether temporarily or permanently, an intake is conducted to determine clinical needs.

The first meeting between the therapist and the client is called an intake. During the intake, the therapist collects precise details to address the client's urgent needs, such as the client's complaint, support network and financial status. The therapist also discusses confidentiality, fees and what to expect during the treatment with the client. Confidentiality refers to the therapist's ability to keep confidentiality unless required or permitted by law.

The therapist and the client will collaborate during the intake to discuss therapeutic goals. Then, typically with clearly defined goals in mind, a treatment plan will be devised. The client and therapist will also talk about how the treatment's success will be evaluated and how long the treatment will take. Individual therapy, family therapy, couples therapy and group therapy are the most common forms of therapy.

Personal Therapy

Individual therapy, also known as psychological counseling or individual counseling, is a one-on-one meeting between the client and the physician (usually lasting 45 minutes to 1 hour). These meetings are usually held once a week or every other week and are private. Clients will collaborate with the practitioner to explore their emotions, work through challenging situations, define personal, familial and work-life elements that they want to change and create objectives to help themselves make these changes.

Group Therapy

In group therapy, a physician meets with a group of clients who have similar issues. When it comes to placing children in group therapy, it's especially important to align clients by age and problem. One advantage of this kind of counseling is that it can help a client feel less ashamed and isolated about an issue while also providing needed assistance from the counselor and other people in the session. A group with a prescribed curriculum to nurture particular skills would tremendously benefit a child with poor communication skills. Being in a group with other women suffering from postpartum depression can make a woman feel better about herself.

There are some drawbacks to group therapy as well. People in the group may be hesitant to share their stories in front of others because it can be stressful and challenging to share secrets and difficulties with unfamiliar people. There could be irreconcilable differences and disagreements among the group members, which could inhibit the development of rapport. There might also be misgivings about confidentiality. People might feel exposed or vulnerable when sharing intimate details of their life.

Couples Therapy

Couples therapy is for two emotionally bonded people who are having problems that they want to solve. The couple can be dating, partnered, committed or married. Cognitive-behavioral therapy is the most common therapeutic approach used in couples therapy. Couples meet with a marriage counselor to talk about their disagreements and/or facets of their marriage they are trying to work through. The therapist helps them recognize how their respective backgrounds, ideologies and behaviors affect their relationship.

Sometimes a couple will recognize that their issues are irreconcilable, even after collaborating with a psychiatrist, and will decide to divorce. Some couples go to therapy to work out their issues, while others seek therapy to determine if breaking up is the best option. It can be hard to counsel couples who are in a high-conflict, dysfunctional relationship.

Family Therapy

This kind of counseling is a type of group therapy in which one or more families participate. The systems approach is one of the most common theoretical inclinations in this kind of counseling, despite the fact that there are many other suitable methods in existence. The family is regarded as a well-organized system, with each member of the family contributing to the system's creation and maintenance of processes that shape behavior. Each family member has an impact on and is impacted by the others.

Family members' poorly functioning social interactions can frequently lead to conflict. A family with this structure may prefer to attend therapy as a group rather than independently. In many cases, one member of the family has issues that have a negative impact on everyone else. The traditional family or the nuclear family and anybody else living in the family participate in family therapy. Family therapists work with the entire family unit.

Kinds of Family Therapy

Family therapy can be done in many ways. In structural family therapy, the counselor observes and explains the family's limitations and structure, such as who tends to make the rules, how judgments are based and the family's limits. In some families, the parents refuse to collaborate to establish rules, or one parent may embarrass the other, causing the children to misbehave. The therapist helps them resolve these issues and improve their communication skills.

Assessing Trauma

The most evident emphasis of assessment in any trauma-related situation is whether the client is in impending danger of losing life or bodily autonomy or if he or she is at risk of injuring others. This includes determining whether the client is clinically fit in the event of an immediate disaster, calamity or physical attack. In cases of continuing physical abuse, it is also critical to determine whether the client is at risk of being victimized by others in the immediate future.

In general, the assessment structure is as follows:

1. Is there a risk of death (for example, bleeding, severe bruising, toxic or contagious agents) or an immediate risk of loss of limb or other significant physical functioning?

2. Is the client immobilized (for example, by intoxication, brain injury, delirium or drastic psychotic symptoms) to the point where he or she seems unable to safeguard his or her own security (for example, roaming the streets or being unable to access available food and housing)?

3. Is the client suicidally depressed?

4. Is the client a threat to others (for example, deranged or making serious threats to harm someone), particularly when threatening objects or means (such as a gun) are available?

Assessing Trauma Exposure

Once the clinician has evaluated that the client is secure and fairly stable, the particulars of traumatic stress and response can be investigated.

In many instances, the clinician begins by inquiring about the distressing event or events, such as the nature and scope of the trauma (for example, severity, duration, frequency, level of life threat). Because it is logical to begin with events and then move on to consequences, trauma exposure is introduced here before trauma consequences.

However, in some instances, the client's emergent emotional state is clearly a greater initial issue. Except in some forensic situations, the assessment of an acute rape victim will frequently focus on psychological well-being and psychiatric disorders rather than the particulars of the rape itself. In other cases, particularly when the trauma is more distant in time and the client is not in acute distress at the moment, it is sensible to begin with a trauma history.

General Guidelines

In light of these concerns, the following general protocols for assessing trauma exposure are provided:

- Before assessing trauma, develop an honest initial rapport with the client.
- At the start of the interview process, spend some time exploring the client's observable rationale with respect to medical care, whatever it may be.
- Pose questions empathically and nonjudgmentally.
- Practice talking about specifics of sexual assault and violent experiences with clients; survivors of psychological distress may be particularly susceptible to intricacies in the clinician's facial expressions and body language, so care should always be taken while conversing with these individuals.
- Keep in mind that trauma is incredibly personal, and the client may be afraid of being ostracized. During a trauma-focused interview, clients may reveal information that they have never told anyone before. The clinician should keep this prospect in mind and should respond to such revelations with visible support.
- Be aware that disclosing a traumatic history may elicit strong feelings of shame, humiliation and rage. Clients may react in a number of ways, including crying, becoming agitated or apprehensive and withdrawing. Others may become grumpy, if not hostile, toward the interviewer.
- Gentle assistance and affirmation of the client's feelings and responses may be extremely crucial in trauma exposure situations.
- Repeat evaluations as needed—some clients may not divulge certain trauma-related information during the initial assessment but may do it later when they are more at ease with the therapist and the treatment plan.

Assessing Substance Use Problems

The main objective of substance abuse screening is to identify people who have a greater likelihood of developing alcohol- or drug-related issues and, within that group, to define patients who require additional evaluation to diagnose their material use illnesses and develop treatment plans.

Specificity and Sensitivity

The ability of a screening device to identify accurate cases of the target condition in a population group is referred to as sensitivity. The more sensitive the test, the closer there is a 100% chance that a screen will recognize those with drug and alcohol problems.

The ability of a mechanism to target people who do not have a disorder is referred to as specificity. False positives (identifying people who do not have a disorder as having it) tend to rise as sensitivity rises, while false negatives (missed cases) rise as specificity rises. Because screening tools are imperfect, aligning sensitivity and specificity is a case-by-case issue.

Cost

The cost of administering a screen is determined by whoever performs the screening (e.g., a physician, nurse, registered nurse or medical doctor), how long it takes, what proper training (if any) is required, whether the screen can be administered to the patient using pencil and paper or a laptop and how long it takes to evaluate the screen.

Administration Ease

The layout of the written series of questions is self-explanatory, whereas the interview format involves a practitioner asking the patient a series of formulated responses. Computerized versions of authenticated paper questionnaires, such as the CAGE, are gaining popularity, and preliminary research on their effectiveness is showing promise.

Acceptance of Patients

Simply bringing up the topic of substance abuse with patients can be beneficial. According to research, asking questions about alcohol or other drugs "primes" patients to reveal information.

Instruments for Screening

To facilitate screening and increase the probability of accurate information, physicians should ask questions concurrently, beginning with legal drug alcohol use. However, there are a couple of exceptions to this rule. Adolescents should be asked about drug use, particularly cannabis use, even if they do not admit to drinking. Expectant mothers, women over the age of 60 and females who have gone through a major life transformation (e.g., the death of a spouse or retirement) should be asked about their psychoactive prescription medication use and use of over-the-counter sleeping pills.

Alcohol Screening Devices

Alcohol screening instruments ask patients how much and how frequently they drink, as well as the repercussions of their drinking. The replies to quantity/frequency questions imply whether a patient was, is or will be at risk of becoming a chronic alcoholic, binge addict and/or alcoholic, the distinctions of which are significant in deciding the clinician's response. Despite negative consequences, the sustained use of a substance is a defining feature of alcoholism (and drug addiction). Questionnaires focusing on repercussions are generally quite effective at detecting reliant users; however, without quantity/frequency queries, these instruments have a tendency to miss initial stage problem drinking.

Instruments for Drug Screening

Although testing for drug use in the clinical setting can cause patients and clinicians to behave unpleasantly, asking about illegal drug use is just as important as asking about other personal experiences that can impact a person's condition (such as sexual behavior that put patients at increased risk of getting sexually transmitted infections).

Screening can also reveal whether a participant in the patient's family has an issue with alcohol or other drugs, so clinicians should be aware of this possibility too.

Many primary health-care clinicians have ongoing, long-term contact with patients and their families. This provides them with a unique responsibility to encourage the patient's non-substance-using family and friends who are upset by their spouse, partner, child, parent or sibling's substance abuse issue.

Conclusion

Counselors must be able to determine the same fully accessible, cooperative, therapeutic relationship with individuals suffering from substance abuse issues that they do with other patient populations. This ability is a requirement for achieving a successful outcome in any counseling setting.

Counselors must guide the counseling relationship and build rapport between themselves and clients to allow clients to discuss their problems and to determine the aspects the clients want to change.

Chapter 8: Choosing the Appropriate Kind of Care

Screening and Assessment

Screening and assessment are techniques used to recognize a client's strengths and weaknesses. They are typically performed at intake, and both procedures continue throughout the duration of the therapy. Routine screening programs can help identify issues that may manifest after the initial intake, as well as a client's strengths, such as successful relationships or family ties, ambition or the lack of pressing crises.

Routine management of these processes is critical because the counselor's knowledge of a client's abilities and problems significantly impacts the selection and duration of the treatments used on the clients.

Screening and assessment are frequently confused, but they are two separate processes. Screening is done by an official who conducts tests and/or interviews the client using documents that outline areas of a client's life that may require additional investigation. It checks for the existence of a disorder but does not diagnose or assess the severity.

Assessing a man for substance abuse, for example, might entail asking him a few questions in interviews about drug use and associated problems, as well as using a brief cognitive scale for drug addiction and/or substance reliance. When favorable indicators are discovered, therapists should make an appointment for the individual to be evaluated.

Screening and Assessment in Men

Despite the fact that there has been little investigation into the dissimilarities in men and women's reactions to screening and assessment, some literature (e.g., Cochran 2005) implies that men present unique challenges. Masculine gender role socialization can cause some men to mitigate or underreport problems, and some problems, such as depression, can manifest differently in men, masking the disorder and leading to underreporting or misinterpretation. Furthermore, different screening or evaluation settings (prisons, outpatient programs and primary health-care offices) impact how men present their problems.

Screening, problem analysis and individual evaluation are the three steps in a thorough substance abuse assessment. The procedure starts with a screening to identify men who require a problem evaluation. Any primary care counselor who has been prepared in the screening process can provide screening. Problem appraisal records patterns of use, clinical signs of drug dependence or abuse and the social, spiritual, cognitive and medical repercussions of use. Typically, problems perceived as being important in the drug treatment or behavioral health-care system are noted.

Within health-care services, the initial contact with patients or clients allows service providers to gather critical information about symptomatology and complaints. The critical data will be used to shape diagnostic perceptions and guide subsequent medical information. Intake procedures used by medical doctors, psychiatrists and nurses include medical interviews, psychiatric interviews (MacKinnon, Michels and Buckley, 2010) and triage (Briggs, 2011; Briggs & Grossman, 2005).

Similarly, counselors undertake clinical assessments in order to obtain critical clinical information about the client and incorporate clinical judgments in order to advance the counseling processes.

Dealing With Patients with Co-Occurring Diagnoses (CODs)

Counselors working with co-occurring diagnoses (COD) clients frequently want to know which disorder appeared first; the answer is not always straightforward because the spatial nature of CODs can be inaccurate.

In some cases, it may be readily apparent that a mental disorder caused the development of a substance use disorder, such as when a person with a long-standing major depressive disorder begins drinking excessively to cope with the symptoms and develops an alcohol use disorder. In other cases, such as someone with a cocaine-induced psychological illness, it may be evident that substance use caused the mental disorder. Therefore, in many cases, it will be difficult to determine which disorder took place first.

Additionally, CODs can be transitive. For some clients, a third category may be interfering with both or either of the two psychotic symptoms (e.g., HIV, chronic pain). External conditions, such as homelessness or emotional stress, can also have an impact on one or both abnormalities.

As a result, even if it is clear which disorder came first, the causal relationship may be unknown. Regardless of the perceptual causal relationship between a client's substance use disorder and mental problems, the two are likely to come into conflict with one another. This implies that both must be treated with the same level of seriousness.

Six Guiding Principles for Dealing with COD Clients

1. Adopt a recovery mindset.

2. Take a multifaceted approach.

3. Create a treatment plan that is phased.

4. Address specific real-world issues early on in treatment.

5. Make plans to accommodate the client's progressive cognitive impairments.

6. Make use of support systems to preserve and broaden treatment efficacy.

Labor force participation is beneficial for addicts recovering from mental disorders or substance use disorders not only because of its economic benefits but because it can also help improve self-efficacy, self-identity (e.g., helping people feel "normal" rather than "like patients"), offer a sense of belonging to society in general, provide a way for people to make connections with others and improve coping skills. A review of the impacts of employment programs for patients with substance use disorders discovered that employment was linked to lower substance use.

Solving economic, housing, vocational and other everyday issues is frequently essential to achieving patient participation in ongoing treatment. Engagement is a critical component of substance use disorder treatment in general and of COD diagnosis in particular because staying in treatment for a sufficient length of time is vital to improving behavior.

What Is the Purpose of Self-Reports?

Therapists can use self-reports to learn more about their clients' symptomatology, thoughts, personal traits, feelings, behaviors, beliefs and self-perception. Self-reports are frequently prescribed during clients' preliminary therapy sessions as a way for counselors to explain the treatment options to their clients. This allows counselors to implement the best treatment plans for the clients.

The information counselors glean from these reports will help them understand their clients and become aware of the steps they need to take in the clients' care. It will also provide counselors with a starting point for developing a course of treatment that will solve these problems and concentrate on the symptoms clients are experiencing.

Advantages and Drawbacks

In counseling, self-reports can provide the following advantages:

- They are simple to obtain, and the findings are immediately available to the psychiatrist.
- They are reasonably priced to administer and score.

- Typically, information from these findings can be acquired during a single session with the client.

- The self-reports can be completed in private, which may motivate clients to be more honest.

- Once a client has completed a self-report, the counselor can go over the responses right away and start talking about them with the client. This availability and confidentiality can benefit both the counselor and the client.

Self-reports may also be subject to the following limitations:

- **Dishonesty**: Clients will frequently respond with responses they believe are culturally acceptable or answers they think will be acceptable by the counselor.

- **Invalidity:** Clients may overstate their symptoms to seek treatment, or they may underreport the seriousness of their symptoms out of worry or humiliation or to avoid further medication.

- **Lack of self-awareness:** Clients may have difficulty in accurately evaluating themselves.

- **Inaccurate interpretation:** Some questions may be perplexing or have different meanings for different clients.

- **Inaccuracy:** Clients frequently respond based on what they are experiencing, which may not truly represent how they feel most of the time.

Components Counselors and Other Service Providers Should Follow

The core principles discussed earlier serve as the basic blocks for successful therapy, but ensuring appropriate treatment necessitates counselors and other providers attending to other variables.

The six key components that comprise the ideal delivery of addiction counseling for COD clients are as follows:

1. Getting access.

2. Completing a comprehensive evaluation.

3. Providing a sufficient level of care.

4. Achieving integrated care.

5. Providing all-inclusive services.

6. Maintaining patient care.

Criteria for Evaluation

Counseling outcome metrics must be both accurate and valid in order to be an effective analysis. Reliability indicates that the measure yields the same result both over multiple applications (presuming no alteration in what is being evaluated) and when used by various researchers. Validity implies that the measure evaluates the outcomes it intends to represent and provides data that is generally applicable.

Neither reliability nor validity are intended to be theoretical concepts; rather, they are established by evaluating the measurement equipment.

Patients' Measures

One common important primary outcome is patient reports and ratings of their actions, thoughts and feelings. Such information is frequently gathered through questionnaires and interviews. These measures, which include paper-and-pencil indicators of personality and adaptation, structure conversational reports of the patient's capacity to adapt to various issues. Although clinical care measures provide valuable information, they are not without limitations. Social desirability effects and response bias are examples of these limitations.

Another type of measuring is psychometric surveys or personality quizzes, such as the Minnesota Multiphasic Personality Inventory (MMPI). Such instruments, possibly the most common type of measuring resource for prognostic and evaluation purposes, ask a range of questions about the respondent's feelings. Patients with severe psychological distress, for example, are shown to respond to all these questions in predictable ways.

Measures Obtained from Family and Friends

Friends, coworkers and family members of patients are frequently expected to provide feedback about a patient's ability to function, and such documentation about patient conditions and implied mental states has been used to evaluate treatment outcomes. The importance of these initiatives may be due to the in-depth knowledge that family, friends and coworkers have about the patient's ability to function. These people have the opportunity to observe the patient in a variety of scenarios and may, thus, have a large amount of data on which to support their questionnaires.

Therapists' Measures

Another common source of study results is data collected from the therapist and others associated with the therapy relationship. While the therapist can provide firsthand information about the therapeutic process, such information may be biased because the psychologist has a vested advantage in developing positive results. Despite this, there is extensive research literature on such diagnostic decisions, and there is some scientific proof that health professionals can provide helpful and fairly impartial reports. There is proof that counselors can provide reliable data, especially in evaluating patients' ability to function.

Measures Contributed by Community Members

More widely, information on the result of psychotherapy can be gathered from members of the community or other organizations. These measures could include customer records on criminal incarceration rates, work-related measures or medical therapeutic ways (from non-psychiatric illness).

The spectrum of possible community measures is very broad and, while often cumbersome, appears to represent essential information that is required to analyze the influence of psychotherapy adequately. Such factors are critical to evaluate in order to conduct proper budget and cost-benefit analyses.

Conclusion

The length of psychotherapy is determined by several factors, including the particular problem or disorder, the patient's character traits and history, the patient's objectives, what is happening in the patient's life outside of talk therapy and how quickly the patient can make progress.

It is important to note that counseling is not a long-term commitment, and it ends with a mutual agreement between the client and the therapist, which could be after weeks or even months.

Chapter 9: Geriatrics

Regardless of gender and health preferences, almost every country has an expected average life expectancy of 70 years for its citizens. It is expected that by the year 2050, the population of individuals aged 60 and above will be two billion.

Geriatrics is a compilation of studying various aspects of human behavior in terms of physical, emotional and psychological changes, which are observed during aging. It is studied to initiate and observe treatment, identify various problems that arise with aging and diagnose and prevent various diseases that afflict the human body at an older age. There is no exact age when an individual needs to consult a geriatrics expert.

Aging/Geriatric Concerns

Since 1985, there has been an increase in the average life span from 60 to 65+ as of 2017. Aging is a natural process that can be delayed but not stopped completely. As people grow older, some look positively toward their middle and later years, while others have difficulty adjusting to this change. As individuals age, regardless of gender, they are likely to suffer various health problems. Problems that arise in a person above 60 are known as geriatric syndrome.

Aging's root cause has been observed at the biological level when there are clusters of various cellular and molecular damage within the body. This results in deterioration of physical and mental capacity, a high risk of disease and many more factors. A large majority of old individuals require care at later stages.

Apart from obvious biological changes, other instances such as stress, work-life, personal life, relocation and/or the death of loved ones also play an important role in speeding the process of aging.

Below are some of the most commonly observed health problems that affect older people:

Subconscious Loss

Various diseases, such as Alzheimer's, Parkinson's and dementia, are often observed at an older age. It is best to watch for early warnings and signs and start appropriate treatment.

Poor Balance

Older people can trip, fall or slip more, and these imbalances can sometimes result in major injuries. This is why people restrict their movement as they grow older, to avoid such occurrences.

Oral Health Issues

Decay and loss of teeth and increase in sensitivity cause various types of oral infections in older adults. This may cause difficulty chewing and eating hard foods, and switching to softer foods or a liquid diet may help people to avoid the pain.

Diabetes

An estimated 30% of adults aged 60 and above develop diabetes. When diagnosed, individuals usually lessen their intake of sugar and make better lifestyle choices.

Heart and Lung Disease

The leading cause of death among individuals aged 60 and above is diseases of major organs such as heart attacks, kidney and liver failure, etc. To avoid further complications, medications for cholesterol and blood pressure may be prescribed.

Sensory Loss

Loss of touch, smell, taste, vision and hearing often occurs in older people. Regular screenings and doctor checkups are important.

Caregiving Concerns

There are two classifications of caregivers: professional and personal (usually a family member).

Professional Caregiver (Paid)

Individuals seeking help in a facility and looking for long-term guidance and support are placed with a professional caregiver. These caregivers are usually trained extensively and hired through agencies or hospitals.

Family Caregiver (Personal and Unpaid)

Children may act as caregivers for elderly people in the family or friend circle. They provide care, comfort and support to elderly people, who can be handicapped, aging or ill.

Problems observed with caregiving are described below:

Anger

When you put more dedication into caring for someone else's life than your own, you get frustrated. Even the smallest things (recriminations, lack of gratitude, asking for too many things) can make you feel annoyed, so getting upset becomes easy.

Stress and Worry

Common worries caregivers think about are health, financial stability or even the fear of their patients getting worse.

Loneliness and Sadness

Seventy percent of caregivers experience the loss of a social life. This can lead to depression.

Guilt

Caregivers may feel that they aren't doing enough to make the elderly person feel comfortable and may, as a result, feel guilty. They may also feel bad as they are prioritizing someone else's life over their own family and friends at certain times.

Lack of Physical Activity

Caregivers usually spend all their time caring for their loved ones, so eating, sleeping and physical activity may take a backseat.

End-of-Life Issues

In many cultures and societies worldwide, it is considered taboo to discuss death. Although it is an uncomfortable topic to discuss, it can lead to understanding a person better and implementing individuals' decisions later, when they are unable to do so themselves.

Common symptoms for a person nearing death include a loss in appetite, extreme weight loss, limited physical activity and movement, lack of interest in surroundings, isolation from the real world and much more.

An end-of-life issue that is frequently overlooked is communication. Patients must know what is wrong with them, how to move forward from it, the dos and the don'ts, any medications to be taken and the possible options of support and care.

Sometimes, if people are near death, they refuse to take any medical advice or support and would rather enjoy their last days resting, saying their goodbyes, making memories or simply preparing for death. People sometimes reminiscence about life and wonder if it was satisfactory. They remember all the things they did, the things they couldn't do, the joys of life and the sorrows, etc.

Grief/Loss

The loss of a loved one causes many distressing symptoms. Some may experience loneliness, numbness, sadness, anger and even guilt. Others may show extreme reactions, either not accepting the death of the loved one or making drastic decisions that could be harmful.

Some individuals move on as time passes, but others don't. Usually, the latter group is holding onto feelings such as love, hate, resentment and other strong emotions.

There are various ways a person could move on, such as:

- Accepting and understanding the loss
- Adjusting to life after a loss
- Finding new relationships.

However, there are some factors that make people unable to get over their grief, such as:

- Feeling immense pain over the loss of a loved one
- Avoiding acceptance of a loved one's death
- Detachment
- Lack of trust in others.

Stages of Grief

A person may go through various stages of grief when the loss of a loved one occurs:

- Denial
- Anger
- Bargaining
- Depression
- Acceptance

There is no specific time frame for when a person will move through all the stages of grief.

Retirement Concerns

When you think about retirement, various risks arise, such as a sudden illness, market collapse or the death of a spouse.

Outliving Your Savings

The main concern of many people upon retirement is whether they will have enough money to live comfortably. Many do not have enough retirement savings, and they often have to look for a job or rely on someone else.

Unsatisfactory Investments

Sometimes investments fail to provide the retirement cushion a person was depending on. To avoid losses, people need to invest in better opportunities.

Sudden Illness

With the rise of medical expenses, a sudden surgery or complication could empty a person's life savings. A solution for this could be to consider life insurance coverage and seek help from a financial advisor.

Death of Spouse

The sudden loss of a spouse may cause great trauma and numbness, especially if a person was planning retirement.

Terminal Illness Issues

When people are suffering from diseases for which there is no cure, they are classified as terminally ill patients. A terminally ill individual usually experiences various emotions, such as sadness, regret, loss of hope, etc. Those who are in the circle of a terminally ill person also are affected by the diagnosis.

There are various preventive methods for coping with death and not becoming numb to the pain and other emotions. Upon receiving news of their condition, patients may become numb, calm or not show any emotion at all. They may feel uncertain and terrified.

Processing the Pain

Many loved ones find it hard to cope with the process of accepting the imminent loss of a loved one and often have a hard time saying their goodbyes. This results in depression for both the patient and the loved one. Those who suffer from a terminal illness often face dilemmas on how to spend their remaining time.

Therapy

Therapy may be a helpful alternative for those who are looking for a way to talk about their feelings. This could involve sessions with counselors, religious leaders or family members to ease communication and seek clarity.

The goals of a terminally ill individual may vary. Some may seek to communicate their wishes to their loved ones, have honest conversations, remove any bad blood between themselves and other people and go with a clear conscience, etc.

Chapter 10: Parenting and Its Effect on a Child's Development

It is a fact that children mimic their elders. Being raised in an overly strict household can cause resentment in a child, which then impacts him or her in adulthood.

Adoption Concerns

People often choose adoption if they can't have children naturally or when fertility treatments aren't effective. Adopting a child is a very long and complicated process that can take years. There are various concerns that must be addressed regarding the process.

Adopting a child is extremely rewarding. However, families must do thorough checks on the adopted child's health before, during and after adoption.

Stress and Complications

For first-time parents, this process can be difficult, tiresome and emotional. Parents feel scared of how the child will feel upon hearing the news that he or she is adopted. Sometimes, as a child grows up, a medical condition might be discovered which was not known before, and the parents may have a hard time accepting this.

Financial Costs

Adoption is extremely expensive. The cost of legal assistance, among other fees, can make adoption prohibitive for some people.

Intrusion in Personal Space

There is a completely different schedule and routine for a person's life when a child is in the picture. All energy and effort have to be dedicated to the safety and well-being of the child. Parents have to put the child's needs before their own.

Failed Adoption

An adoption can fail when the birth parent does not want to continue after everything has been finalized or when the parents applying for the adoption do not meet the standard requirements.

Issues With Blended Families

In the US, 55% of remarriages include children from a previous marriage. This results in the creation of blended families. Sometimes, when entering into a new relationship, it can be hard for the other partner to accept children that are not his or her own. Issues may also arise between step-siblings. Arguments and disagreements occur in all families, but this can be more challenging in blended families.

Lack of Attention/Sharing

When a family adopts a blended lifestyle, a lot of changes have to be made. Sometimes it becomes difficult for the parent to provide the same time and energy to every child or to his or her spouse.

Sibling Rivalry

With new family members in the house, a child may feel threatened. Sibling rivalries may develop as children figure out their new positions in the household.

Identity Crisis

Children or individuals in a blended family often don't understand why their birth parents are not together anymore and may harbor resentment toward their new family and blame them for change. If a child's mother remarries and has children, the difference in last name could make the child question his or her identity and whether he or she is even still part of the family. Also, children may face bullying from others and keep their feelings inside without discussing them with anyone, leading to further misunderstandings.

Financial Setback

Raising multiple children often increases household expenses. School fees, health care and clothing can all strain a household budget.

Conflicts Between Ex-Spouses

Many parents, after a divorce, opt for co-parenting, which is important when there is a child involved. Usually, the biological parents make key decisions, but in blended families, spouses may feel as if they don't have a right to their own opinion.

Concerns About Child Abuse

Child abuse is very common, with most victims being under one year of age. Thirty percent of victims are under 10 years old, and 20% are preteens. There are various types of abuse that children face, including physical, sexual and mental abuse.

Physical Abuse

Three in 20 children are physically abused. Some red flags are:

- Bruises on various parts of the body

- Child is distressed when out with a person in public
- Child is shy and refrains from conversation
- Child informs someone about the abuse
- Weight loss.

Sexual Abuse

More than 90% of sexual abuse victims have direct ties to their abusers and usually live with them. The most common acts of sexual abuse include:

- Sexual intercourse
- Oral-genital contact
- Inappropriate advances and touching parts of the body.

Mental Torture

Oftentimes, a disruptive household may not exhibit any signs of physical or sexual abuse but still causes major distress to a child psychologically. Periodically, this is linked to child neglect when parents or guardians fail to provide necessities such as clothing, food, education, medical support, etc. Also, when a parent fails to provide emotional support, such as love and comfort, the child is usually very guarded and proceeds not to interact with others.

Concerns About Children's Development

Parents play a very important role in their children's development.

Cognitive Skills

It is vital for children to learn cognitive skills. They must possess the capability to think about information and have the confidence to speak about it. As children grow older, their focus increases and various skills also improve. Children must learn how to connect ideas, determine cause and effect and then put it into practice.

A child might not be able to develop basic cognitive skills if he or she is suffering from a medical condition that impacts the brain, such as Down syndrome, shaken baby syndrome (a result of physical abuse), seizures, etc.

Motor Delays

Delays in motor skills development may affect a child's ability to move his or her muscles. Infants may have difficulty when trying to roll over, walking for the first time, or crawling; as the children grow older, they may still have these problems, which may cause difficulty with balance, walking or climbing stairs.

Behavioral Aspects

Recently, there has been a spike in the observation of related neurobehavioral disorders in children such as autism, hyperactivity, lack of social interaction, etc. This leads to a gap in the development of the child's communication, interaction and learning skills.

Difficulty in developing emotional and social interaction skills is common for children who go through developmental delays. In some cases, they may feel difficulty in initiating a conversation, understanding what the other person is saying, etc. Depending on the environment, children may start to throw tantrums out of frustration. Parents may have a hard time controlling their children in an environment away from their comfort zone.

Language and Speech Functionality

Children may have problems when trying to speak, understanding what is being said or thinking due to various language disorders. Some examples include when a child has difficulty identifying color, shapes and body parts. Such children have a very limited vocabulary. At times, there may be an oral motor problem that could cause difficulty or weakness in the movement of the mouth, which could result in difficulties with speech production.

Disconnection from Primary Care Providers

There has been a great disparity in the advocacy of strong family and care providers for a long time. Health-care providers and adults have contradicted each other in many ways. To change the way current primary care providers work, strategies need to be strengthened for better guidance for an individual approach, establishing trust, advocating and spreading information about various health-care services, etc.

Conflicts Between Parents and Co-Parents

Co-parenting is different for every family; even the most amicably separated couples may have difficulty in co-parenting and establishing limits. A conflict between two co-parents is only worsened by communication gaps and misunderstandings.

Contradicting Parenting Styles

After living separately, parenting a child could be different. The mother may be stricter in some cases, whereas the father may be more lenient or vice-versa. Parents need to establish certain household rules. Discussions of likes and dislikes when it comes to parenting methods should be raised, and alternatives should be discussed. Here are some examples:

- Food intake
- Religious beliefs and practices
- School
- Bedtime.

Worry for Child When Not in a Parent's Presence

It is common to worry about what children are doing when they are with an ex-spouse. In such cases, parents should give their children the freedom they deserve with the other parent. Basic communication, such as updates about the children, is acceptable, but requiring information on every move the children make while with the other parent is unacceptable.

Using Children to Hurt Others

It might be unintentional or planned, but it is not acceptable to use children as a middle ground to have arguments and spread false narratives about the other spouse. Spreading hatred about an ex-spouse or his or her current family and blaming the ex-spouse for the separation are signs that one parent hasn't let go of the past relationship.

Emotionally Unstable Reaction

Sometimes it becomes difficult for parents to emotionally distance themselves from a child when in the presence of the ex-spouse. Thoughts arise in the mind that the child should only remain with one parent and that only that parent's parenting preferences should be followed.

Impact on Children

Many studies have determined that 97% of households with co-parenting issues take a toll on the children involved. Children witness various instances where their parents are not in sync, which causes them to become depressed, stressed out and have drastic behavioral changes. Worst-case situations are when parents fight in front of children. This can have long-term effects on the children.

Conflict Resolution

Co-parenting is not an easy task and usually takes time to adjust to. Once co-parents discuss the problems and identify possible solutions, progress may be made. But sometimes legal professionals should be consulted to make matters more streamlined.

Conclusion

Families are influenced by the changes that occur around them, be it cultural, economic, geographic, etc. With proper communication, parenting is much easier. However, there are shifts at a macro level, such as divorce, death, change in job, etc., that may all impact a family.

Chapter 11: Relationships of a Romantic Nature

Communication is of utmost importance in a romantic relationship.

Importance of a Relationship

Romantic relationships include premarital and marital couples, such as couples dating, live-in relationships, casual friendships, etc. As a couple becomes more serious, they may move in together before marriage.

It is important to note that as people are growing up, they are more prone to adopting the attachment style that they observed as children. Individuals who witnessed a loving relationship between their parents are more invested in their own relationships. Individuals raised in a disruptive household, on the other hand, usually adopt the same style and take it out on their future partners.

When two individuals are in a relationship together, a transverse effect is taken on their age and health. Individuals who are currently studying at the university level will find it difficult to get sick if in a satisfying relationship, whereas those above 40 would find it tiresome, stressful and a heavy load on the shoulders. A recent study suggests that those couples who maintain a healthy and active relationship and surround themselves with positive friends and coworkers are likely to stay married.

Problems With Dating and Relationships

All relationships, at one point or another, go through bitter disagreements and stressful moments due to conflicting points of view, beliefs and ideas. But, for those couples who suffer from chronic conflicts, maintaining a relationship can cause many problems in their personal and professional lives. Children who are raised in a house with constant conflict are at a high risk of developing behavioral problems, depression, anxiety, etc. Couples should use effective, respectful methods to communicate with one another, for the benefit of everyone around them.

The most effective way of overcoming relationship problems is by discussing them openly with one's partner.

Past Experiences

It is important to reiterate that a person's upbringing and childhood play a critical role in establishing future relationships. Children raised in dysfunctional families are likely to repeat the same behaviors they observed in their families. However, there is no definitive answer as to whether relationship problems are directly linked to one's upbringing.

Stress and Other Changes

Living together, dividing finances, having children and caring for them, changing careers, etc., could all cause a couple to drift away from each other and/or to develop conflicts.

Behavioral Factors

Various things can lead to a shift in the dynamics of a relationship. Couples must observe and identify behaviors that cause negative changes. Disrespect, criticism, judgment and lack of trust are red flags that suggest a communication breakdown.

Divorce

Divorce is a topic that is mutable and means different things to different people. For some, divorce means regaining the freedom or independence they lost when they got married. For others, it is a change a person needs in his or her life after trying all available options to stay together. For a couple who has no children, divorce can be liberating, but divorce can have negative effects for a couple with children.

The reasons for divorce can be varied, but the most common are listed below:

Lack of Interest

After a couple is together for a long time, spouses may become distant from one another. This could be due to various reasons, such as increased workload, not spending enough time with the spouse, developing different hobbies, etc.

Abusive Relationships

The leading reason for divorce is physical, sexual or mental abuse of a spouse. In such situations, if children are involved, the parents keep the child separate to protect him or her. Children are also at times deprived of the education they deserve.

Conflict in Finances

Division in finances and hidden assets often lead to fights between couples. Offshore accounts and business registrations in the spouse's name may result in distrust as to where a couple's potential earnings are coming from. Simple financial considerations such as rent and groceries may be a divisive issue between a couple. Financial conflicts may result in separation.

Infidelity

Spouses catching their significant others in affairs is one common reason for divorce.

Statistics

- Since 2016, the United States has observed a decline in marriage and divorce rates. The younger generation is more career-oriented and financially thoughtful—they want to marry at a later stage of life.

- The marriage rate in the United States is 6.8 per 1,000 people; this is a rapid decline from a previous marriage rate of 24.2.
- The divorce rate among individuals has increased in people aged 20–35, with a spike of 4.2 per 1,000 people. However, it is to be noted that the older (50 years and older) generation's divorce rate has declined.

Abuse and Violence in the Family

All of the following may be perpetrators or victims of abuse:

- Parents or stepparents
- Children
- Siblings
- Grandparents, grandchildren
- Uncles and aunts
- Nephews, nieces or cousins
- Close family friends
- Business partners
- Domestic help
- Caregivers
- Medical experts.

The most common types of abuse are:

Physical

Family violence may include sudden outbursts of anger, which could be both intentional and unintentional. In the US, women are most susceptible to physical abuse by either a spouse or immediate family members, such as parents, siblings or close relatives.

Emotional

Emotional abuse can have a long-lasting effect. A family member could bully someone for being fat, not studying enough, talking differently and not being pretty enough, etc. The victims of this bullying often end up depressed at a later stage of life and often perform badly at school, take drugs, start fights, etc.

Sexual Abuse

Individuals raised in families who are in constant conflict are most likely to face sexual abuse. Teenagers, especially girls, tend to be affected the most. Often, this abuse isn't discovered, and the victims aren't believed when they report the abuse.

Statistics

According to research, the United States has reported that:

- 25% of females who are or were in a relationship experience emotional and sexual abuse.
- 48% of females ages 14–18 experience emotional abuse from their parents.
- 32% of females experience physical and sexual abuse from their spouses.

It is also reported that:

- 5% of males experience sexual abuse in their households.
- 32% of males experience emotional abuse from friends, teachers and family.
- 20% of males reported experiencing abuse from their female spouses and family.

Recent cases suggest that abuse toward women has increased compared to men. Also, only 10% of abuse victims contact higher authorities.

Concerns About Partner Violence in Relationships

The United States is exhibiting an all-time high in domestic violence rates. A person is a victim of domestic violence when his or her spouse tries to exert force or authority in the relationship, whether physical, sexual or mental. There is no gender, age, religion or race most associated with domestic violence; anyone can fall victim to it in the form of abuse, negligence of finances, nonconsensual sexual activity, etc. This also takes a toll on individuals if they belong to a different socioeconomic background and education level.

Health Concerns

An estimated 45 million (38%) women in the United States have reported they have faced physical violence, rape and mental torture while being in a relationship. These women usually have health problems such as eating disorders, low confidence, poor social interaction skills, depression, etc. Abused women are highly likely to get pregnant and abort the child or leave it in foster care. In the case of men, their spouses are more likely to lash out based on predominately jealous behavior and emotionally and physically attack them. Five in 10 women report partner violence, versus one in 10 males.

Problems With Communication Between Spouses or Partners

Before entering into a relationship, it is important for couples to talk about any concerns they have and problems they would like to avoid in the future.

Why Is Communication Important?

Most challenges that couples face involve understanding how and what to communicate with one another. Communication is not a debate; it is a simple chat to understand the other person's point of view.

Reasons Couples Fail to Communicate

Failure to communicate often boils down to underlying issues with one individual or the other. One partner may be more open about his or her thoughts and feelings.

Some of the reasons couples fail to communicate properly in their relationship include:

- Lack of individual time to talk about the issue
- High expectations and assuming one partner should know about the other person's needs and wants without communicating
- Showing a lack of interest in the other partner's concerns
- Avoiding talking to each other in hopes of avoiding conflict.

Confrontation is never the answer, but neither is avoidance.

Concerns About Sexual Function

Another leading cause of problems in a relationship is sexual dysfunction, present in both men and women. Such conditions are caused by medical problems such as hormone imbalance, depression and after-effects of trauma.

There are four main categories of sexual dysfunction:

Desire Disorders

Such disorders may change an individual's sexual desire and interest in physical and sexual activity, known as libido disorders. Many factors, such as hormonal changes, depression, anxiety, work stress, dissatisfaction and high estrogen levels, may cause this to become a problem. It is also possible that an individual is simply not interested in his or her partner anymore.

Arousal Disorders

With arousal disorders, it is very difficult for an individual to get physically aroused. For men, the most common type of disorder is erectile dysfunction, which is the inability to develop an erection. Both men and women face problems of arousal. They are interested in the activity but cannot perform it.

Orgasm Disorders

During intercourse, many women experience a delay in orgasms, which can be caused due to stress or other health conditions. This can leave one partner feeling unsatisfied and may lead to emotional disconnection.

Pain Disorders

Sometimes, during intercourse, an individual might feel pain. This is usually caused by yeast infections, urinary tract infections, vaginal dryness, menopause, etc. For men, Peyronie's disease causes physical damage to the penis, as do urinary tract infections, herpes, sexually transmitted diseases, etc.

If an individual experiences any signs of sexual dysfunction or dissatisfaction, it is advisable to visit a medical expert and discuss various treatment options. Lack of intimacy may cause a rift between a couple and may become a reason for ending the relationship.

Second marriages/Recommitment

An increase in blended families suggests that second marriages have become popular as spouses move on from their exes. Statistics show that individuals who get married for the second time end up with a divorce rate of 60%, whereas for third-time remarriages, the divorce rates are 70%.

Age

Research suggests that 70% of divorced individuals (aged 40 and above) have gotten married a second time compared to the younger generation (whose remarriage rate is only 12%).

Learn from Previous Mistakes

People delay getting married again as they do not want history to repeat itself and end up in similar situations that they are now trying to avoid.

Fixing the Wrong

In some cases, existing married couples renew their vows and get remarried as they want to strengthen their relationship with their spouse. This type of recommitment may feel like a fresh start.

Financial Dependability

At times, marrying again is the only option left for some people. Those who were victims of abuse from their family or a previous spouse have no other choice but to find someone they can depend on. In cases where children are involved, a father or mother figure is needed to look after the child. As a result, the divorced parent may remarry.

Conclusion

Compatibility is an important factor when determining if two people are meant to continue in a relationship. If the individuals involved in the relationship share a common vision, they can work around conflicts. A new identity is established, which is a combination of both individuals' feelings, thoughts, concerns and personalities.

Chapter 12: Mental Stress and Its Manifestations

Suicidal Ideation In Patients

Realizing suicidal ideation in clients and responding to their specific needs requires training and knowledge of suicide preparedness and detection and a certain amount of professional instinct. Suicide is a complicated issue, and counselors must do everything possible to ensure quality care and maintain client trust while probing people's darkest moments.

Above all, suicide is a subject that counselors should not avoid or be afraid to discuss. It is the responsibility of professionals to screen for suicidal thoughts and to address the issue sensitively.

Even the most experienced therapist may find it difficult to work with clients who have suicidal ideation or plans. Identifying the client's experience of feeling suicidal, realizing how to respond appropriately in the therapeutic relationship and making conscious choices about the consequences for confidential information, where possible, all pose challenging dilemmas for practitioners. When dealing with someone who is suicidal, practitioners may experience a variety of emotions, including fear, anger and negative thoughts, as well as a feeling of professional ineptness (Reeves and Mintz, 2001; Richards, 2000).

What Are the Signs That Something Is Wrong?

There is no such thing as a "typical suicidal individual." There are, however, a number of behaviors that can indicate that someone is seriously considering suicide.

Here are some of them:

- Talking about suicide and having a morbid fascination with death and dying
- Having difficulty eating or sleeping, as well as a visible change in appearance
- Withdrawing from social events, friends and family
- Showing a lack of interest in work, school or leisure activities
- Experiencing or anticipating a major personal loss (spouse or other)
- Displaying a significant shift in behavior
- Frequently taking huge risks as if the person doesn't care about the consequences

- Escalating use of alcohol and drugs
- Making funeral plans or giving away treasured possessions
- Expressing intent to self-harm is the most important indicator.

Any combination of these behaviors could indicate to family and friends that a person is contemplating suicide.

Protective Factors

Most of the research on working with suicidal people focuses on the risks associated with counseling patients with psychological problems. However, prevention efforts (those that may make suicidal behavior less probable) are also important. Protective factors can frequently provide a path forward for clients and help them consider how they can keep taking responsibility for their own safety and health where practicable and how they might provide themselves with assistance.

The following are some of the most important suicide safeguards. However, it is important to remember that, as with risk factors, many will be unique to each individual. It is always essential for therapists to feel comfortable enough to talk transparently with their clients about any threats they've experienced and how the clients have assisted themselves up to this point.

Protective Factors in Suicide Prevention

- Some ability to express emotions
- A willingness to discuss one's thoughts and emotions
- Presence of informal support systems (e.g., friends, family)
- Presence of formal assistance networks (e.g., mental health support, counseling)
- Participation in hobbies and activities
- Established, effective coping mechanisms
- Options for "after-hours" assistance
- Exercise or some other kind of physical activity
- Key attachment figures that have been identified and talked to already

- A crisis plan that has been agreed upon collaboratively
- Taking part in counseling.

Recognizing the Possibility of Suicide

Practitioners are frequently concerned that discussing suicide will "put the idea into the client's mind" or that it will be "offensive or clumsy." These fears can make it difficult for professionals to feel comfortable discussing suicide openly.

There is no proof that asking clients if they have suicidal thoughts will prompt them to start considering suicidal ideation if they haven't already. There is, however, a growing body of evidence that suggests that being able to communicate to clients about suicide is critical in providing a safe environment for them to express their feelings.

Clients frequently express relief at being able to discuss their suicidal thoughts. Some clients, on the other hand, will be unable to express their suicidal thoughts, either consciously or unconsciously. Others may experience suicidal thoughts but have no inclination to act on them. Still other clients claim that simply knowing they have the option of suicide is enough to help them manage troubling or overpowering feelings.

Risk Assessment and Investigation

While suicide risk analysis (distinguishing and adjusting risk behaviors) is important, therapists should also concentrate on suicide risk exploration (assisting clients in interpreting their feelings). The importance of discovery, which remains at the core of the interaction between a therapist and a client, is frequently undervalued in scientific literature.

When assessing suicide risk, practitioners must consider whether the client has sufficient capacity or cognitive competence to make a choice to end his or her own life. Suicidal ideation is rarely enough to violate confidentiality against a client's wishes in a vast majority of cases. Bond (2009) provides a useful summary of the individual aspects that practitioners should consider in such situations, focusing on three main scenarios:

- The client is capable of making his or her own treatment decisions and taking control of whether or not he or she wants to live or die.
- There is skepticism about the individual's psychological condition and, as a result, about his or her ability to make suicidal choices.
- The client lacks the basic ability to comprehend the implications of his or her possible actions, putting him or her at a high risk of committing suicide.

Ascertaining a client's "capacity" or "mental state" is extremely difficult, and it's often only possible with the help of specialized mental health services. Counselors are not expected to conduct a thorough examination of a person's mental state or capacity; however, when making decisions about a client's safety, counselors must be able to show that they weighed the client's right to self-determination and confidentiality against the risk of suicide discussed in the session.

Responding to the Threat of Suicide

There are several effective ways for a therapist to discuss suicide with a client. It can be helpful to ask clients to rate the severity of their suicidal ideation. A 0–10 scale (where 0 indicates no intention to act and 10 indicates imminent action) can aid in the evaluation of the risk urgency. If the evaluative score is high, the counselor should inquire how the client intends to kill him or herself or consider whether the risk is more likely to come from a more unexpected or impetuous act.

Counselors should also seek to identify whether clients feel able to endure suicidal urges if they are at risk of suicide due to an irrational decision, perhaps by talking it through with them.

One of the most important resources in handling suicidal thoughts is a client's own treatment options, also known as protective factors. Inquiring about how clients have kept themselves healthy and how they have kept themselves from acting on their thoughts may aid in the development or reinforcement of long-term coping mechanisms. If clients refuse or are unable to recognize and use such strategies, it may indicate that they are no longer able to protect themselves.

Some professionals use plans designed for times of emergency. These plans, which are developed in collaboration with clients, provide clients with knowledge about their stressors (to help them recognize when they are at higher risk) and protective factors (specific things clients can do to support themselves in times of crisis between sessions, including how to get extra assistance).

Creating a Crisis Plan With Others

A crisis plan will:

- Concentrate on the client's associated risk factors (what makes suicide more probable).
- Concentrate on the client's individual protective factors (what makes suicide less probable).

- Recognize “times of danger” when risks are higher or more difficult to balance with protective factors.

- Provide a detailed list of both structured and additional unstructured services, including chat and online contact information.

- Be written in collaboration with the client—a client’s refusal to collaborate on such a plan may signify a degree of risk that needs to be addressed further.

- Promote a client’s sense of “ownership” and “control” over the plan, i.e., he or she helps draft the plan and can take a duplicate plan home.

- Be presented in a way that the client can comprehend even when he or she is not in the session.

- Be reviewed at least once a week or on a regular basis.

- Be sensitive to the client’s age and depth of understanding and perhaps share with others if suitable.

Risk assessment is an imprecise science—it is hard to anticipate how an individual will respond in a difficult situation.

Therapists should not believe they must accomplish the impossible or foresee the future. Whenever possible, all things should be decided in collaboration with the client and implemented with the client’s clear and specific written permission.

One of the most difficult choices for practitioners is whether or not to reveal details about a session/consideration to a third party. An important overarching consideration is that, whenever possible and realistic, practitioners should not go against a client’s known desires in isolation, even when it comes to suicide. That is, such decisions must be made in collaboration with others, such as a superintendent, manager or senior therapist. Another person’s viewpoint can be crucial in ensuring that decisions are made in the client’s long-term interests rather than in reaction to the therapist’s anxiety.

Contacting the client’s general practitioner to express particular issues about the nature of the suicidal ideation and to discuss how to react to the client may be appropriate. In some areas, contacting a mental health crisis team may be possible. The team can discuss a variety of options with the health-care professional and the client. At the start of therapy, some therapists and clients agree on the name of a person who should be contacted in case of an emergency. If the emergency contact is a family member or friend, therapists must still ensure that they have enough information from clients to consult a professional for extra specialist help if necessary.

Confidentiality and Documentation

Practitioners use various approaches when working with suicidal clients, taking into account the complexities of the client and rehabilitative relationship. When a client is at risk of death, one of the most difficult decisions for therapists is divulging information and sharing their concerns with another person, such as the client's personal physician. Given the significance of confidential information in developing and maintaining a therapeutic relationship, the initial contract must include an agreement between the parties about the circumstances in which information may be disclosed.

Three factors, according to Daines et al. (1997), may be crucial in evaluating counselor actions:

- Whether the client's suicide could have been prevented
- Whether the therapist took appropriate preventive measures if the suicide risk was recognized by the therapist
- Whether the therapist provided reliable and trustworthy assistance.

Given that it is impossible to predict whether or not clients will act on their suicidal ideations, therapists must explain their actions to their clients, supervisors and line managers, as well as draft them in any notations they may keep. These may include the following:

- The reasons why the therapist believed that disclosing the information was in the best interests of a client
- The reason for the transparency, such as a referral for psychiatric evaluation
- Why obtaining client consent was impossible. This could be due to the client's inability to give explicit consent at the time based on emotional and/or physical anguish.

When collaborating with suicidal clients, taking notes can help counselors keep track of what interventions were made and why. It may be useful for the practitioner to keep track of the following:

- The manner in which the client conveyed suicidal ideation or intent
- How the therapist reacted (in detail) to the patient's expressed risk of suicide, including what he or she said and did
- The factors that indicated a higher risk of suicide
- The factors that indicated a lower risk of suicide
- The session's end result, such as whether any intermediaries were consulted, i.e., a superintendent, whether confidential information was maintained and whether the client agreed with the outcome.

Following a meeting with a suicidal client, the above may assist practitioners in structuring any notes.

Self-Care and Monitoring

According to research, working with suicidal clients has been linked to traumatic stress (Fox and Cooper, 1998). When discussing how working with suicidal clients impacts them, Fox and Cooper identify numerous factors that practitioners should consider, including:

- Remorse for ostensibly failing to recognize warning signs
- Apprehension of one's irresponsibility
- Shame resulting from a sense of "failure"
- The threat of legal action
- Fear of retaliation from the client's family/friends and coworkers.

All of these factors have the potential to stifle the strategies that are typically used to support practice. Fear of being blamed, for example, may make it difficult to seek peer support from coworkers. It's critical for practitioners to think about how they'll support themselves. The discourse for therapists working in a professional setting may also include how the team can support ongoing work and how they would respond if a client died. All practitioners should think about what might be preventing them from using standard support systems and what they can do about it.

The importance of supervision in working with all clients, especially suicidal clients, cannot be overstated (Reeves, 2015). In addition to supervision, practitioners frequently look to their overseers for support and encouragement.

When possible, consulting with a supervisor in the event of a pressing issue about a client can be extremely helpful in keeping the practitioner focused on the client rather than on his or her own anxiety. It is beneficial to discuss hypothetical scenarios with a supervisor before they occur in practice. In addition to essential practical issues, such conversations can include common goals, opinions and feelings.

Counselors' reactions to suicidal clients can be influenced by their personal opinions on suicide, which are influenced by religious, societal, intellectual or ethical standpoints. It's important that before accepting a client, counselors take the time to consider their own thoughts and feelings, as well as how their reactions to their clients correspond to their own situations.

Conclusion

When clients' distress is so severe that they are contemplating suicide, the relationship that therapists build with them can be extremely valuable. However, the therapist must take proactive measures to ensure that the restorative process is backed. The fear of being sued and of "making an error" can be incredibly powerful. It is an ethical requirement that decisions about the counselor-client relationship's safety and anonymity be made with the client's best interests in mind.

Chapter 13: Adjustment Disorders

Overview of Adjustment Disorders

An adjustment disorder is a reaction to a traumatic incident or change in a person's emotional or developmental life. Within three months of the incident or change, the behavior is called an undesirable or unnecessary response. A big move, divorce or separation, the loss of a pet or the birth of a sibling can all be particularly stressful for a child or adolescent to adjust to. An adjustment response may be triggered by a sudden illness or a child's development limitation due to severe disease.

Adjustment disorders are most commonly diagnosed in children and young adults. Adult women are more vulnerable to adjustment disorders than men.

Underlying Causes of Adjustment Disorders

Sudden major life changes or major shifts in life, such as marriage, illness, relationship breakdowns and work issues, can cause anxiety and serve as stressors, but even positive times can cause emotional issues too.

Diagnosis

The detection of major stressful situations, symptoms and how they affect a person's ability to behave properly is used to diagnose adjustment disorders. Counselors should inquire about patients' clinical and mental well-being and social background. They can use the criteria from the DSM-5 to make a diagnosis.

The DSM-5 includes the following criteria for diagnosing adjustment disorders:

- Experiencing emotions linked to a traumatic experience, even 12 weeks after the incident
- More anxiety than what is normal as a response to some kind of change that might be considered stressful
- Symptoms aren't caused by another mental health condition or aren't part of the normal bereavement process.

Symptoms of adjustment disorders include:

- **Downbeat mood** – Feeling depressed, tearful and helpless and lacking enjoyment in things that previously gave someone pleasure.

- **Fear** – Nervousness, worry, trouble focusing or recalling information and feeling exhausted are the most common symptoms. Children with an anxiety-related adjustment disorder may be terrified of being torn away from loved ones.
- **Depression combined with anxiety** – A mixture of depression and anxiety are common symptoms.
- **Disturbed behavior** – Behavioral issues, such as picking on children or aggressive driving, are the most common symptoms. It is possible for teenagers to skip school or destroy school property.
- **A variety of emotional and behavioral disturbances** – A combination of anxiety and depression, as well as behavioral issues, are common symptoms.
- **Unspecified** – Medical symptoms, fights with parents or loved ones, issues in the workplace or school are common symptoms that don't align with the other types of adjustment disorders.

Duration of Symptoms

- **Acute adjustment disorder** – Signs and symptoms last for six months or less. Once the source of stress is removed, the symptoms should subside.
- **Tenacious (chronic) adjustment disorder** – The signs and symptoms can last up to six months.

Treatment of Adjustment Disorders

Adjustment disorders are treated in a variety of ways.

An individual's care provider will determine the appropriate treatment for adjustment disorders based on the following factors:

- Age, general health
- The severity of the adolescent's signs and symptoms
- The adolescent's tolerance to certain therapies
- Goals for the treatment's outcome
- Parent and adolescent's point of view or preference.

The following treatments may be used:

- **Cognitive-behavioral approaches** – Used in individual psychotherapy to enhance age-appropriate issue skills, interpersonal skills, emotion regulation, anger management skills and emotional competence.
- **Therapy for the whole family** – Family therapy is frequently used to help families make necessary changes, such as improving communication skills and

family interactions. Increasing the support network among close relatives is another area of focus.

The most common treatment for an adjustment disorder is therapy. If a doctor believes a client needs medication, he or she may refer the person to a psychiatrist or a mental health nurse practitioner.

Adjustment disorders are treated with a variety of therapies. Among these treatments are:

- Hypnotherapy (also called counseling or talk therapy)
- Intervention in a crisis (emergency psychological care)
- Counseling services specific to the reason for the adjustment disorder
- Behavioral therapy, or CBT, which is supported through family and group therapy
- Interpersonal psychotherapy (IPT), which is short-term psychotherapy
- Peer-to-peer counseling. Peer group therapy frequently focuses on the development and application of interpersonal and social skills.
- Medicine. The use of medications to treat adjustment disorders is extremely limited.

Identity Formation and Adjustment Issues

Identity formation is a crucial stage of adolescence. While identity can be defined as a person's positive personality traits and values, it is a dynamic, immersive relationship-based process that changes dramatically during adolescence (Huffaker and Calvert, 2005). Adolescents go through a period of sexual growth as part of their identity development (Rosario, Schrimshaw and Hunter, 2008). Adolescents are strongly encouraged by society to presume a gender identity and sexual preference toward others as their private parts mature during adolescence (Grotevant, 1998).

Adjustment Issues in Children

The research on identity formation has become more cognizant of how teenagers think about their social and economic and racial-ethnic identities. One way to examine the consequences of these evolving identities is to use the status-based identity structure, which is extremely effective as people approach early adulthood. For children from low socioeconomic backgrounds, economic and social flexibility can be accompanied by an aversive feeling of confusion about their own SES (status uncertainty), which can negatively affect their educational processes and attitudes.

Ethnic Identity and Adjustment Issues

Considering the significance of identity formation issues during adolescence, ethnic identity plays a significant role during this stage of development (Phinney, 1990a). While precision of self-definition is the primary concern for young children, during the teenage years, the major concerns are the labels one chooses to identify oneself with, the extent to which one investigates one's cultural identity and the extent and essence of group identity (Phinney, 1990a).

According to research, adolescents with a well-defined ethnic identity have a better psychological adjustment than those with a limited ethnic identity. During an interview, those adolescents who had reached more thoughtful stages of cultural identity had a stronger level of skill and more social connections than their peers with small amounts of cultural identity (Phinney, 1989).

Dementia and Alzheimer's

Although Alzheimer's disease is a common diagnosis in clinical practice, there is still a lack of information about its true diagnostic category. There are no treatment efficacy surveys available. The use of psychotropic drugs, such as antidepressants, in people with Alzheimer's disease—especially those who have an anxious or depressed mental state—is not well supported and should be prevented, whereas medical data better supports psychotherapies. Randomized-controlled trials, even for the blended use of drugs and psychosocial interventions, are critical for better determining the correct course of treatment.

Social Circle and Adjustment Issues

Most human social interactions are encapsulated in five social settings: home, school and/or work, local groups, relationships with friends and community members. When civic contexts vary greatly from one another or a person's identity is in some way vague, this last socioeconomic context is key because it may contest a person's understanding of who he or she is.

Being a Minority

Despite the country's diversity, most US citizens are of European descent and identify as Christians. Given the accepted centralized racial framework in the United States, which disregards rights and opportunities through ethnic, societal and class isolation, all racial minorities are denied access to resources (Abrafdo-Lanza, Florenz, Armbrister and Aguirre, 2006; Grewal, 2003; Portes and Rumbaut, 1996).

Psychosocial Identity Formation

Most analysts believe that the host culture's identity formation reflects a cognitive-developmental path, similar to Erikson's theory of psychosocial identity formation. The experiences associated with migration herald a recycling of the neurocognitive method in the host culture, even if the immigrant is not an infant. From infants to the elderly, Erikson observes, stages of developmental psychology are brokered.

Stereotypes, Culture and Adjustment Disorders

Another factor that influences how people adapt to a new society is basic traditions and presumptions, which can be as similar or dissimilar to the preconceived stereotypes as they are to the host culture. According to research, our identities are deeply embedded in a historical environment that structures them, and this system is related to individual identity, roles, position and networks. Because they are in a social structure where they have no primary contacts, migrant workers from collectivistic systems, especially when they arrive alone, face much greater isolation in the United States and the West than people socially conditioned in western cultural systems.

Conclusion

The assessment of this immersive life experience, filtered through the interaction of the multiple viewpoints posed by hereditary influences, characteristics and cultural situations, aids our understanding of ethnic and racial heritage identity in the perspective of race and sexuality. These ideologies, in turn, serve as a lens through which to view life. Racial and ethnic identity can impact what is passed down through the generations.

Chapter 14: Physical Illnesses

Physical Manifestation of Anxiety

Patients with mental illnesses, such as depression and anxiety, frequently present with idiopathic physical ailments. These symptoms are typically comprised of pain and other physical symptoms that are medically inexplicable. While conventional psychopathology previously stressed the importance of somatic manifestations for disorders such as depression, recent research suggests that the "somatic element" has been overlooked in the assessment and treatment of mental health patients.

Anxiety can cause physical symptoms as well. Consider a time when you were anxious—perhaps your hands were sweaty, or your legs shook; your heart rate may have increased, or you might even have been sick to your stomach. You may have associated these symptoms with your uneasiness. Perhaps you weren't sure why you were feeling ill.

Many people experience anxiety on a regular basis. Anxiety can be dangerous and could develop into a disorder if left untreated for a long period. It causes significant discomfort and can disrupt a person's life.

Anxiety can be classified into the following types:

- General anxiety disorder (GAD) or anxiety disorder in general (GAD)
- Anxiety caused by separation
- Obsessive-compulsive disorder.

Generalized Anxiety Disorder

Generalized anxiety disorder is characterized by a prolonged worry that disrupts everyday activities. This constant sense of fear and looming dread may be affected by additional symptoms such as anxiety, feeling tense or being easily startled, as well as having a hard time focusing, having muscle spasms or sleeping difficulties. Worries about everyday things like job duties and obligations, family health or trivial tasks like grocery shopping or appointments are common.

Panic Disorder

Repetitive panic attacks, an overpowering mixture of psychosocial discomfort, are the primary symptom of a panic disorder.

Several of these symptoms occur in tandem during an attack:

- Palpitations or a rapid heartbeat (symptoms of a heart condition)
- Sweating
- Quivering or trembling
- Chest ache
- Dizziness or lightheadedness
- Choking sensation
- Tingling or loss of sensation
- Brain fog or chills
- Nausea or stomach pains
- Concern about losing control
- Fear of dying.

Many people often mistake the symptoms of a panic attack for a heart attack. Panic attacks can be anticipated, such as a reaction to a feared stimulus, or they can be unexpected, occurring seemingly out of nowhere. The average age of onset of panic disorder is between the ages of 20 and 24. Panic attacks can occur in conjunction with other mental disorders.

Phobias

A specific phobia is an abnormal and enduring fear of a certain object, scenario or activity that is not inherently dangerous. Patients are aware that their fear is extreme, but they are unable to rise above it. These concerns cause so much distress that some people will arrange their whole lives just to avoid that one catalyst of paralyzing fear.

Agoraphobia

Agoraphobia is the dread of being in situations where leaving is difficult or humiliating or where help is unavailable in the incident of panic symptoms. The fear is out of proportion with the actual situation, lasts for six months or more and interferes with functioning.

A person who has agoraphobia is terrified in at least two of the following situations:

- Making use of mass transit
- Being out in the open
- Being in confined spaces
- Being in a crowd
- Being alone outside the house.

The person goes to great lengths to avoid a certain situation, requires company or suffers from intense anxiety. Undiagnosed agoraphobia can progress to the point where a person is unable to leave the house. A person is diagnosed with agoraphobia only if the fear is extremely distressing or interferes substantially with normal activities.

Anxiety Disorder in Social Situations

A person suffering from social anxiety disorder experiences intense anxiety and discomfort when he or she is embarrassed, rejected or treated poorly in social situations. People suffering from this disorder will either try to avoid the situation or withstand it with high anxiety. Excessive fear of public speaking, socializing or eating/drinking in public are typical examples. The fear or anxiety interferes with daily functioning for at least six months.

Separation Anxiety Disorder (SAD)

A person suffering from a separation anxiety disorder is abnormally fearful or worried about being separated from loved ones. The feeling is excessive for the person's age, lasts for a long time (at least a month in young kids and six months in adults) and interferes with normal functioning.

People suffering from separation anxiety disorder may be relentlessly concerned about losing the person closest to them, may be hesitant or refuse to leave the house or sleep away from that person or may have nightmares about being away from that person. Physical symptoms of distress are common in childhood, but they can persist into adulthood.

How Does Anxiety Affect Your Body?

Anxiety can cause physical symptoms that interfere with one's health and daily life.

If you are experiencing a panic attack, you may:

- Have a fear of death
- Have difficulty breathing or feel as if you're choking
- Have a numb or tickling sensation in areas of the body
- Have a muscle pain
- Have shivers
- Feel woozy, lightheaded or overheated.

Anxiety, the body's response to stress, is how the body warns a person about potential threats. This is referred to as the fight-or-flight response.

When the body reacts to danger, a person breathes quickly because the lungs are attempting to move more oxygen through the body in order to prepare it to flee. This can cause people to feel as if they're not getting enough air, leading to even more anxiety or panic.

Who Is at Risk of Developing Anxiety Disorders?

Anxiety disorders can be caused by an interaction of genetic and environmental factors. People may be more vulnerable if they have experienced:

- Certain personality traits, such as social anxiety or behavioral problems, feeling uneasy around and avoiding strangers or certain situations
- Childhood or adulthood stressors or traumatic events
- Anxiety or other mental health conditions that run in the family
- Certain medical conditions, such as thyroid issues and heart arrhythmias (unusual heart rhythms).

Treatment and Diagnosis

The first step is to consult with a doctor to ensure that there is no physical issue causing the symptoms. If a person is diagnosed with an anxiety disorder, a therapist can help him or her find the best medication. Unfortunately, many people suffering from anxiety disorders are unaware that they have a disease for which there are effective treatments.

Although each anxiety disorder is distinctive, the majority respond well to two methods of therapy: psychotherapy, also known as "talk therapy," and prescription drugs. These treatments can be administered singly or in combination. Cognitive-behavior therapy (CBT), a type of counseling, can help people learn a new way of thinking, reacting and behaving to help them feel less anxious. Medications will not cure mental illnesses, but they can provide significant symptomatic relief.

Antidepressants and anti-anxiety treatments are the most commonly used medications to treat physical symptoms. Beta-blockers, which are commonly used to treat heart conditions, can also be used.

A mental health provider may do the following to assist in the diagnosis of an anxiety disorder:

- Provide a psychological evaluation. This entails discussing a patient's thoughts, feelings and behavior to narrow down a diagnosis and rule out any potential complications. Anxiety disorders frequently coexist with other mental health issues, such as depression or substance abuse, making diagnosis more difficult.

- Contrast a patient's symptoms against the American Psychiatric Association's Diagnostic and Statistical Manual of Mental Disorders (DSM-5) to make a diagnosis of anxiety disorder.

Physical Symptoms of Depression

Fatigue or a Consistent Decrease in Energy Levels

Fatigue is a common side effect of depression. Depression-related fatigue can cause difficulty concentrating, moodiness and apathy.

Pain Tolerance is Reduced

Depression and pain frequently coexist together.

One 2015 study found a link between depression and decreased pain tolerance, while another 2010 study found that pain has a bigger influence on people who are depressed.

Although there is no clear cause-and-effect relationship between these two symptoms, it is crucial to analyze them together, especially if a doctor prescribes medication.

Back Pain or Aching Muscles

While frequently associated with poor posture or injuries, backaches can also be a sign of depressive symptoms.

Pain is the Way the Body Communicates

If a person is uncomfortable identifying and discussing troubling emotions such as sadness, rage and shame, this may cause feelings to materialize differently in the body. Depression can be caused by several factors, including genetics, childhood anxiety or trauma and chemical imbalances. People suffering from depression frequently require professional assistance, such as medications and psychotherapy.

Trauma-Related Physical and Emotional Problems

Trauma can have long-term consequences for a person's mental, physical and emotional well-being. People who have experienced abuse or other trauma are more likely to develop mental health problems such as:

- Anxiety problems
- Depression
- Post-traumatic stress disorder (PTSD)
- Abuse of alcohol or drugs
- Borderline personality disorder (BPD).

Abuse may have occurred as a child or as an adult. It could be emotional, verbal, physiological or sexual in nature.

Trauma can include extremely stressful situations such as sexual harassment, war, a natural catastrophe, the unexpected or violent death of a loved one or a severe medical problem.

The following are some of the long-term consequences of abuse or trauma:

- Nervousness, stress or fear at an extremely high level
- Alcoholism or drug abuse
- Anxiety
- Eating disorders
- Self-injury
- Suicide.

Trauma affects people differently, whether it is a specific moment, a chain of events or a long set of circumstances. Some individuals will clearly show signs of PTSD, but many others will exhibit resistant reactions or relatively brief idiopathic health consequences or implications that fall outside of diagnostic criteria.

The effects of trauma can be sophisticated, pervasive or outright harmful. Many factors, such as the individual's actions, the type and quality of the event(s), external influences and the impact of the trauma and social factors, influence how an incident affects a person.

Survivors' initial reactions to trauma are very complex and usually influenced by their own encounters, the availability of natural support systems and guardians, their resilience and life skills and the reactions of the greater surrounding community. Although reactions vary in severity, even the most severe reactions are organic responses to trauma and are not indicative of psychiatric disorders. How a patient copes with such an incident ranges from action-oriented to introspective and emotionally evocative to hesitant behaviors.

Clinically, the extent to which coping efforts effectively enable one to continue specific functions, manage emotions, maintain self-esteem and retain and enjoy interpersonal contacts is important. A previous mistake in traumatic stress psychology, especially with regard to collective or mass traumatic events, was the presumption that all survivors need to express and discuss their trauma-related emotions; more recent evidence has shown that survivors who choose not to handle their trauma are just as mentally healthy as those who do.

The most important recent consultation models suggest respecting the individual's coping strategies rather than favoring one over another.

Childhood Trauma and the Risk of Future Adversity

While tragic experiences can befall anyone, people are more likely to be deeply impacted by their experiences if they have been under some kind of pressure or stress, or if they have suffered from some other kind of trauma in the recent past.

Traumatic experiences can occur as a result of anything that interrupts a child's sense of safety, such as:

- An unstable or dangerous environment
- Separation from a parent
- Serious illness
- Invasive medical procedures
- Abuse, whether sexual, physical or verbal
- Neglect.

Childhood trauma can have serious and long-lasting consequences. When childhood abuse is not resolved, a feeling of dread and helplessness follows the child's growth and development, laying the groundwork for future trauma.

Even if trauma occurred many years ago, some steps can be taken to surmount the pain, restore psychological balance and help a person learn to trust and connect with others again.

Conclusion

Symptoms due to abuse or trauma and anxiety or depression are typically treated with various types of talk therapy, medication or both. Therapy with a professional counselor can help people work through their feelings and learn healthy coping strategies. Antidepressants and anti-anxiety medications may be prescribed in order to manage symptoms.

Complementary mind-body therapies—such as mindfulness and yoga—can now be used alongside conventional therapies, such as medications and mental therapy.

Chapter 15: Communicating with Patients About Their Course of Treatment

In this chapter, we will discuss the relationship between the health-care worker and the patient, specifically during the time of prescribing treatment. This chapter will highlight the various hurdles a physician might face during this phase and how to solve them. Also included in this chapter are tips for establishing a treatment plan with the patient.

Establishing Aims and Outcomes of Treatment in Collaboration With the Client

During the first discussion of treatment with the patient, a physician is required to provide information about the treatment plan in layman terms. The salient features of this discussion include the outline of the treatment and the expected outcome. This discussion aims to make sure the patient fully understands the doctor's recommended course of treatment.

When it has been established that the patient is aware of the textbook course of treatment, then the new goal of this discussion is to listen to the patient's concerns and adjust the treatment plan accordingly. However, physicians must keep in mind the actual priority of the treatment plan. They must not be swayed by minute patient concerns and must devise a convenient treatment route while also fulfilling the therapeutic goal of the treatment plan.

During this discussion, the physician needs to employ communication skills. For example, the physician should be comfortable with confronting any possible aggressive or annoying behavior exhibited by the patient. Furthermore, physicians should also display adequate empathy toward the patient's concerns.

Keeping the above in mind, the conclusion of this discussion should educate the patient about the treatment plan and what he or she can expect its results to be. Additionally, it should satisfy the concerns of the patient. Lastly, any appropriate adjustments should be made at this stage so as not to confuse either party later.

Setting Short- and Long-Term Counseling Goals That Are in Line With Patients' Diagnoses

Setting goals during the treatment phase of patients helps educate patients about their illness and how the treatment will alleviate their symptoms. A technique that yields even better results is adapting chronology into goal setting. All of this is to be done in accordance with the diagnosis.

It is important to understand that this strategy usually does not affect the functional outcome of the treatment but is actually utilized for fostering better understanding and stronger compliance between the patient and the therapy, which occurs because patients experience an enhanced sense of autonomy over their treatment. This practice also helps patients better manage their treatment.

Chronological goal setting involves dividing goals into short term and long term. Short-term goals are those that are to be achieved at equal intervals throughout the duration of treatment. They tend to be simpler and more repetitive. For example, during occupational therapy, patients are required to set small goals for themselves that they can achieve daily, e.g., taking a shower, making breakfast, etc. In the same example, a patient can set goals to make new friends, repair old relationships or switch jobs. These are examples of long-term goals, which are usually set to be achieved at the end of the treatment or during much longer intervals.

Identifying Hurdles Related to Goal Achievement

As discussed previously, communication is of utmost importance between physician-patient interactions since the whole principle of understanding the treatment and its goals depends on it. Therefore, gaps during communication are one of the first hurdles to be addressed.

Misuse of Medical Jargon

A skilled physician is able to measure a patient's level of understanding and adjust wording accordingly. But even then, it is safer to stick to using layman's language during patient interaction.

Language Barriers

Sometimes patients are unable to understand English; therefore, a skilled translator must be provided to correctly convey the physician's orders.

Dialect Barriers

It is possible that a patient might be well-versed in English but unable to understand the physician's accent or dialect. Therefore, it is the physician's job to identify any confusion and use paper and pencil as necessary to clearly convey the point.

Speech/Hearing Disability

Usually, differently-abled patients have translators with them when they make hospital visits, but if they don't, it is up to the physician to provide such aid. Also, the physician needs to make sure the medical advice is conveyed and understood correctly in case of any speech impairment.

Inability to Read/Write

Physicians may come across illiterate patients, and they should then identify a coping mechanism, such as using a pictogram for prescriptions.

Another obstacle during goal achievement is the personal outlook of a patient toward health-care workers. This can be attributed to a number of reasons, i.e., a previous bad experience in a health-care setting. To overcome this obstacle, the physician must first identify the discrepancy in the patient-physician interaction. Then the physician must counsel the patient, so he or she understands that not all hospital visits have to be the same. This can be done by showing empathy and humility during the conversation.

Further obstacles can be in the form of a hesitance to follow the treatment plan due to religious beliefs. Some religions prohibit certain things for their followers. This must be taken into account when treating patients. Respecting the differences between patients should be a priority. For example, a Hindu patient in need of a heart-valve transplant should be provided with an alternative to using bovine valves.

One more reason for hesitancy in following the treatment plan can be when a patient suffers from a prior illness or chronic illness. The fear of interaction between the two therapies is common. Therefore it is the patient's duty to inform his or her physician of any ongoing treatments.

Factors That Facilitate Goal Achievement

When interacting with patients, physicians must present themselves amicably by displaying kindness and compassion. During the interaction, the patient must feel like he or she is understood and respected. Additionally, when patients present concerns about the treatment plan, physicians must patiently reassure them and be clear and concise.

Health-care workers should be careful about keeping patients' information confidential. Strict laws are in place to protect patients' privacy, and the consequences of breaking those laws are severe.

Treatment should not be forced upon the patient. It is a basic rule for physicians to explain all possible treatment options but respect patients' wishes if they decline to adhere to any of the advice.

All of the above is significant because the image of the physician plays a great role in patient compliance and, consequently, in goal achievement.

In a contemporary clinical setting, one of the challenges that a physician faces is differentiating patients on an individual basis. Physicians should try to limit this practice as it is incredibly important to see each patient as an individual. This recognition is greatly beneficial when establishing the margins of a treatment plan. A physician should pay special attention to traits like ethnicity, religion, circumstance and financial background as these traits can influence a patient's adherence to the treatment plan.

Levels of Treatment

Primary Care

This term refers to the level of care a patient seeks in the initial stages of an illness. For example, the care the patient seeks when he or she visits the outpatient department. The illness is usually mild at this stage. However, when a patient goes to the emergency department for immediate intervention, this is also termed primary care. This kind of care can be provided by the outpatient department of any hospital or clinic.

Secondary Care

Secondary care is care given by a specialist through a referral from the primary care professional. The need for this kind of care usually arises when the illness is chronic and will not subside after a few visits. Therefore, the physicians that cater to these patients specialize in different fields related to the illness to provide broader knowledge and tailor the treatment plan accordingly.

Tertiary Care

This is the term used when a patient has been hospitalized. The illness is usually quite severe at this point. The key difference between secondary and tertiary care is that tertiary care patients cannot be managed at home. There is a need for special equipment and medicine that cannot be administered over the counter or orally. Examples of tertiary care procedures include renal dialysis, coronary artery bypass, neurosurgery, etc. All of these procedures require skilled personnel and specialized equipment, which can only be found at specialized medical centers.

When patients with chronic illnesses receive tertiary care, it is recommended that their primary care providers should be informed of these procedures to facilitate long-term management of their illness.

Quaternary Care

This term refers to diagnostical and therapeutic procedures that are not found in a conventional medical center. The equipment and/or medicine is highly specialized and is usually kept in a controlled facility, e.g., a laboratory. Additionally, this care is usually experimental and not widely used yet.

Conclusion

This chapter highlighted how a physician should communicate with a patient during the treatment phase. However, all of this knowledge and practice can go to waste if the patient does not adhere to the plan for the prescribed amount of time. There are numerous reasons that can contribute to noncompliance. The strategies mentioned to negate them must be practiced thoroughly. Above all, patients should be informed of the ill effects of their noncompliance. The physician must mention the course the illness is likely to take if left untreated. This should be done in a civil manner; the aim of this exercise is not to force patients to comply out of fear but rather to educate them, so they are able to make the right decision on their own. All of this is extremely beneficial in the case of long-term treatments.

Consider the following scenario: a patient is being counseled to have a laparoscopic gall bladder removal due to acute cholecystitis. The patient is hesitant to undergo surgery and is stubbornly asking for medicinal treatment. The physician then calmly explains that medication temporarily alleviates the pain but does not fix the problem, which is a malfunctioning gallbladder. The physician should explain that if the patient decides to opt out of the surgery, numerous events of emergent proportions could take place, e.g., gallbladder empyema, gallstone ileus, cholangitis, etc. However, the physician should end the explanation by stating that the final treatment decision rests with the patient.

Chapter 16: Guiding the Treatment Plan

Outline of a Basic Treatment Plan

History and counselor's assessment: This section includes information regarding what demographic the client belongs to, history of prior symptoms and respective diagnoses and details of previous diagnoses, e.g., onset, severity and treatment history.

Presenting complaints: This section refers to the current mental health complaints experienced by clients and any problems they are facing that prevent them from living normally.

Treatment contract: The treatment contract includes future references, such as a list of goals clients should ideally achieve if the therapy is to take place. It summarizes the treatment's advantage and is also a direct outline of the counselor and client's input.

Strengths: This section talks about the qualities of clients that will empower them in rough times. It is important to highlight such qualities to motivate clients to achieve their targets.

Modality, frequency and targets: Modality refers to what resources will be used to achieve a certain goal, and frequency refers to how often this goal is to be achieved, e.g., short-term goals are usually set daily, while long-term goals can be monthly or yearly.

Treatment goals: Setting goals is what makes the treatment plan succeed. These goals must be realistic and clear so clients can use them as stepping stones throughout the course of treatment. It is important that these goals be measurable.

Objectives: Objectives are a subcategory of goals. Dividing goals into smaller categories will help make the targets more attainable. It will also heighten clients' motivation toward achieving larger goals.

Progress and outcomes: It is up to counselors to meticulously document clients' progress throughout the course of treatment. This is done in order to provide adequate information when setting future targets. Also, it is helpful when briefing clients about their progress and using their input in establishing future outcomes. Furthermore, keeping track of progress will help identify redundant modalities, which will then be eliminated in future planning.

Stages of Group Therapy

This section will discuss the advantages of group therapy and the different roles of the counselor and the group members during the four stages of group therapy. The division into four stages is necessary because, throughout therapy, purposes and expectations change, and it is important to acknowledge these changes when they arise.

Initial Stage

This is the first stage of group therapy. This stage is initiated through introductions between the different group members as well as the counselors. After the basic greetings, the counselor explains what the different members can expect from the group, e.g., trust roles and goals. Any issues that arise need to be addressed by the counselor at this stage. These issues can manifest as cultural/religious concerns as well as concerns about confidentiality.

The counselor needs to explain the process and the expected milestones of the therapy. This is done to clarify any confusion and set a clear expectation for group members.

The above techniques are employed throughout therapy, but it is critical to establish them during the initial stages so that everyone knows their place in the coming meetings.

Transition Stage

This stage is the most difficult for both the group members and the counselor. It involves active participation from all the members, while the counselor plays the role of mediator. It may be difficult because members are nervous and anxious about sharing personal information with strangers. They naturally fear a breach of confidentiality—which has been addressed during the initial stage—and also the judgment of others. This can manifest as many kinds of aggressive or passive-aggressive behaviors among the group members.

Members will initially tend to compete for attention and recognition. They will carry this out by influencing beta group members and enforcing their opinion strongly. This usually leads to confrontation and conflict. And as a result of this, divisions might form in the group. Unsolicited comments and a harsh tone of voice can bring about overly emotional responses by some members. Tensions can also manifest when group members are present involuntarily or have social anxiety tendencies.

All of the above are a normal part of the transitional stage. The outcome of such events depends entirely on how the counselor mediates the situations. The right steps can be taken by allowing underlying tensions to surface and assisting in solving them collaboratively. The counselor should also learn to identify smaller non-issues and curb them at the right time and with the right tone of enforcement.

Working Stage

After the transitional stage, the real purpose of group therapy is addressed. During this stage, group members will feel more comfortable around each other. Offensive remarks and overly emotional responses will be minimal. The strategy will start to become more cohesive as deeper issues start to surface and various members start to feel a sense of relatability toward each other. Confrontations will become rarer.

Behaviors that are more commonly seen at this stage include appreciation and acceptance of opinions, a suggestion of practical approaches and pinpointing toxic traits or issues without upheaval. Members will usually wait for their turn to talk, and quieter members will actively participate in the discussions.

At this stage, the counselor's task becomes much easier. A skilled counselor will have a minimal say during this stage. He or she will allow the group to identify and solve issues on its own. The counselor will only participate in directing the flow of conversation and highlight points that might otherwise be missed. He or she will encourage the building of a positive group identity and will challenge the boundaries of the group. All of this can only be done if the counselor can pick up verbal and nonverbal cues during the meetings.

Final Stage

This stage includes working on the ideas and behaviors learned from the previous group discussions. Members of the group will begin to actively make changes in their lives according to the group's direction and provide feedback and accept critique. The reviews are more frequent in this stage as the changes are being brought about. Diversity blooms and is not only accepted but also welcomed.

At this point, the counselor can guide the members toward positive reinforcements that haven't been discussed yet. He or she may choose to help the members to self-critique. Additionally, the counselor must make newer members feel at home. Some counselors organize small ceremonies or celebrations when members achieve certain milestones.

The final stage also consists of the adjourning practices in a group. A sense of finality falls upon the group. It is the counselor's job to give feedback and encourage others to do the same. Sometimes certain group members want to continue with group therapy. The counselor should then provide an additional resource for them to be transferred elsewhere.

The group is asked to reflect on its experiences and to address unfinished issues. Group members can also choose to share how they will apply their experiences in their daily lives.

The counselor should remind all group members of the confidentiality they discussed in the earlier sessions. A feeling of sadness is natural at the end. The counselor must address this and share coping mechanisms.

Issues With the Termination Process

The termination process is the term used to refer to the ending of the relationship between the counselor and client. The nature of this ending can be surprising or scheduled.

It is important to differentiate between termination and abandonment. The term abandonment is used when a therapeutic relationship is ended inappropriately. It fails to provide the client with the correct treatment during or after the termination.

The following are methods employed to avoid the termination process turning into abandonment.

Provide Informed Consent

Informed consent refers to getting permission from the client and sharing all relevant information about the services being offered. It is vital to share information with the client that pertains to the time the counselor is available. This should be made clear in terms of weeks or months.

Informed consent is crucial because it allows clients to be prepared when it's time to end meetings or to refrain from counseling if they feel the abrupt conclusion might not work in their favor.

Besides this, any factor that is likely to affect the course of treatment must be disclosed in the initial session of therapy.

Set Criteria for Completion

Setting goals related to the client's concerns is a must in order to gauge the closure of sessions so that when that time occurs, no discrepancies will appear between the client and counselor's point of view.

These goals should be modified throughout therapy to keep up with changing circumstances, but this does not excuse either party from establishing these goals in the first place to avoid problems.

Make Arrangements for Counselor-Initiated Interruptions

Interruptions of any nature are only natural. However, it is the counselor's job to prepare for any such events before they occur.

Skilled counselors are able to gauge when clients are benefitting from treatment. If counselors sense that something is amiss, it is their ethical duty to terminate the process. Other ethical concerns that can lead to termination include developing or discovering multiple relationships between the client and counselor.

Sometimes the client or another person related to the client can hold ill will toward the counselor due to the nature of the relationship between the counselor and client, as well as the confidentiality aspect. This can lead to threatening situations in which the only resolution is to terminate the process.

Of course, issues like counselor illness, disability or fitness can also lead to termination. In all of the situations above, the counselor must provide personnel for the client to be referred to.

Make Arrangements for Client-Initiated Interruptions

Just like counselor-initiated interruptions are natural, so are client-initiated interruptions. Clients can run into multiple problems throughout their tenure with a counselor, such as personal problems that the counselor has no control over, such as financial limitations (due to a loss of job) and loss of insurance coverage. While it is difficult to anticipate such events at the beginning of the counseling process, it is up to the counselor to behave appropriately when faced with these situations and to offer adequate alternates.

Another reason for client-initiated termination includes personal dissatisfaction with the counselor or the client moving to a different locality.

Follow-Up Care

This term can refer to follow-up after termination or follow-up after discharge from a facility.

In terms of termination, if the client's issue has been resolved, the need for follow-up is minimal. But in any other case leading to termination, the counselor is obligated to provide the client with a list of appropriate alternatives that can come in the form of colleagues or facilities.

While discharge from a facility is more complicated, the solution, again, is to not only provide alternate counseling but to ensure the client benefits from it. This can be challenging because the client is leaving behind an intense support system.

Chapter 17: Aligning Treatment According to Patient Profile

Psychodynamic Theory

This theory is also sometimes called the "historical perspective." It is based on the buildup of unconscious forces (from past experiences and relationships) that drive a person's present behavior. Unfinished thought processes from dysfunctional relationships and detrimental experiences become the unconscious drive behind a person's actions.

Sigmund Freud was a prominent name in the development of this theory. He designed the techniques that are still used today to perform psychoanalysis on a subject. Some examples of these techniques are dream analysis (using the subject's dream to find clues about the person's unconscious thought process), free association (conversing with the subject without hindering the flow of conversation, no matter what the topic of discussion) and transference (encouragement of projection of feelings toward the therapist).

Today, psychoanalytic counselors practice this theory by encouraging their patients to realize the connection between their conscious and unconscious minds. They help their patients explore the negative influences in their past events, such as traumatic childhood experiences, to help reveal connections that could be altered to strengthen the healing process.

This theory has been researched and practiced vigorously throughout the years. As a result, now we are aware of this practice's positive effects on the patient's brain. But these changes aren't achieved in the short term; rather, it takes months and years to make these changes. Thus, psychodynamic theory is a long-term strategy because it addresses the root cause of the problem, not superficial issues. Moreover, it strives to help clients understand themselves–and that is not always so simple.

Below are some extensions of psychodynamic theory:

Attachment Therapy

Attachment therapy was first theorized in the 1960s by British psychologist John Bowlby. This kind of therapy was thought of as a process-oriented type of counseling. It involved a strong client-therapist relationship, which was used to improve the client's trust levels in relation to their family. Such a relationship was Bowlby's idea. He suggested that a person needed to have a significant attachment to at least one caregiver in childhood to live a fully functioning life with healthy physical and emotional relationships in adult life. This therapy is usually used to treat anxiety disorders and depression.

Attachment therapy can be exercised through numerous types of therapy, e.g., individual, family, couples and group. It is also commonly used with children who have PTSD from their childhood experiences (sexual abuse, physical abuse, etc.). For instance, children in foster care, adoptees, children of depressed parents and children with divorced parents may exhibit signs of PTSD and require counseling. This theory has also been proven helpful for teenagers who are dealing with depression or have suicidal ideations.

The therapist works with both the child and his/her family in personal and group therapy, respectively. This is done to gauge the success of the personal therapy and strengthens the child-parent bond.

When the client is an adult, the family is not conventionally involved, so the therapist establishes a firm bond with the client. This bond encourages the client to open up about past experiences and address these issues' influence on present problems in the person's life.

Object-Relation Therapy

The theory of object-relation therapy is not very different from attachment therapy theory. It states that a person is motivated by the urge to have contact with other people, in other words, to form relationships. This varies from Freud's belief that people are primarily motivated by sexual urges.

Like attachment therapy theory, object-relation therapy aims to address trauma from the early stages of life that contribute to present-life issues. These issues usually show themselves as problems in social interactions. Another similarity between the two approaches is the need for a strong client-therapist bond.

In the term object-relation therapy, the word "object" does not refer to inanimate objects but rather to significant others or parents. However, sometimes "object" can also be used to refer to a part of a specific person.

Object-relation therapy helps clients recover suppressed objects from their past that are then incorporated into their daily lives to make their living experience more grounded. This process of self-discovery often uncovers different facets of past objects (positive and negative). In this situation, the counselor helps clients come to terms with both aspects and integrate them into their lives for a more realistic perspective. Furthermore, these assets lessen the internal conflict a client might be facing.

The techniques the counselor uses in object-relation therapy are not all that different from the previously described therapies. In the beginning, counselors listen to clients talk about themselves and topics that the clients feel are important, such as family background, needs, fears and hopes. Sharing such information strengthens the client-counselor bond. Consequently, counselors can move on to more sensitive or carefully guarded topics that might be the cause of present problematic tendencies. Counselors can then guide their clients to use this information to promote greater self-awareness and understanding.

During the course of therapy, counselors are able to gauge how their clients interact and react around other people in their lives by observing their general behavior. As a rule, counselors should always respond empathetically toward clients during their sessions. This technique strengths clients' ability to form healthy relationships outside of the counseling sessions. Therefore, the success of this kind of therapy is greatly influenced by the client-counselor relationship.

It is now understood that object-relation therapy is better used synergistically with pharmaceutical support, as it is a lengthy process on its own. The delayed results are seen as a setback in certain cases where clients are dealing with substance addictions, suicidal tendencies, etc.

Psychoanalytic Therapy

Austrian psychologist Sigmund Freud first coined the term "psychoanalytic therapy" back in the late nineteenth century. All of the above-mentioned theories of therapy have been created by psychoanalysis. Freud was the first to establish that present psychological issues are deeply rooted in a person's past unconscious internal conflicts. In psychoanalysis, along with deep introspection, another technique of amplifying the ego's functioning is used to lessen the control of biological drives that are causing present-day issues.

Traditionally, counselors took a completely anonymous role in their clients' treatment. They almost never disclosed or discussed anything about themselves. This is because the focus of psychoanalysis (at that time) was to revamp the core personality of a client rather than alleviate present symptoms. This usually took place over a long period of time. Nowadays, counselors no longer take this approach because the goal of therapy has changed.

The following techniques are now used when practicing psychoanalysis:

Free Association

This technique was highly recommended by Freud. It involves clients speaking freely about anything and everything that crosses their mind during the session. While a client is speaking, counselors are advised not to pass any judgment or offer any input but instead pay full attention to every detail of the client's words and feelings. Furthermore, counselors should observe clients' behavior and other unconscious cues hidden behind their words and slips of the tongue (known as a Freudian Slip in psychoanalysis, this can indicate unconscious conflicts).

Another behavior counselors need to watch out for is self-interruption, which could indicate the development of anxiety-inducing thoughts. After noting all these behaviors, counselors should help clients gain greater insight into their thought processes. Classically, free association therapy was practiced with the client lying on a couch while the counselor sat out of sight, but this is no longer the case.

Dream Analysis

Freud believed dreams were "the royal road to the unconscious" because they revealed people's unconscious desires and fears that were considered unconventional to their conscious minds. In the exercise of dream analysis, clients are asked to vocalize every detail of their dreams and any reflections they have about them. Counselors then help the clients differentiate between the conscious and the unconscious signs in the dream. These signs are used as a clue to learn more about the unconscious mind. These are called "manifest content" and "latent content," respectively.

Resistance Analysis

In psychoanalysis, resistance is defined as the attempt to suppress anxiety-provoking thoughts from entering the conscious mind. This suppression can manifest in many forms, such as when a client is consistently late for an appointment or when someone refuses to answer questions during the session. This is normally seen as a hindrance, but in resistance analysis, counselors can use these cues to gain insight into clients' internal conflicts. Counselors can then assist clients in understanding and overcoming this resistive behavior to fully benefit from the therapeutic process and work through the internal conflict.

Transference Analysis

Transference analysis is one of the more popular techniques that Freud developed. It is commonly used in other kinds of therapies too. Essentially, it calls for counselors to offer themselves as a blank canvas for clients to project their feelings and thoughts upon. This process takes time, and it is of utmost importance for counselors to accept these projections without any resistance; rather, they should encourage it by presenting themselves as empathetic and attentive listeners. This attention leads to clients relocating unconscious feelings that may previously have been attached to a significant other (e.g., parent) onto the counselor. This specific action is called transference, and through this, clients reexperience past emotions and events. Counselors then help their clients dissect these behaviors and relate them to their present issues. In this way, the clients become more aware of the effect of their past experiences on their present problems.

Classic forms of psychoanalysis are rarely used nowadays. Modern changes include limiting the time period of the therapy, increasing client-counselor interactions, shifting the focus from identity to how the ego functions and alleviating current symptoms instead of treating early childhood problems. Now, psychoanalysis is used to treat people who suffer from phobias, anxiety disorders and depression. However, it is important to mention that it is still not the first-line treatment for such disorders—cognitive-behavioral therapy is used instead.

Adlerian Therapy

This type of short-term therapy was developed by psychologist Alfred Adler. His goal was to understand the growth of a singular personality while also focusing on the interconnections between humans. Adler's research was dedicated to inferiority complexes and the effects of encouragement and disapproval on a person's psyche. He believed there was a fine line between the amount of inferiority felt by a person. Too much could result in neurotic behavior, but just enough acted as a great motivating tool.

Adlerian therapy has no limitations on its use. Because of its ideal time frame, it can be used to treat a number of disorders. It has also proven beneficial for multiple age groups.

Like all kinds of therapy, the first stage of Adlerian therapy is establishing a strong bond with the therapist. This is called "engagement." In the second stage, the counselor then uses the information exchanged in this phase to assess the client's personal history, emphasizing the number of siblings, childhood experiences and birth order. The third stage is called "insight." This is when the counselor helps the client build perspective on his or her own life. And then, in the "reorientation" stage, the counselor encourages the client to apply the newly developed perspective to his or her current situation. This exercise helps the client change his or her outlook to a more positive one, which helps during interpersonal interactions.

The major focus of Adlerian therapy is on the client's ability to fit into society. Adler believed that the root causes of social anxiety are deeply rooted in the client's place in a family. This is why Adlerian therapists normally practice in places like schools, clinics and corporate offices. These counselors specialize in encouragement and in bringing about a positive outlook.

Addiction Therapy

The process of substance addiction recovery is a difficult one. Substance abusers usually find it very difficult to seek help, so a counselor must take time to form a strong counselor-client bond. The therapy will only be beneficial if a client trusts the counselor fully.

Recovery from substance addiction is difficult, and one of the main reasons for this difficulty is the failure of clients to recognize their patterns of abuse. It falls to the counselor to guide clients through the stage of acceptance so that clients learn to acknowledge their problems before fixing them.

After clients have reached the acceptance phase, they can motivate themselves toward recovery with the counselor's help. At this stage, the counselor plays a mostly supportive role by displaying warmth, friendliness, respectfulness, empathy, kindness, etc. The counselor should avoid abrupt and confrontational behavior as studies have shown this kind of persona can have a negative impact on the client's motivation.

Relapse is a major issue during substance abuse therapy. Studies have shown that 40–60% of patients relapse after their first round of abstinence. Therefore, it is the counselor's job to recognize if a client has truly made the decision to abstain. When this has been achieved, the counselor can create a thorough relapse-prevention program that is designed exclusively for the client.

A relapse-prevention plan should include a detailed account of the patient's involvement with drugs. It should also include the client's previous relapses. More details about relapses include warning signs and targeted management of these warning signs once they are seen. The counselor should list family members and friends as a part of the client's support system since, sometimes, targeted management includes resorting to such people for advice or help. Specific lifestyle changes that promote the well-being of the client should also be mentioned in the plan. Lastly, the relapse prevention plan must contain an *emergency* relapse plan.

As mentioned before, the family takes on a big role during a client's recovery from substance abuse. It is important for the counselor to address the members who are in close contact with the client and offer them the support they need. The counselor can do this by briefing family members about the process, keeping them updated on the client's recovery and informing them about how they can address this issue at home. It is common for family members to be hesitant about confronting a client about his or her problems. The counselor's job is to teach family members techniques that are not too aggressive but, at the same time, not too evasive. Furthermore, the counselor can provide information on local support groups and hold family therapy sessions.

By providing the client's support system members with adequate information on how to help the client during the different phases of recovery, the counselor greatly increases the chances of a successful recovery.

Group therapies like Alcoholics Anonymous and Narcotic Anonymous can act as conjunctive therapy for the clients. These groups can add an additional tier of answerability, as well as provide different perspectives on their own problems. Meeting people who suffer from the same problem often motivates the client to act in the right direction too.

Family Therapy

Family therapy is a term that refers to solving familial issues and nurturing healthy relationships between family members. Some situations in which family therapy is beneficial include major life transitions, sickness of a family member and behavioral problems in family members. The fundamental principle of family therapy involves understanding an individual's problem in relation to his or her role in the larger family unit. In order to understand the full scope of such a problem, it is vital to understand the dynamic of the group, i.e., how family functions influence the client's problem. The techniques to combat such issues can be varied, depending on the client's needs. They include interpersonal, behavioral or cognitive therapy.

A common reason to seek family therapy is behavioral issues in children. Children are sometimes unable to express themselves fully. In cases like these, it is helpful for family members to step in. During the course of therapy, these members provide the context for the child's problem, as well as gain advice from the counselor on how to assist with the child's treatment. It is essential to note that family members are not exclusively blood relatives of the client but can also be people who play a prolonged supportive role in the client's life.

The following are types of family therapy suited for the different needs of the client:

Bowenian Therapy

This type of therapy focuses more on gaining insight into the client's issue rather than resolving it. Bowen believed there were two forces at large in a relationship between family members: togetherness and individuality. According to him, these two forces need to be in balance for a person to form healthy relationships in the future. As a result, Bowenian therapy focuses on balancing these two forces in family units.

Structural Therapy

This kind of therapy concentrates on strengthening and correcting the structure of a family. It ensures parents have full autonomy and that all members of the family form appropriate boundaries. In this type of therapy, it is common for the counselor to closely observe the family's daily workings. Then the counselor uses his or her observations to help the family navigate their issues and strengthen their ties.

Systemic Therapy

This model focuses on the unconscious cues exhibited by the family and their explanations. The counselor plays a distant role; he or she doesn't hinder the family's movements, even if they're detrimental. Instead, the counselor allows the family to reach a civil conclusion on their own. This resolution can have positive effects on the existing problems between family members.

Strategic Therapy

Strategic therapy is short-term therapy because it is more direct than the others. The counselor takes the leading role, allowing the leading family members to express themselves more openly without any tension or obligations. The rest of the members are advised to change their behaviors to shift the dynamic of the family. This advice usually helps the family members gain insight into why they each behave a certain way, helping them understand each other better.

The Aim of Family Therapy

The broad goal of family therapy is to strengthen the ties between all family members equally while simultaneously solving any major issues causing tensions between them and the client. The goal is also to enhance the mental and emotional well-being of the client in relation to the family.

Counselors achieve these goals by promoting open communication between family members, which is the key to solving and understanding family conflicts. It creates an amiable environment for all the members.

Below are some scenarios in which therapy is helpful:

- **A family member has been diagnosed with a mental illness, such as schizophrenia or Alzheimer's disease** – The counselor's role is to educate the family members about the illness. He or she should give them a detailed description of how the illness will proceed, as well as a list of support groups for the respective illness.

- **Issues stemming from cross-generational gaps** – Sometimes parents and grandparents live together, a couple raises their children and takes care of their parents under the same roof or children are raised by their grandparents. The goal is to provide effective tools for communication and encourage family members to employ these tools to set boundaries and maintain healthy relationships.

- **Families that do not fit into social norms, such as unmarried parents, gay couples, single parents** – In this example, the core issues are external, not internal. Problems can arise in the form of problematic neighborhoods, judgmental society, etc. The counselor should recommend coping mechanisms to deal with such problems.

- **Family members who come from mixed backgrounds, such as parents of different races, religions, etc.** – It is common for the children of such couples to have an identity crisis at some point in their lives. A counselor should help prevent such occurrences by advising the parents on how to deal with their differences and not to project their beliefs on their children.

Chapter 18: Counseling Interventions

Therapeutic Alliance

The term therapeutic alliance (or working alliance) refers to the characteristics of the interaction between a counselor and a client. Therapeutic alliance is a vital part of the therapeutic process and can significantly influence treatment results. Once a strong therapeutic alliance has been established, the counselor can then take steps toward offering patient-centered care. This is when the counselor steps down from the decision-making role and becomes a mediator for clients to accomplish their targets. The counselor further facilitates clients by encouraging them to play a more active role in their treatment so that the road to recovery is a result of collaboration.

The following is a list of factors involved in establishing a strong therapeutic alliance:

A Judgment-Free Zone

A therapeutic alliance is based on security and nonjudgment. In order for clients to accomplish their targets—this could vary from recovering from childhood trauma to achieving inner peace—it is vital for them to know they can share all their thoughts and emotions with the counselor. Clients must realize that they can be vulnerable in their therapy sessions. It is common for clients to seek therapy because of hypercritical experiences. The inducers of such a situation can sometimes be the clients themselves.

The therapeutic process will only be effective once the counselor provides a safe space in which there are no obligations or deadlines for clients to meet. The counselor must treat patients at their own desired pace.

Adequate Communication

Therapy sessions are not only ways to address trauma but also ways to learn life skills. One of these skills is communication. People who seek therapy often have problems communicating with their loved ones. This has a detrimental effect on their relationships. To counter this, a counselor can encourage open conversation within therapy sessions. This will allow clients to exercise their communication ability, which will improve in time. Certain traits of conversation prove particularly difficult to encourage, e.g., assertiveness, confrontation and criticism. It is up to the counselor to pay special attention to these areas. Note that a counselor must also have good communication skills in order to achieve a successful relationship with clients.

Collaboration

It is vital to a strong therapeutic alliance that the nature of the relationship between the counselor and client be collaborative. A therapeutic alliance in which the counselor plays the figurehead is now obsolete. Today, both the client and the counselor need to work as a team to come up with solutions and see them through. This reinforces the concept that the actual action needed for the betterment of the client's life is up to the individual. The counselor's role in the sessions is only to assist, guide and ensure a safe and confidential environment for the exposure of the client's emotions and thoughts. It is critical for clients to understand that they alone hold the key to their successful recovery.

Amiable Termination

At the end of the therapeutic process, it is the counselor's duty to make the parting with the client as amiable as possible. After all, the therapeutic alliance was also one of the relationships in the client's life, and the counselor must address the different needs of the client at the end of such a journey. For example, sometimes clients want to continue therapy but are restricted by financial ability. In this scenario, the counselor should provide the client with suitable alternatives.

Support Systems

A support system is a casual network an individual relies on for emotional and practical support. This support network usually includes family, friends, coworkers, teammates, voluntary organizations and religious groups, etc.

The following are some benefits of an adequate support system:

Social Support

Often a person suffering from mental illness does not do well in isolation. The brain naturally works in an antagonistic manner during vulnerable moments. This results in detrimental ideations that highlight insecurities, heighten anxiety, depression and other conditions.

The above scenario can be prevented by securing an adequate support system for clients. This shifts the conscious focus of clients onto something other than themselves. This can be achieved in many forms. For example, just a simple interaction at a grocery store can distract the mind, but an even better strategy would be a prolonged interaction with a close companion. Not only will this act as a distraction, but a companion can serve as an advisor in the time of need. Furthermore, companions might be in need of advice themselves, so the client can exercise problem-solving skills with them.

Unprompted Check-Ins

It is common for a client who's going through a particularly tough mental health episode to become unwilling to interact with the outside world, even in times of need. Clients might find themselves increasing their isolation by missing their appointments, canceling get-togethers, etc.

A good support system will allow clients to deal with their situation alone at first since it is of utmost importance that clients follow their own time frame. However, they must also be aware of the fine line between healthy isolation and social withdrawal.

It falls to the support system to check up on clients when they refuse to reach out to anyone. This wake-up call is sometimes necessary to jolt clients out of a bad mental health episode.

Positive Influence

Unprompted check-ins usually cause a positive shift in the client's behavior because they act as encouragement. Examples are not just limited to surprise visits or texts but can also include a spouse making breakfast, a coworker sharing a drink after work, etc.

It is important to note that these actions are not always welcomed by clients. Sometimes their mental health episodes make them feel irritated by such behavior. But a good support system refuses to back down until the client is on the right track again. The support system, as well as the client, needs to understand that these actions can be lifesavers.

Healthy Distractions

Not all clients are the same. Some value their privacy more than others, so the intrusions caused by family therapy may cause them distress. This is usually caused by the fear of confronting their loved ones about the problems they are facing. This is a valid concern as it is not always easy to explain mental health episodes. Sometimes clients are unsure of what the cause is.

In this situation, it is important for the members of the support system to handle their visits tactfully. They should present themselves as a healthy distraction (offering the client a trip to go hiking or asking him or her to join a yoga class, etc.) rather than unhealthy distractions, i.e., alcohol abuse, illegal drugs, etc.

Referrals and Feedback

Once a therapeutic alliance is formed with the client, a counselor must constantly evaluate the client's behavior for positive and negative changes. The counselor must then analyze these changes and give feedback to the client. During the feedback process, the counselor must gain input from the client's point of view too. This will help the counselor assess further progress and to determine how accurate his or her analysis is.

A counselor can receive feedback on the client's progress through many routes. If the client allows it, the counselor can contact members of the client's support group to seek their opinion of the client's well-being. Or a spouse or family member can contact the counselor to seek advice on how to handle the client during mental health episodes.

Furthermore, the counselor can refer the client to support groups that provide specific help for his or her problems. Clients benefit from such groups as they are able to relate to other people who are dealing with the same problems. Additionally, the counselor can contact the group therapist to find out more about the client's progress.

Chapter 19: Ensuring the Health, Safety and Comfort of Patients

Multicultural Counseling

Multicultural counseling came into existence in the late seventies when the Association for Multicultural Counseling and Development (AMCD) was established. The goal of this establishment was to recognize that there is a large human diversity in the country, and the same quality of care provided to the majority should also be available to minorities.

Multicultural counseling is the practice of addressing issues like racism, ethnic cleansing, historical oppression, etc. A counselor should be able to come up with adequate solutions to a client's problem. The fact that the client's challenges are different from those of the counselor's own challenges should not be a hindrance in this practice. Therefore, it is critical that counselors in this field understand that minorities have different perspectives and work with their clients to accommodate this perspective.

The counselor needs to understand the various factors that lead to different perspectives, such as religious beliefs, traditional practices, socioeconomic status, disabilities, sexual orientation and more.

It is important to note that multicultural counseling is not exclusive to a specific type of counselor but is a mindset that counselors of all types can employ in their practice to better assist their clients.

A counselor's journey toward successful multicultural counseling starts in undergraduate school. During the course of their learning, counselors are exposed to different therapeutic strategies that are aligned with the different ideas and beliefs of various minorities. They are then able to bring this theoretical knowledge into practice during their tenure as certified counselors. Additionally, counselors must also examine their inner thoughts and biases, which are a result of their background influences and upbringing. Counselors must keep revisiting these biases throughout their education and career to make sure they provide a consistent level of care to their clients.

Issues Dealt with in Multicultural Counseling

Systemic Racism

Racism is rooted in America's foundation, dating back to the arrival of the first slaves. Even today, the majority of the prison population is of African American descent. This pattern of racism can be seen in government institutions, corporate offices, schools and many other communities.

Ableism

Ableism refers to people who suffer from discrimination due to disabilities. This is yet another issue multicultural counselors are faced with. Although the outlook on people with disabilities has changed, they can still be victims of discrimination in the workplace, society, etc.

Religious Differences

A wide variety of belief systems are practiced in America. Multicultural counselors are specially trained to make sure they don't violate their clients' rights to believe as they choose.

Importance of Cultural Competence

Cultural competence is necessary to better understand a client's specific problems. An example of this would be when a client presents a problem relating to socioeconomic status. The person might be suffering financially. A counselor's solution to the client's problem might not be adequate because the counselor comes from a wealthy background. The failure to recognize the difference in their experiences is a shortcoming on the counselor's part. In order to avoid this, the counselor must determine a solution by keeping a client's needs and cultural competency in mind.

Multicultural Counseling Skills

As mentioned above, the multiple skills needed to practice multicultural counseling correctly are gained through the education and work experience of a counselor.

Interpersonal Abilities

Counselors must be able to connect to their clients on a fundamental level. This not only ensures a better therapeutic experience for the client but also allows the client to open up more easily, providing the counselor with further insight into the client's struggles. These findings are obviously beneficial for the overall therapeutic process. Skills like listening, responding and thoughtful inquiry are very important in order to achieve a fruitful conversation. The topic of conversation can easily vary due to the influence of a person's background, feelings, emotions and views. During the conversation, it is important for the counselor to be able to read body language and identify hidden cues.

Cultural Awareness

Cultural awareness is a particularly important skill for a counselor to possess as it is a gateway to understanding how different communities shape a person's view of the world. It specifically refers to the understanding that characteristics of culture do not only include physical appearance or skin color but also beliefs, interests, traditions and so much more. A counselor must understand cultural differences and the effect they have on their clients' relationships and experiences. In order to better understand such a phenomenon, counselors must look within themselves and understand how their own culture has affected their personal growth.

Sensitivity

It is up to counselors to uncover the trauma and suffering their clients have gone through. Counselors must approach sensitive topics with tact and care. They must make sure the client's wishes are always respected. If the issue is too sensitive, or the client is not forthcoming with his or her experiences, the counselor must find alternate methods to coax the client into opening up.

Understanding

Implicit in all of these skills is an understanding of why they are important. Multicultural counseling is about more than practicing these skills and being kind. It is also about understanding clients on a deep level—not only being sensitive but also recognizing why that sensitivity is necessary for the counselor-client relationship, as well as outside of the office.

In order for counselors to become successful, they must acquire a basic understanding of why all of the above-mentioned traits are of importance. Counseling is not limited to being a skilled and respectful listener; it is also about comprehending the client's issues and experiences and how they all relate to each other. Counselors are only able to provide successful solutions once they are able to connect the dots themselves.

Empathy

For counselors to practice cultural competence properly, they must be able to adequately understand their clients' perspectives. Once they understand this, they can then share the clients' feelings and develop the strong bond needed to yield positive results. A counselor must know how to use empathy in a professional yet understanding manner.

Counseling During Time of Crisis

In counseling, the term "crisis" refers to a traumatic event or experience in an individual's life and the person's response to it. Examples can vary from going through puberty to suffering from the aftermath of a natural disaster.

Crisis counseling's purpose is to offer assistance to people living through the traumatic experience as well as coping with it in the future. This practice dates back all the way to WWI. Before this practice was established, soldiers with symptoms of psychological trauma were seen as weak, disloyal or unfit for service. When crisis counseling became the norm, people realized that veterans who got counseling coped much better than the ones who did not.

Elements of Crisis Counseling

Crisis counseling is similar to psychotherapy in the sense that it also involves meticulous assessment and analysis to provide clients with suitable treatment, but the major difference is that the field is more specific. Psychotherapy is suitable for long-term clients who are unsure about the origin of their issues and require a long, slow healing process that is devised by assessing a large range of information and past history. In comparison, crisis counseling addresses the most immediate event and a client's thoughts and reactions toward that event only. Great care needs to be taken concerning the client's safety and immediate needs during this time.

There are many different techniques used in crisis counseling.

Analyzing the Situation

Counselors should be able to sense the nature of the problem when talking to the client while also presenting themselves as empathetic listeners. Counselors must show acceptance and support and should not pass judgment on the content of the client's conversation. Again, safety should be the top priority, and it is the counselor's duty to provide this secure environment.

Education

It is vital for counselors to provide clients and their support systems with adequate information on how to cope with a client's current situation. A counselor does this by reassuring clients that their response is completely normal and temporary. Furthermore, counselors advise their clients on how to reduce the damage resulting from their current problems.

Offering Support

Offering support is a practice that is not limited to just crisis counseling; clients may seek counseling for this sole purpose. The counselor's ability to provide stabilization, support and helpful resources is of great benefit to clients. This could make the key difference in the time frame of their road to recovery. If a counselor identifies the right time to offer the appropriate support, a client may achieve a better quality of life much sooner.

A counselor can practice this by actively listening to clients and providing an empathetic and nonjudgmental response. This will reduce clients' tensions, which will improve their coping skills. It is a fact that when clients are in crisis, it is beneficial for them to depend on supportive individuals. This is a healthy dependency, unlike that of drugs and alcohol.

Developing Coping Skills

The support and resources provided by a counselor are an effective way of dealing with the situation in the present. However, counselors must equip their clients for dealing with the event and its memories in the future too. Traumatic events tend to have a lasting effect. If these effects are not dealt with properly, they could cause clients to relapse into their trauma again.

Improving clients' coping mechanisms involves assisting them in exploring multiple solutions to their problems, such as using different techniques to manage a panic attack, stress reduction techniques and encouraging a positive outlook.

Teaching clients these skills will help them in a temporary situation, but it is important to instill within them a commitment to recover from the event and let that chapter of their life close.

Psychoeducation

This term refers to the practice of delivering information and education to those receiving counseling services, i.e., individuals who suffer from mental or terminal illnesses and their families. This concept dates back to the twentieth century, but only now has it come into common practice.

Aims of Psychoeducation

The primary goal of psychoeducation is to assist clients in understanding their illnesses and learning how to cope with them. Clients with a clearer understanding of their illness tend to be better equipped for facing difficulties. For example, a study showed that integrating psychoeducation into a schizophrenic client's treatment process reduced hospitalizations.

Many clients know very little about their illness at the time of diagnosis. Sometimes clients turn to the internet to find out more. However, not all the information they come across is accurate and it may intimidate them, put them off of therapy or have a detrimental effect on a patient's recovery. This is why counselors must take over as the font of knowledge for their clients. Counselors can provide reference materials after assessing their patients' mentality.

The following are some ways counselors can integrate psychoeducation into their practice:

- Inform clients about how their health condition might impact their future life and help them develop coping mechanisms to aid a better quality of life
- Ask the prescribing psychiatrist to explain the workings of the medication prescribed, side effects and when the client can expect results
- Provide the client's support system with helpful material that will guide them about what to expect during different phases of the client's recovery
- Refer the client to classes or groups designed to enhance the therapeutic experience by creating an environment in which the person can share strategies with people like him or herself
- Recommend educational material to further increase the client's knowledge about the illness. This material may also contain solutions to some of the person's issues.

Telemental Health

This term refers to the practice of providing health care to clients with mental illnesses through telecommunication and video conferencing. It can also be called telepsychiatry or telepsychology.

The following are some ways in which a counselor can ensure a smooth telemental health service for clients:

- Counselors should take time out to research the laws and regulations of their practicing location and their clients' locations to prevent any unnecessary legal damage. They should also inform the clients of these regulations.

- Counselors should adjust the procedure of informed consent according to the platform they are using. This includes social media policies, time zone differences, language barriers, etc.

- At the beginning of each meeting, counselors should allot a certain time to clearly go through the verification process with clients. This can be done through graphics, number codes, etc.

- Counselors must make sure clients are emotionally, physically and linguistically capable of using the platform being used for the therapeutic process.

- Counselors must inform their clients about the method of record-keeping and the assured confidentiality of all of their information. They must make sure their practice falls within the relevant laws. This includes the kind of encryption used to protect records.

Chapter 20: Managing Emotions

Managing emotions can be defined as the ability to recognize, readily acknowledge and constructively handle both positive and challenging sentiments in oneself. When they are felt and understood, this helps people manage triggering situations and adapt to the valuable information and encouragement emotions provide.

Emotions are perceived at every stage of human social affairs and can significantly determine people's experience in their home, workplaces, with family and friends and influence their well-being, daily routine, job satisfaction, motivation and performance.

As human emotions are directly connected with social life, individuals typically adjust their emotional expressions to align with the expectations of their surroundings. The ability to manage and control emotions commences during childhood and normally improves with age.

Developing Communication Abilities

Communication abilities are interpersonal skills that mainly include but are not limited to effectively communicating ideas and thoughts while patiently listening to others, making an attempt to acknowledge and understand their opinions and giving and receiving critical feedback. Communication abilities help people understand and be understood by those around them.

The ability to communicate effectively is significant in a relationship, work and education. The language of leadership is the art of communication.

The fear of offending others, nonverbal behavior, lack of knowledge about the topic being discussed and feeling uncomfortable about expressing one's concerns are some hurdles individuals face while communicating with others.

The following are some key skills for effective communication.

Active Listening

Active listening involves listening attentively when a person is talking. Active listeners are usually well-regarded by their colleagues.

Altering Communication Style to the Audience

Before expressing their ideas and thoughts to an audience, speakers must try to understand the audience first. Different ways of communication are suitable in different situations. Some common barriers while listening to others are jumping to conclusions, filtering out unimportant parts of a conversation, arguing and debating, having a response ready before a person is done speaking and diverting attention while the other person is talking.

Confidence

Making persuasive arguments is likely to get more people to respond to the speaker's ideas. Delivering these arguments with confidence by making eye contact, adjusting one's tone and sitting with shoulders straight are three ways to appear confident.

Empathy and Respect

Understanding the sentiments of the individuals the speaker is communicating with and forming an appropriate response to acknowledge these sentiments is called empathy. Respect is knowing when and where to initiate conversations and when to pause to let others speak. Empathy and respect make up two qualities every person must remember while interacting with people.

Responsiveness and Feedback

Fast communicators are regarded as more effective than those who take time to respond. These communicators are likely to handle critical feedback well and will provide constructive input to others on time.

Creating Conflict Resolution Techniques

Conflict resolution techniques are formal or informal methods by which two or more parties reach a peaceful resolution to a dispute. The creation and application of these techniques vary from situation to situation. Patient, confident and emotionally intelligent individuals are capable of designing effective conflict resolution techniques.

The following are common types of conflict.

Pseudo Conflict

A pseudo conflict usually takes place when a misunderstanding leads to a difference of opinion, when one person involved in the problem ridicules the other person and when the parties involved in the fight believe they have different goals when in reality, they have similar goals.

Pseudo conflicts can be solved with patience. An individual needs to understand his or her own goals and then align them with the goals and viewpoint of the other person.

Fact Conflict

A fact conflict is often called a simple conflict. It exists when two individuals or groups disagree on factual information. It can be resolved by checking a credible source for truth.

Value Conflict

This sort of conflict arises when different personal values lead to disagreements. Disagreements on religious beliefs or abortion rights can be classified under value conflicts. Value conflicts do not always have a straight path to resolution because people can have extensively varying private values and beliefs.

Policy Conflict

Policy conflicts happen when parties cannot settle on a problem-solving plan. It can happen between parents who are deciding on ways to discipline their child or when coworkers have different ideas about to address a project.

Ego Conflict

Ego conflicts commonly happen when issues get personal. They are difficult to navigate. In such conflicts, the involved parties don't try to solve the problem with their intelligence but with emotions and ego.

Meta Conflict

Meta conflicts take place when a person is conflicted about his or her conflicts. To resolve this sort of conflict, better communication and active listening are needed.

Conflicts reduce productivity at work and lead to a difficult work environment, resulting in an unwanted turnover in staff and fallen morale. Conflict resolution techniques in a workplace involve recognition of the existence of the problem by the parties or individuals involved. Then, a mutual agreement is brought in to address the problem and look for a solution. Efforts are made to understand the concerns and viewpoints of the opposing party. After that, triggers that led to the conflict are recognized, along with changes in behavior that will reduce the negative sentiments.

The human resources representative of the company is the one who negotiates through the turbulence caused by the conflict. A desire by one or both parties to compromise and an agreement on a plan to address the differences is required. If the parties agree to a solution, its impact is examined. If the employees resist or continue with the conflict, they might be terminated.

Managing Systemic Changes

Systemic change permeates all parts of a system and accounts for interrelationships and interdependencies among those parts, i.e., a change in the organizational system. Systemic changes can be social, economic, political, etc.

Change management is a systemic approach that deals with the transformation of an organization's aims, procedures or technologies. It exists to implement plans for effecting change, controlling change and helping people to adapt to change.

Effective communication skills are significant at every point of a change project. Communication is the key to clarifying queries and making the best decisions. It takes time to understand the individuals involved in the change. Quick judgments and decisions during or right after a systemic change can be damaging.

Increasing the Likelihood of Empathetic Responses

Empathy is the ability to sense other people's emotions, together with the skill to imagine what someone else might be thinking or feeling. When people are good at managing their emotions, they are more likely to respond empathetically to situations. Empathy helps people avoid conflicts and presents them in a good light.

Talking to new people, asking them about their issues and imagining and feeling the situation they are in is an important step toward building empathy. The core of empathy is curiosity. To be in someone's shoes, you need to know what their condition is and how they are feeling.

Using Meaningful Confrontation and Self-Disclosure

Confrontations usually remind us of arguments and are perceived as negative actions; however, they are not meant to be negative. They are meant to bring an issue to the table to obtain a clear understanding of the problem. When confrontations are managed properly, they can provide a more positive outcome in relationships and communications. The art of confrontation allows for honesty and is a sign of maturity.

Self-disclosure is the process of passing on information about oneself to someone else—a partner, colleague, friend, etc. It can be both intentional and unintentional. There are two types of self-disclosure: verbal and nonverbal. We self-reveal verbally when we tell others about our hopes, fears, etc. We self-reveal nonverbally when we disclose our values and viewpoints through our body language, attire and expressions.

Self-disclosure plays a vital role in forming strong relationships, making other people feel closer, understanding others better and aids in cooperating more efficiently.

Emotional disclosures are significant for boosting empathy and building trust in relationships. Opening up or ranting about a bad day to a friend or colleague helps a person manage stress and emotions and avoid burnout. Self-disclosure also aids in resolving conflicts, building productive teams and strengthens a person's relationships with colleagues and clients.

In workplaces, people have to be careful about sharing and receiving personal information. Sensitive information should not be shared with anyone.

Increasing Awareness of Current Interactions

When people are able to manage their emotions, they are also able to understand the emotions of the others communicating with them. They more easily observe the nonverbal hints people around them might exhibit.

Emotional management leads to emotional intelligence. People with high emotional intelligence are good decision-makers, better conflict resolutioners and problem solvers, have greater empathy, do not lose their cool, and listen, reflect and respond to constructive criticism positively.

Promoting Interpersonal Problem Solving

Interpersonal problem solving is a subcategory of socially acceptable behavior, which is projective of successful life adjustment. It aids in confronting problems in a manner that shows respect for the other person and the relationship.

An interpersonal problem is any type of disagreement between two or more people. It is unlike an intrapersonal problem, which refers to an internal conflict with oneself.

Recognizing the type of problem or conflict people are facing is the first step toward resolving it. Deciding on a resolution strategy is the second step. Withdrawing is only an option if the emotions involved are high. Withdrawal or avoiding problems can cause more issues in a relationship.

Accommodation involves placing the needs of someone else first. This makes the other person feel positive and respectful. However, healthy relationships must always include some give and take.

Compromise also promotes interpersonal problem-solving. When people compromise, they each let go of some of their wishes. It's a balanced situation between both parties. People in conflict should always look at the problem they're having as an issue that can be resolved if they work together, not as a competition that they can win individually.

Processing and Managing Strong Emotions

The procedure of processing and managing emotions starts from recognizing them. One of the most important ways to manage emotions is to understand the reason behind the emotion—we need to know what it is and what it is trying to tell us. When we have recognized an emotion, this recognition helps us feel more in control of a situation and shifts our focus from negative thoughts. It motivates us to ask for help and build better bonds with our peers.

Processing and managing emotions requires several quick and easy exercises. Regular meditation is a supportive way to calm yourself down and build a good relationship with yourself. It helps you feel more connected to yourself and brings mental peace. Taking 10 deep breaths when your feelings are taking over and you're losing control helps a lot!

Distractions, self-care, self-soothing strategies, mindfulness and anger management techniques are all required in a balanced blend to cope with strong emotions over time.

Providing Distance Counseling

Distance counseling is a type of telemedicine that permits clinicians in the mental health field to offer therapy without being face-to-face with a client in an office. It can be delivered through communicating and providing services through phones, video calls and using secure email and electronic medical record (EMR) platforms to share information.

Online therapy is a suitable choice for those who cannot access care because of health, remote location or transportation issues. Meeting in an office is also a source of discomfort for some people, so distance counseling allows them to get help within their comfort zone. Many aspects of mental health can be addressed through distance counseling, such as stress, anxiety, parenting issues, depression, food and eating issues, relationship issues and obsessions and compulsions (OCD).

However, there are psychological conditions that can limit (or prohibit) the use of distance counseling. For example, when a person is experiencing severe psychological or emotional issues like schizophrenia, severe depression, suicidal thoughts or bipolar disorders, then he or she may not be allowed to register for distance counseling, mostly because these issues may be best matched to face-to-face services.

Distance counseling has proved to be beneficial due to its reduced costs, ability to maintain regular sessions wherever the client feels comfortable and ease of access.

Chapter 21: Group Therapy

Group therapy is a situation when a clinician meets with several clients with similar problems. It creates a feeling of togetherness and comforts the clients by making them feel accompanied. Being a part of a group with a similar goal can help members gain a sense of belonging. It reduces their shame and isolation about the problem they are facing. For instance, a cancer survivor may be relieved when expressing his or her emotions in a group of survivors, and a woman going through postpartum depression could feel less embarrassed and more supported by being around women with similar experiences.

Group therapy is, however, not for people who have a fear of speaking in public or those who don't like to share their issues with others, as opening up around strangers can be quite stressful and overwhelming. Personalities of members in a group might clash, so conflict is also likely. Someone from the group could share the experiences and stories of another participant with people outside the group; this insecurity can hinder therapy.

A clinician's main focus is to make sure that all participants enjoy the same benefits and participate in the discussion. During the session, the entire group could reflect on the difficulties of a member and share their similar experiences, but the sole focus should never be just one member. This might make others feel excluded, and the member who is the focus of the discussion could be overwhelmed.

The main objective of group therapy is not just to prevent discomfort and distress in the future but to help people become more able to handle the issues and frustrations they are experiencing. Sharing their emotional states, experiences and grief with a group of people who are there to listen, comfort and give advice can help people release anger and pent-up emotions.

When children are placed in group therapy, it is important to match their ages and problems in order to allow a rapport to be established.

Group therapy sessions generally last for 1 hour and 15 minutes and take place every week. They can help with an extensive variety of psychological difficulties, including:

- Post-traumatic stress disorder symptoms
- Anxiety
- Phobias
- Panic disorder
- Attention deficit hyperactivity disorder (ADHD)
- Domestic violence
- Addiction

- Weight loss
- Cultural trauma
- Anger management
- Depression
- Relationship difficulties.

Procedure

People are assigned to group therapy after two to six sessions of psychotherapy with a counselor. During these sessions, the counselor tries to understand a client's difficulties and the sort of personality he or she has. These sessions give the counselor an idea of whether group therapy will work for the person or not. If the client is offered group therapy, he or she may have to wait for a vacancy in a suitable group. During this wait, the client should be offered appropriate support.

The group therapist leads the group and ensures that each member's participation is central to his or her own and other members' treatment. The therapist helps members develop an understanding of the mindsets of the people present and their situation.

During the sessions, group members are exposed to diverse opinions and are given a chance to learn from others and to give and receive feedback. Each member comes with his or her own history and personality, which makes the individual unique and creates a group situation. Understanding that each member is different can reduce confusion, judgmental behavior and misconceptions.

Group therapy may be intimidating at first, but members usually overcome this worry as they benefit from sharing and listening to others with the same experiences.

Using Structured Activities

Structured activities can be defined as goal-oriented actions that require proper directions to be followed in order to be completed.

Group facilitators usually organize activities between the participants of a group to break the ice and to encourage them to speak. Activities help members believe that they are all able to have fun and motivate them to reach a solution for their issues.

Group members often make comments that they get more out of a group experience than they had initially thought they would, and a majority of the members find themselves forming deep emotional bonds with other people throughout the treatment. As a result of these activities, members tend to exhibit a greater sense of empathy and understanding for other people, as well as develop a sense of being understood and accepted. Their communication skills improve.

Structured activities help with issues that relate to family and relationships with others. Group counseling activities deal with common interpersonal issues that include trust, reassurance, isolation, intimacy and abandonment. As humans are social creatures, being around people who are not judgmental and are ready to listen can prove to be very healing.

A few group activities are explained below.

About Your Partner

This activity is particularly for couples therapy groups. One partner asks the other questions from the section below. These questions don't probe too intensely but are a good reminder of the couple's emotional bond and relationship history.

The questions are divided into six categories:

1. You and me – i.e., Can you describe a time when your partner was proud of your achievements?
2. Careers – i.e., How does a normal weekday look for your partner?
3. Fun and games – i.e., Which singer/band is your partner listening to these days?
4. Feelings – i.e., How does your partner relax at the end of a long day?
5. The future – i.e., What is your partner's retirement plan?
6. Other people – i.e., Apart from you, who can your partner confide in?

By answering these questions, a couple can remember the memories they've made together, what they have in common and what they are supposed to work on to sustain their relationship.

Couples can also share fun memories with the group during the activity.

Categories

This activity is designed particularly for teens. The group is divided into subgroups based on similarities between members, such as favorite color, number of siblings, favorite musician or film, etc. This can help teens get more comfortable interacting with each other and enable them to have a good time.

Human Knot

A human knot is usually used in teen or child therapy groups. It is a physical activity, so it may not be appropriate for all groups. All members get in a circle and take the hand of someone who is standing far from them, then try to untie the knot without letting go of anyone's hand.

Influence of Social Support Networks

A social support network is made up of family, friends and peers. It is different from support groups because it is not structured or headed by a mental health professional.

Mental health experts often discuss the importance of social support networks in a person's life. Having support to lean on is essential for people to achieve their goals or deal with a crisis. Lack of social support has been linked to depression and loneliness, alters the functioning of the brain and increases risks of cardiovascular disease, alcohol use and suicide.

One of the most prominent traits of social networks is knowing what another person knows and when to turn to them for information. Friends and family are usually always there for help. For instance, the need for personalized advice regarding health matters can be an important reason that people ask questions within their social support network.

Interactions With Groupmates

Communicating with groupmates reduces the feelings of loneliness in members. They are encouraged as they share their progress with everyone in the group and feel empowered when they share their stories. Giving and receiving support from others can boost the overall health of members as well. The interaction prompts members to talk about their feelings, knowing others are there to do the same thing.

As members connect, it helps them articulate their feelings. It builds their confidence and motivates them to work toward a positive change in their life. Interactions with groupmates allow the members to try and discover new ways of communicating and socializing. They enable them to overcome their social anxieties and fear of public speaking.

Group members may sometimes bring up issues that strike a chord with members who did not know how to bring up those issues themselves. They have an opportunity to lean into feeling accepted by others and to challenge themselves in making their needs known.

Group therapy is also a time for participants to explore painful existential factors, such as loss and death. Group members can help each other to develop a strong sense of self-reliance by educating them to understand that they are the eventual regulators of their behaviors, actions and choices.

Relationship With Group Facilitator

Better relationships between the counselor and patients lead to better outcomes. A positive relationship is important to helping clients connect with, remain in and receive the most from therapy.

One major shift in psychotherapy lately is toward greater mutuality—the concept that psychotherapy is a two-way association in which therapist and client are equal partners in the process. Therapists show this attitude in an ongoing manner, for instance, revealing their feelings when appropriate and actively inviting feedback from patients about the effectiveness of the therapy.

A better relationship among the facilitator and members leads to them working together to define and actualize therapy goals and setting the direction the therapy is taking and should take in the future. A good relationship enables the facilitator to tell the difference between when a group member might be acting out or resisting and when the therapy is not working for some reason.

Using feedback and incorporating it into treatment is an important way to boost therapeutic relationships along with improving patient outcomes.

Including Psychoeducation in Group Process

Psychoeducation is the process of imparting education and information to those seeking or receiving mental health services, such as people in group therapy and their family members. It is considered to be an essential part of all therapy programs, with the aim of helping people understand mental health conditions. People who have a detailed understanding of the issues they are facing, as well as knowledge of their personal coping abilities, are better at handling problems, feel more in control of their situation and have a superior internal capacity to work toward mental and emotional happiness.

It is quite common for individuals with mental health conditions to know very little or nothing about the condition they have been diagnosed with, how therapy works, the impacts of therapy on their health and the medicines they might be prescribed.

Psychoeducation is offered in both individual and group sessions. It can benefit the diagnosed individuals, their families, friends and caregivers. Psychoeducation is not a part of the treatment itself; rather, it is necessary for early treatment as it gives information to caregivers on how to handle patients, how to understand what they are going through and how counselors can maintain their own mental and emotional well-being.

Psychoeducation, whether highly specified or general, can be provided in numerous ways, mainly comprising of the transfer of information, medication and treatment provision, training and support in self-help and self-care and the facilitation of a safe place to vent emotional frustrations. It is put forward when therapists explain to clients the ways their condition might have an impact on their life, the symptoms of medicine, etc.

Psychoeducation can be administered in schools, hospitals, clinics, webinars and more. It results in increased obedience to treatment rules. When people understand what they are going through and are able to identify their illness, they are more likely to view their illness as a treatable condition rather than some shameful diagnosis.

Apart from a better understanding of mental health issues, psychoeducation also helps to destigmatize mental health conditions, a major goal of mental health experts worldwide.

Stages of Group Therapy

Group therapy is normally divided into four main stages. Once a group is formed, counselors generally have a pre-group meeting to make sure that each individual fits into the group.

At each stage, different purposes and expectations must be addressed. The role and functions of the counselor and group members also transform as the group changes.

1. Initial Stage

The initial stage establishes the expectations of what the group is going to be like. Counselors usually work on building trust, constructing goals and explaining roles. Confidentiality and conflict are addressed to avoid negative situations in future sessions, and cultural concerns (if any) are also dealt with. The counselors support each member when dealing with confrontation and explain the process. Counselors also encourage group members to participate and involve themselves in the discussions and activities.

2. Transition Stage

The transition stage is difficult to get through. At this stage, most members feel anxious about sharing their sentiments and life stories with strangers. Some participants are defensive and resistant, while others may appear shy and fearful. Counselors are sometimes belittled and attacked at this stage. If the counselor is experienced and good at his or her job, the group will learn to trust and respect the counselor during this stage and cancel the negativity out. For members to obtain the most out of therapy, they must participate, listen to their peers and give advice.

3. Working Stage

Once the counselor has successfully led the group through the transitional stage, group members will start to feel comfortable and get ready to talk about the issues that concern them at a deeper level—the issues the therapy group was set up for. This is called the working stage. The members become capable of exploring their thoughts and emotions, especially those that may be triggered by someone else's words. The counselor guides the members through this process by using techniques and activities that bring out emotions.

An expert will know how to guide the group through the minimal use of language on the counselor's part and be able to read and interpret verbal and nonverbal cues of all the participants in the group. The participants need to be completely honest about their situation and sentiments during this stage and must speak their minds. The counselor's job is to make group members feel welcome and address any issues they are facing.

4. Understanding Stage

The final stage of group therapy is when the members understand they will no longer be together. Members usually reflect on their therapy experience and decide how they will use the knowledge that they obtained from the sessions in the future to overcome their issues and improve their lives. This stage often comes with the sadness of separation. The counselor must not forget to collect feedback and remind the participants of confidentiality.

Linking and Blocking

A good group counselor will always use a comprehensive set of skills to lead a group and facilitate progress and change. Linking and blocking are two of these skills.

Linking can be defined as promoting interactions between members of a group by pointing out similar themes among them, whereas blocking can be defined as discontinuing counterproductive behaviors in a group in order to establish rubrics or to protect participants. Linking is used mostly in the beginning to make the participants feel comfortable around each other. Blocking is normally used when a participant says something inappropriate—something that could offend or hurt the personal beliefs of the rest of the members.

Effective Therapy Leader

All leaders face difficulties, but in chemical dependency groups, the members might still be adjusting to sobriety, so their thoughts, actions and judgments may be clouded. As an effective group leader, one of the most important actions a counselor can take is to conduct proper screening of the personalities of patients before forming a group. The counselor must take time and understand all of the patients' personas, so they don't face any unexpected problems in the group sessions.

Knowing how to handle conflicts, resistance and how to guide everyone in a meaningful direction is a leader's job. Group members can belong to different cultures, so a leader must be able to understand diversity and help form bonds of trust between all cultures present in the group.

Therapists can help group members feel hopeful by recognizing and sharing how current and former members have grown toward their aims.

Common Misconceptions About Group Therapy

Many times, when they first join a group, clients are afraid that they will be forced to tell all of their deepest thoughts, feelings and secrets to strangers. The leader must assure the members that it is an individual's decision about how much and when someone shares with the group. No one can force group members to talk or reveal anything they don't want to. Counselors must encourage, but not pressure, people to speak by informing them how personal sharing aspects about themselves will be fruitful for both the group and their personal lives.

Another misconception about group therapy is that it takes longer than individual therapy. During private sessions, counselors must inform new members that group therapy is often more efficient than individual therapy.

Individuals may be afraid that they might be verbally attacked by the group leaders and by other group members when they open up about their experiences and share their opinions. This is why it is so important for the members to feel safe during the sessions.

Receiving feedback from other group members is also a difficult process because the feedback can feel like a personal attack. Being vulnerable is difficult for people who are trying to piece themselves back together, so they may lash out when they feel threatened. This is why fostering an environment in which members can trust each other and can speak without fear of judgment is so crucial.

As a leader, the mental health expert must work on building a supportive and comfortable space. The leader must ensure members of care and respect and explain to them how group sessions are the best place to receive feedback if they are not comfortable receiving it from their family and friends.

Rules for a Therapy Group

The counselor must put the following regulations into effect as soon as the group begins.

1. Members must inform the leader if they intend to miss a session.
2. Members must adhere to the group schedule set by the leaders.
3. Members must remember that having a feeling and acting on it are two different actions.
4. It is a group member's responsibility to talk about the reason for his or her presence in the group.
5. The group's work is supposed to be done within the group during the allotted time. Thus, the leader must ask that members not socialize with other members of their group when they are present in the group.
6. The group sessions are confidential. Members and leaders are bound both legally and ethically to not disclose the contents of the group sessions.
7. If a member has decided that he or she has benefitted as much as possible from the group or believes that this is not a suitable treatment for him or her, then the leader(s) must ask the person to come to the group and say goodbye.

Chapter 22: Positive Attributes of Every Effective Counselor

Counseling can be defined as the application of mental health, psychological and developmental philosophies through an efficient intellectual, behavioral or systemic intervention approach. The main focus of counseling is helping people make changes and deal with issues in their life. A counselor, hence, is a person who gives advice.

Counselors are required to perform their duties in diverse community settings designed to provide a variety of support and rehabilitation services. Their duties depend on their specialty, which is determined by their working experience in a particular community and environment.

To be a good counselor, patience is necessary. It takes time for clients to open up and explain their situation clearly. An effective counselor will always wait, never pressuring or interrupting clients. If clients seem angry, good counselors will ask the reason for their anger and listen tolerantly. They will be observant and interpret all signs of nonverbal communication. Good counselors smile to create an accepting and trusted environment.

Self-Awareness and Influence on Clients

The counseling profession is unique. It requires practitioners to employ interventions outside learned knowledge or acquired skills. Counselors are required to incorporate self-awareness into their practice.

Self-awareness in therapists has been identified as a critical part of psychotherapy and is believed to be a significant aspect of a successful therapeutic process. In multicultural counseling competence, self-awareness is deemed to be of great importance by psychotherapy scholars of all therapeutic orientations.

Counselors are trained to observe the behavior of their clients, yet it is equally vital for them to look within. Self-awareness means having an unbiased knowledge about one's own strengths and weaknesses. During therapy sessions, this ability allows counselors to question their own beliefs and biases. If counselors do not possess this quality, they may voluntarily or involuntarily react to their own or their clients' subconscious programming.

Knowing their personality and thoughts will help therapists manage their internal reactions and stay present with clients. This will benefit the therapeutic relationship and make clients more comfortable while discussing their problems, thereby limiting any possibility of harm.

This is specified in The American Counseling Association Code of Ethics (2014).

- A.4.a. Avoiding Harm and Imposing Values:

"Counselors act to avoid harming their clients, trainees and research participants and to minimize or to remedy unavoidable or unanticipated harm."

- A.4.b. Personal Values

"Counselors are aware of—and avoid imposing—their own values, attitudes, beliefs and behaviors. Counselors respect the diversity of clients, trainees and research participants and seek training in areas in which they are at risk of imposing their values onto clients, especially when the counselor's values are inconsistent with the client's goals or are discriminatory in nature."

When diagnosing mental disorders, the American Counseling Association's Ethical Codes (2014) E.5.c Historical and Social Prejudices in the Diagnosis of Pathology states,

"Counselors recognize historical and social prejudices in the misdiagnosis and pathologizing of certain individuals and groups and strive to become aware of and address such biases in themselves or others."

Increasing self-care, practicing mindfulness and meditation, journaling and connecting with support are four ways through which counselors can build self-awareness.

Sincerity and Confidentiality

Sincerity involves speaking frankly about one's sentiments, beliefs and desires. A counselor must show sympathetic understanding and respect with a sincere heart to support the client.

Often, clients are shy and hesitant during their first counseling sessions. They try to judge and understand the personality of their counselor. Clients keenly observe whether a counselor is making a sincere effort to comprehend their point of view. Thus, counselors must always be sincere in their advice and suggestions to clients.

Moments of true mutual sincerity in psychotherapy are calming because of the understanding attained.

Confidentiality is key in health matters. Clients will feel offended if the counselor ends up disclosing any information about them to others, and this will damage the relationship between the counselor and client.

Consistency

Consistency has proven to bring quicker results in counseling and is also considered to be cost-effective. An effective counselor makes the most of the fewest appointments. Long gaps between appointments extend the time of the procedure and delay the results. Delays often increase the communication gap between the counselor and client, which further worsens the problem.

A motivated client makes treatment a priority and saves money by achieving his or her goals from the counseling sessions on time. Delaying appointments only delays the time before both of the stakeholders get results.

Formatting the sessions on a digital device or taking notes manually helps therapists reduce time spent on documenting each session. They also have the benefit of being less frustrated if they are lagging behind schedule. If counselors utilize a consistent template for notes, they will complete notes efficiently and on time.

Compassionate Attunement

Compassion is an important healing element in therapeutic concepts of acceptance, empathy and unconditional positive regard. It can be defined as connecting with the client's grief and promoting change through action. Compassion is broader and deeper than empathy, makes the client feel understood and eases symptoms.

Factors that usually facilitate compassion in therapy are counselors sympathizing with clients' pain, understanding client dynamics, involvement of clients, identifying with and liking clients and a healthy and positive overall therapy relationship.

Counselors must always try to cultivate true feelings of compassion for their clients. Without a sense of where clients are coming from, it will be impossible for counselors to advise their clients or help them heal and recover.

Empathetic Responding

Empathy can be defined as the skill of being understanding, aware and sensitive and being able to experience the thoughts, experiences and feelings of someone's life without having the sentiments communicated in an objectively explicit manner.

An effective counselor is able to exercise empathy during client-counselor communication. Clients feel at ease when counselors are empathetic toward them; they feel that they are being heard.

Some problems for counselors to consider that make them unempathetic are intensity, context and selective responding. It is essential for a counselor to respond to feelings expressed at the appropriate level of intensity. If this is not done appropriately, clients will become distant as their counselor is unable to reflect accurately on their emotions.

The second problem is context. Effective counselors take all aspects into account, not just a word or a client's nonverbal behavior. They must understand that people belong to diverse backgrounds and have gone through different difficulties in their lives. Clients may act in ways counselors might find inappropriate, but when taken in the context of people's history, their actions may be more understandable.

Thirdly, when counselors respond selectively to a feeling or behavior, clients may feel uncomfortable discussing their feelings. So, a counselor must always respond to experiences and behaviors appropriately.

It is easy to recognize if the counselor's empathetic responses have been beneficial. If the client nods or gives some verbal response, the counselor's response was helpful. If the client becomes frustrated or exhibits nonverbal indications of irritation, annoyance, or anger, the counselor failed to be receptive.

During a counseling session, facilitators must give themselves time to think, listen and understand clients' perspectives. They must be themselves while responding and use short responses.

Counselors must also refrain from using sympathy excessively, asking inappropriate questions, making judgments about clients, giving early and unasked advice, pretending to understand and parroting clients' exact words.

Nonjudgmental Attitude

Nonjudgmental listening is about trying to understand the client's perspective. It is about going beyond just hearing the words spoken and involves interpreting exactly what the client is trying to communicate—reading between the lines. Mental health professionals and counselors are trained to be nonjudgmental listeners.

Counselors must always put aside their personal viewpoints when listening to clients. Silence is the best practice in this case. The aim is to not criticize or judge clients but to simply hear and take in what they are trying to express.

Being nonjudgmental does not mean that counselors are ignoring their sentiments or being blind to clients' behavior. It means that they are choosing to separate the clients' behavior from who they are as people.

Acceptance and genuineness are two conditions necessary to form a safe environment where the client is comfortable and can talk openly without the fear of being judged. An effective listener is understanding of clients' experiences and respects them. The counselor's body language matches what he or she says to show the client that whatever the counselor is trying to communicate is genuine.

Children are able to detect judgment from another person quite quickly. If they don't feel comfortable around a counselor, they might stop opening up and being authentic.

Respect for the Client-Counselor Relationship

Respect and tolerance are two significant components of the client-counselor relationship. Respect is an expression of acceptance, admiration, consent and loyalty.

Regardless of the background, personality and behavior of the client, counselors are honor-bound to respect their clients, who have come to them for assistance and deserve to be treated as people of value and worth. An effective counselor shows respect for clients by seeing the good in them, recognizing and respecting their spirit.

As a sign of respect, counselors must not impose personal beliefs and opinions upon clients. They must respect and accept who their clients are and where in their lives they currently are. Respect is also shown through the use of fitting and professional language. Counselors have to be aware of their language in relation to the context and client. For example, they might have to counsel patients who have been raised in households where swearing is common.

A counselor must show respect through drawing and practicing boundaries to protect the client's privacy. Clients are in a vulnerable state when they visit a counselor. They are highly emotional. If the counselor is too open, the client could perceive him or her to be very caring and giving during the sessions. Unavoidably, the relationship can then progress toward genuine familiarity as the client opens up. While counselors study to be compassionate and empathic, the client-counselor relationship can become closer than is appropriate for a professional relationship. An effective therapist shows respect to the client by keeping in mind that the objective of treatment is for the client to be an independently operative person and not to remain emotionally dependent on the therapist.

Chapter 23: Channeling Empathy into a Counseling Session

Empathy in counseling is about counselors perceiving the world as they see and observe it. It is to view what the client is communicating from the person's point of view and deliver understanding and advice back in a manner that makes the client feel understood. If counselors can do this, they complete the empathic circle of compassion, nurture, caring, understanding and relating.

Therapist empathy is acknowledged as a vital generic factor in treatment and is known to exert variable effects on client outcomes. The channeling of empathy into a counseling session is considered a complex process comprised of several components that include, but are not limited to, effective response to the client's sentiments with similar sentiments, rational understanding of the client's experiences and demonstration of warmth and esteem.

While empathy is essential throughout the process, it is an obligation in the initial stages of a therapeutic connection. It builds an early connection and rapport when deliberating problematic subjects.

Other ways to express empathy within a counseling session are setting aside one's own opinions as a counselor to enter the client's world without judgment or bias and attune to momentary nonverbal changes in the client's attitude and persona.

There are several therapist empathy assessment methods. In self-report rating, therapists rate themselves on how empathetic they think they have been during the session. Note that therapist reports are unreliable, as therapists may intentionally or unintentionally overrate themselves as compared to the client's ratings.

Secondly, the client reports therapist empathy. In these reports, the client rates the therapist. Therapists who exhibit nurturance and self-disclosure are labeled as empathic by clients.

Thirdly, there are written assessments of therapist empathy. These are not associated strongly with straight measures of empathic reflections in therapy sessions and are considered a less favored substitute to direct observational assessment.

Promoting the Development of Group Therapeutic Values

A counselor in charge of a group during therapy encourages the growth of therapeutic values to receive positive outcomes from the sessions. Unconditional acceptance, confidentiality, the skills of the leader and the responsibility of group members are some of the therapeutic values a counselor works on.

Unconditional acceptance is a significant issue that has been highlighted in counseling. For clients, feeling acknowledged in the group will create a sense of relief and allow them to feel that they have the same rights as other members. It gives members a chance to learn that to be accepted, they have to first accept those around them.

Compliance with confidentiality during the sessions can help members express their ideas, sentiments and experiences without any reservation. The group facilitator needs to discuss the significance of confidentiality at the beginning of the group counseling and ensure that all members are on board. Confidentiality also affects the personal development of members. Each member needs the support of the group counselor to come forward and participate during the sessions.

Group counseling requires facilitators who can ensure that sessions run smoothly. Group leaders must be able to determine the effectiveness of group sessions, whether they are successful or not. They should be empathetic and pay consistent attention to nonverbal movements and changes in members' words.

Along with the leader, the group members are also supposed to carry the group forward. Participation of members encourages demotivated or shy members to speak up.

Demonstrating Conflict Respect

Professional counselors guide clients through painful situations and grief and help them process the difficulties of life. It is the first and foremost responsibility of a counselor to respect clients' dignity and promote their welfare. To be an effective and ethical counselor, one must be ethnically sensitive and respectful of the diversity that clients bring to the client-counselor therapeutic relationship.

Counselors can respond effectively to challenging clients by calming down, practicing mindful meditation, not escalating the situation by reacting to it, expressing empathy, reframing resistance, cultivating patience, seeking support from their peers or terminating the relationship.

When counselors and counselors-in-training experience conflict between their personal values and beliefs and the necessities of ethical guidelines, they are confronted with three ethically approved options. They can choose not to engage in the practice of counseling. They can choose to practice in a setting that does not require a license and faithfulness to a code of ethics for licensed professional counselors. Or they can follow the "both/and" viewpoint.

In the third choice, counselors are able to maintain their beliefs, follow ethical guidelines and carry out the role of a professional counselor during a therapy session. In the last scenario, a consultant or supervisor who facilitates the process of achieving a positive environment and acceptable solution between a professional counselor's conflicting personal values and ethical responsibilities is present.

The American Counseling Association does not ask counselors or clients to change their beliefs. Counselors always have clients with whom they disagree for any reason; thus, these clients may cause distress to the counselor. When facing a struggle between individual and professional morals, a counselor must ask for help and guidance from other mental health experts. Counselors should be ready to be tested outside of their comfort zones by clients as challenges result in personal growth.

Demonstrating Sexual Orientation

In sessions with patients who are bisexual, lesbian, gay or have another perceived sexual orientation, the gender orientation of the therapist can never be an unbiased issue to the patient and may influence the treatment. Like any other trait, the therapist must always be carefully deliberate on how the revelation of sexual orientation will affect the treatment. Patients who never express any interest in knowing the counselor's gender identity are of equal importance. The choice of whether or not to reveal one's sexual orientation should be decided on a case-by-case basis.

Demonstrating an Understanding of Multiculturalism

As discussed earlier, multiculturalism has various approaches that revolve around considering different factors that affect ethnic, racial and other types of minorities, including historical oppression and its effect on society. Multicultural psychotherapists understand their clients' background and how it impacts their viewpoint. Counselors must tailor their role to accommodate these perspectives.

The major driving force behind multicultural counseling is that minorities perceive the world through different lenses, and counselors, therapists and psychologists need to be subtle to their unique practices and difficulties. By being committed to empathy and care, multicultural counselors can consider how the life situation of a patient may be diverse from their own.

Race, geographic background, ethnicity and religion are some experiences and systems that impact everything from an individual's values to how a person performs in life around family, friends and colleagues. A vast range of socioeconomic circumstances is to be considered by therapists, as people who grew up in extreme wealth and also those who have endured life well below the poverty line both come and seek therapy.

Multicultural counseling emerged from a growing public awareness that the old ways of performing counseling were no longer applicable or enough for different races, cultures and social minority groups. Becoming a multicultural counselor is an ongoing process as it takes years of education, training and on-the-job experience to become culturally competent. Multicultural psychotherapists are always eager to learn and adapt to new policies that include fresh thoughts and therapeutic strategies.

A challenging yet essential part of developing multicultural counseling expertise is examining one's own biases and privileges. Multicultural counselors must be self-aware about how their upbringing and background impact the way they treat their clients.

Using Basic Listening, Paying Attention and Reflecting Skills

Counseling is about forming strong relationships with clients regardless of their history, beliefs and background. These relationships empower them to achieve effective mental health treatment and motivate them to accomplish their goals. Counselors can guide their clients in attaining optimal mental health through the efficient practice of deliberate counseling techniques and a thoughtful understanding of human nature developed through counseling concepts.

Listening is one of the most important counseling skills in the therapeutic relationship. It can be used by being physically attentive toward a client—giving undivided attention, nodding as a sign of understanding, mirroring body language and making appropriate eye contact. These actions may be minor but mean a lot to clients, showing that the counselor cares for them.

Active listening is also a part of basic listening skills. It comprises listening with the body, ears, eyes, heart and mouth. Verbal listening is a form of showing the counselor's listening by the choice of words used to show attention and to encourage more examination from the client.

Asking questions is supportive in a therapeutic environment because this allows counselors to learn more about their clients. By asking a particular set of questions, a counselor can easily set the flow and tone of the session. It will make the entire process calmer. Closed questions are generally avoided as they do not encourage deeper exploration of the issue. These questions come with either a "yes" or "no" answer. Open-ended questions are important to collect information about the issue the client is facing. They can't be answered with a simple "yes" or "no" as they require reflection or exploration of thoughts from the client.

Reflections are used in the counseling procedure to precisely describe clients' mental state from their verbal or nonverbal signals. Reflecting allows clients to hear their sentiments, but sometimes the counselor has to search for descriptive feelings in a client's statement to construct a reflection. Restating and rephrasing as a part of reflecting can also build a strong client-counselor relationship. Rephrasing a client's statement allows a counselor to understand the client's situation and sentiments in a better way.

Affirmation is also a part of reflecting. It is a method of reassurance that is used to confirm actions or life choices. Affirming the progress of clients makes them feel empowered. As every therapist practices a different therapeutic procedure, it is essential to remain honest in all counseling techniques and verbal and nonverbal signals.

Test 1

Professional Practice and Ethics

(1) Which of the following best describes the client's right to protect his/her confidential therapy information from being revealed in any court proceedings?

(A) Privacy

(B) Client privilege

(C) Counseling

(D) None of the above

(2) When people seek therapy and counseling, they display their thoughts and feelings in a variety of ways. Which of the following is one of them?

(A) Questionnaires

(B) Forms

(C) Nonverbal cues

(D) All of the above

(3) Identify the final step in the research process usually carried out by counselors to solve their clients' problems.

(A) Dissemination

(B) Analyzing

(C) Devising a hypothesis

(D) Designing a plan

(4) A patient sought therapy from a counselor but was left with the same issues he initially presented with. Which of the following could have been a reason behind this?

(A) The patient did not open up about his/her issues.

(B) The counselor did not continuously evaluate the behavior of the patient.

(C) The counselor demanded a high fee.

(D) The counselor breached the patient's privacy.

(5) Psychotherapy is a treatment option for people dealing with a variety of mental illnesses. For long-standing and complex problems, how long should the treatment ideally be?

(A) A few sessions

(B) A few months

(C) Both A and B

(D) None of the above

(6) The counseling process can be broken down into how many stages?

(A) Ten

(B) Seven

(C) Four

(D) Five

(7) According to Carl Rogers, what are the three basic conditions for establishing an effective counselor-client relationship?

(A) Verbal, nonverbal and written communication

(B) Empathy, genuineness and unconditional caring

(C) Problem identification, analyzing and assessment

(D) Influence, talks and behaviors

(8) Identify the second stage of the counseling process.

(A) Problem assessment and in-depth exploration

(B) Goal-setting

(C) Interventions

(D) Initial disclosure and relationship building

(9) According to Schneider, which of the following words best describes the information revealed in counseling?

(A) Legal right

(B) Entrusted secret

(C) Crime

(D) All of the above

(10) It is the responsibility of counselors to adhere to the right to privacy of their clients. However, there may be some limitations.

Which of the following can be a limitation?

(A) Child abuse

(B) Suicidal thoughts

(C) Incest

(D) All of the above

(11) A child opens up to a counselor about her plans of running away from home. What is the counselor's responsibility?

(A) Tell the parents.

(B) Keep the disclosure confidential and try to resolve the problem.

(C) Ignore the disclosure because it is an emotional state that shall pass.

(D) Scold the child.

(12) Which of the following is the biggest drawback when a client's right to privacy is violated?

(A) Counselors lose money.

(B) People feel reluctant seeking therapy and counseling.

(C) Mental illnesses worsen.

(D) Both B and C.

(13) Which of the following is/are essential to pursue counseling as a profession?

(A) Lifelong learning

(B) Competency boundaries

(C) Understanding of ethical standards

(D) All of the above

(14) A court case involves an alleged killer who once sought therapy from a counselor. What should the counselor do when he is asked to appear in court?

(A) He should state all the major and minor facts regarding the alleged killer.

(B) He should not breach patient-doctor confidentiality.

(C) Both A and B.

(D) None of the above.

(15) What should a counselor do if he starts facing problems in his personal life while dealing with a case?

(A) He should immediately take a break.

(B) He should complete the case first.

(C) He should refer the case to a trusted colleague with the consent of the patient.

(D) Both A and C.

(16) When clients lack the ability to give consent, who should be contacted by the advocate to obtain permission for the protection of their interests?

(A) A legally recognized third party

(B) The parents

(C) Any family members

(D) Nobody

(17) According to the Disabilities Act, what are some places people with disabilities in the US aren't allowed to access?

(A) Schools

(B) Public parks

(C) Hospitals

(D) None of the above

(18) Low IQ and attention deficit disorders can affect a client's ________.

(A) Factual comprehension

(B) Treatment

(C) Relationship with the counselor

(D) All of the above

(19) How should counselors regard a patient with a disability?

(A) As people who are physically and mentally challenged

(B) As people with the same rights, demands and desires as everyone else

(C) As people who deserve pity

(D) Both A and C

(20) Which of the following strategies adopted by counselors in dealing with disabled patients can lessen fear in clients?

(A) Compassion

(B) Forgiveness

(C) Both A and B

(D) All of the above

(21) Unethical behavior shown by counselors can appear in a variety of forms. Which of the following can be classified as unethical behavior?

(A) Taking a break due to personal problems

(B) Charging exorbitant fees

(C) Both A and B

(D) None of the above

(22) Why is confidentiality considered relative and subjective rather than an unmitigated obligation?

(A) The conditions and laws regarding confidentiality can change from time to time.

(B) Counselors define their own rules regarding confidentiality.

(C) Patients decide the rules of confidentiality for themselves.

(D) All of the above.

(23) Which of the following is not a step in the counseling process?

(A) Allowing the client to speak

(B) Taking fees on time

(C) Discussing the client's perspectives and goals

(D) Filling in gaps in the client's knowledge

(24) "Assessment should strive to recognize the client's significance and uniqueness." Which psychologist made this statement?

(A) Williams James

(B) Albert Bandura

(C) Martin Seligman

(D) Aaron Beck

(25) Even if the client and the staff move on to the next stage in the counseling process, which stage continues?

(A) All stages

(B) Stage two

(C) Stage five

(D) Stage one

Intake, Assessment and Diagnosis

(26) What does BPS stand for in counseling?

(A) Biopsychosocial

(B) Blood pressure state

(C) Both A and B

(D) None of the above

(27) BPS is broken down into how many components?

(A) Three

(B) Four

(C) Two

(D) Five

28) Who proposed the universal model followed by all clinical interviews?

(A) Schneider

(B) Shea

(C) Seligman

(D) Martin

(29) How many stages make up Shea's model for clinical interviewing?

(A) Five

(B) Four

(C) Ten

(D) Nine

(30) How many questions make up the first part of CFI?

(A) Ten

(B) Five

(C) Sixteen

(D) Twelve

(31) In which of the following situations should a counselor adopt a directive approach?

(A) When the counselor needs to control the interview situation

(B) When the interviewee prefers to manage the situation

(C) Both A and B

(D) None of the above

(32) Which of the following best describes the word *specificity*?

(A) The ability of a mechanism to target people who do not have a disorder

(B) The ability of a screening device to identify accurate cases of a target condition in a population group

(C) Both A and B

(D) None of the above

(33) Which of the following is the most common therapeutic approach used in couples therapy?

(A) Cognitive

(B) Behavioral

(C) Systems

(D) Only A and B

(34) Which of the following is/are the technique(s) used to recognize a client's strengths and weaknesses?

(A) Screening

(B) Behavior

(C) Discipline

(D) Treatment

(35) Which of the following is/are the limitation(s) self-reports are usually subjected to?

(A) Lack of self-awareness

(B) Invalidity

(C) Dishonesty

(D) All of the above

(36) What does COD stand for in counseling?

(A) Call of duty

(B) Co-occurring diagnoses

(C) Cash on delivery

(D) Capacity on demand

(37) Which of the following is a guiding principle for dealing with COD clients?

(A) Adopting a recovery mindset

(B) Reasonably pricing self-reports

(C) Providing a sufficient level of care

(D) Maintaining patient care

(38) Which of the following are the three steps in a thorough substance abuse assessment?

(A) Screening, assessment and evaluation

(B) Assessment, evaluation and care

(C) Screening, problem analysis and individual evaluation

(D) Assessment, evaluation and problem analysis

(39) Identify an advantage that self-reports can provide in counseling.

(A) They can be completed in private.

(B) Some questions may be engaging.

(C) Clients frequently respond based on how they are feeling at the time.

(D) Clients may overstate their symptoms.

(40) Screening and assessment are _______________.

(A) Similar processes

(B) Two separate processes

(C) Both A and B

(D) None of the above

(41) There is a great stigma attached to the mental health of men. What can the implications of this be in the screening and assessment of men?

(A) There is a lack of research in this area.

(B) Men underreport problems.

(C) Screening and assessment are independent of the stigma attached to men's mental health.

(D) All of the above

(42) "Do you consume alcoholic beverages or illegal substances? How often?"

Which component of the BPS features in this question?

(A) Biological

(B) Psychological

(C) Social

(D) All of the above

(43) It is the responsibility of a counselor to close a session in a way that the primary objectives of that session are met.

Identify one objective from the following.

(A) Terminating the session

(B) Ingraining hope

(C) Introduction

(D) Diagnosis

(44) Which of the following can help a counselor distinguish between a variety of systemic diseases as well as neurocognitive disorders?

(A) CFI

(B) BPS

(C) MSE

(D) COD

(45) Identify the third stage of the five-stage Shea model for clinical interviewing.

(A) Body

(B) Closing

(C) Termination

(D) Opening

(46) According to Shea, if a counselor asks direct questions before building rapport and trust, what is the result?

(A) The client's problems are solved in a limited time span.

(B) There is dismissiveness and deception.

(C) A lot of time can be saved.

(D) Fewer resources are wasted.

(47) ___________ is a part of culture.

(A) Language

(B) Religion

(C) Social structures

(D) All of the above

(48) In which of the following cases is it not sensible for a counselor to begin with gathering a trauma history?

(A) Loss of a loved one

(B) Rape

(C) Robbery

(D) Accident

(49) Which of the following is the most common modality of treatment in psychotherapy?

(A) Personal therapy

(B) Couples therapy

(C) Group therapy

(D) All of the above

(50) What is meant by false positives?

(A) Identifying people who supposedly have a disorder as not having it

(B) Identifying people who do not have a disorder as having it

(C) Identification of false tests

(D) None of the above

Areas of Clinical Focus

(51) A person is suffering from a sickness for which there is no treatment or medication. The patient only has a few years left to live. What is this patient classified as?

(A) Near-death

(B) Non-satisfactory

(C) Terminally ill

(D) End-of-life

(52) What is the projected population of individuals above 60 by 2050?

(A) 2.0 billion

(B) 2.3 billion

(C) 2.6 billion

(D) 2.9 billion

(53) People who find it hard to move on from the death of their loved ones often suffer from ________.

(A) Cancer

(B) Depression

(C) Schizophrenia

(D) Asthma

(54) How does therapy help individuals seeking a way to talk their feelings out?

(A) It eases communication.

(B) It helps people to survive alone.

(C) It supports people's goals and intentions.

(D) It forces people to go to gatherings

(55) What does the study of geriatrics comprise?

(A) Initiating treatment, diagnosing and preventing diseases at an older age

(B) Raising awareness, campaigning and diagnosing diseases that arise with aging

(C) Preventing and dealing with emotional changes that come with older age

(D) Estimating values and preventing damage that arises with age

(56) What are the most common health issues a person experiences at an older age?

(A) Diabetes, cancer, hepatitis

(B) Sensory loss, schizophrenia, oral health issues

(C) Sensory loss, improper balance, subconscious loss

(D) Oral health issues, schizophrenia, cancer

(57) When caregivers invest in someone's life more than their own, what sort of problems might they suffer?

(A) Sadness, eating issues, PTSD

(B) Guilt, lack of physical activity, anger

(C) Loneliness, improper loss, end-of-life issues

(D) Anger, sensory loss, guilt

(58) What are some occurrences that hasten the process of aging?

(A) Nutrition, work-life, anger

(B) Diseases, personal life, climate

(C) Stress, relocation, death of loved ones

(D) Anger, climate, absence of motivation

(59) When a person is suffering from diseases such as Alzheimer's, Parkinson's and dementia, this is known as?

(A) Oral health issues

(B) Sensory loss

(C) Improper balance

(D) Subconscious loss

(60) What is not a common reason for adopting children?

(A) Failure to conceive naturally

(B) Lack of results from medical treatment

(C) Fear of childbirth

(D) A child wants a sibling

(61) What are some of the problems that arise with adoption?

(A) Financial imbalance, anxiety, lack of food

(B) Stress, failed adoption, intrusion of personal space

(C) Stress, financial imbalance, lack of love for other kids

(D) Time management, lack of resources, grief

(62) How many families in the US include children from a previous marriage?

(A) 25%

(B) 35%

(C) 45%

(D) 55%

(63) What is it called when an individual in a blended family is not able to comprehend the separation of his birth parents and/or the difference in last names and harbors resentment toward new family members?

(A) Sibling rivalry

(B) Conflicts

(C) Identity crisis

(D) Lack of attention

(64) What are some signs of physical abuse in a child?

(A) Bruises on various body parts and distress

(B) No weight gain and talkative nature

(C) Introversion and preference for books

(D) Sudden weight gain and lack of physical activity

(65) What are some forms of sexual abuse?

(A) Romantic texts and oral-genital contact

(B) Staring inappropriately and shouting

(C) Inappropriate touching of body parts and sexting

(D) Sexual intercourse and oral-genital contact

(66) What is it called when a disruptive household causes major psychological distress to a child by neglecting necessities such as clothing, food, education, medical support, etc.?

(A) Sexual abuse

(B) Physical abuse

(C) Mental torture

(D) Loneliness

(67) What are the statistics for child abuse?

(A) 30% under 10 years of age; 20% preteens

(B) 35% under 10 years of age; 25% preteens

(C) 45% under 10 years of age; 35% preteens

(D) 50% under 10 years of age; 40% preteens

(68) What is it called when either the birth parents or the parents applying for adoption don't want to continue with the adoption after everything has been finalized?

(A) Stress

(B) Guilt

(C) Intrusion of personal space

(D) Failed adoption

(69) For a relationship to function well, what is the basic requirement?

(A) Communication

(B) Money

(C) Poetry

(D) Children

(70) What are some common reasons that could result in a shift in the dynamics of a relationship?

(A) Sleeping patterns and financial issues

(B) Behavior of children and work issues

(C) Lack of evenly balanced division of responsibilities and cultural issues

(D) Past experiences and behavioral factors

(71) If a person catches his or her spouse cheating, what is such a situation called?

(A) Financial conflict

(B) Infidelity

(C) Abusive relationship

(D) Lack of interest

(72) What are some triggers that may lead to abuse and violence in a family?

(A) Illness and malnutrition

(B) Alcoholism and complications at work

(C) Motor vehicle accident and hunger

(D) Loss of a loved one and anxiety

(73) What sort of family abuse is likely to have a long-lasting effect?

(A) Sexual abuse

(B) Physical abuse

(C) Emotional abuse

(D) Financial abuse

(74) When a person in a relationship is threatened, he or she is a victim of?

(A) Domestic violence

(B) Stress

(C) Depression

(D) Mental illness

(75) What are some solutions to a partner's violence in a relationship?

(A) Litigation

(B) Communication

(C) Fighting back

(D) Doing nothing

(76) What percentage of women in the US have reportedly faced physical violence, rape and mental torture while in a relationship with a partner?

(A) 28%

(B) 38%

(C) 48%

(D) 58%

(77) What's the biggest hurdle in learning the art of communication in a relationship?

(A) Poverty

(B) Technology

(C) Children

(D) Inflation

(78) What are some behaviors that indicate suicidal ideation?

(A) Withdrawal from social events and a morbid fascination with death

(B) Experiencing a major personal loss and a natural disaster

(C) A change in sleeping pattern and increase in work

(D) Alcohol consumption and body aches

(79) If a person expresses the intent to harm and increases his or her usage of alcohol and drugs, what should a therapist do?

(A) Identify the client's depressive thoughts and prescribe sleeping pills

(B) Tell the client to calm down and inform the family immediately

(C) Be afraid of the client and call the police

(D) Identify the client's suicidal feelings and respond appropriately while maintaining trust

(80) What sorts of emotions should a counselor experience while dealing with suicidal clients?

(A) Negative thoughts and anxiety

(B) Anger and unconsciousness

(C) Fear and anger

(D) Sadness and curiosity

(81) What are some protective factors in suicide prevention?

(A) Physical exercise, informal support systems, a crisis plan

(B) Emotional expression, counseling, spending time alone

(C) Effective coping mechanisms, mental health support, crime documentaries

(D) Participation in hobbies, emotional abuse, after-hours assistance

(82) How must a therapist respond to a woman who has not stated suicidal intentions clearly but gives off many suicidal signs?

(A) Tell her that she is suicidal and prescribe pills.

(B) Talk to the woman about suicide and make the environment safe for suicide risk exploration.

(C) End the session and give the woman a pamphlet filled with necessary helplines.

(D) Take the woman out and help her cheer up.

(83) What actions could help most while collaborating with a suicidal client in order to make significant future decisions involving a third party?

(A) Setting up a device and recording the sessions

(B) Asking the client to sign papers every time he or she expresses extreme suicidal ability

(C) Asking the client to bring along a person he or she trusts

(D) Taking notes to keep track of the client's manners, beliefs and factors of indication

(84) What does the situation suggest if a client lacks the basic ability to comprehend the implications of possible actions?

(A) The client is at high risk of committing suicide.

(B) The client is at moderate risk of committing suicide.

(C) The client is at low risk of committing suicide.

(D) The client is not suicidal.

(85) What is the most important factor in the success of a therapeutic procedure when a client is suffering from severe distress?

(A) Client-family relationship

(B) Client-counselor relationship

(C) Less consumption of alcohol and drugs

(D) Active participation in sports

(86) What are some reasons for the stress a practitioner goes through while dealing with a suicidal client?

(A) Shame from failure

(B) Failure to recognize warning signs

(C) Involvement of colleagues

(D) Retaliation from a client's family

(87) What sort of sickness or disorder is emotional or developmental?

(A) Post-traumatic stress disorder

(B) Adjustment disorders

(C) Anxiety

(D) Depression

(88) What is not a reason for an adjustment disorder?

(A) Sexual abuse by one's partner

(B) Moving away from home

(C) Divorced parents

(D) Death of a loved one

(89) What disease/disorder/trauma do practitioners identify by the use of DSM-5 criteria?

(A) Aging

(B) Family abuse

(C) Adjustment disorder

(D) Suicidal sentiment

(90) What are some symptoms of adjustment disorders?

(A) Nervousness, gloomy mood, behavioral disturbances

(B) Burn marks, headache, bulimia

(C) Restlessness, lack of sleep, harassing others

(D) Breaking things, respiratory issues, weak eyesight

(91) What is the maximum estimated time length of signs and symptoms of an adjustment disorder?

(A) Two months

(B) Four months

(C) Six months

(D) Eight months

(92) What sorts of approaches are used to enhance interpersonal skills, emotional regulation and anger management skills?

(A) Therapy for the whole family

(B) Social support groups

(C) Cognitive-behavioral methods

(D) Couples therapy

(93) The use of antidepressants should be avoided when treating which disease?

(A) Bipolar disorder

(B) Alzheimer's

(C) Agitation

(D) Childhood enuresis

(94) Identity formation is a crucial stage of ________.

(A) Prenatal development

(B) Childhood

(C) Adolescence

(D) Adultery

(95) What is IPT an acronym of?

(A) Internet protocol

(B) Interpersonal psychotherapy

(C) Intellectual property

(D) Ingress protection

(96) What anxiety disorder is categorized by extended and excessive worry that disrupts everyday activities?

(A) Obsessive-compulsive disorder

(B) Separation anxiety

(C) Panic disorder

(D) Generalized anxiety disorder

(97) What are some symptoms of a panic disorder?

(A) Choking sensation, chest ache, sweating

(B) Palpitations, nausea, laughter

(C) Brain fog, stomach pains, excessive sleep

(D) Loss of sensation, loss of balance, loss of hair

(98) What condition might a client have if he has a fear of being in situations where it is difficult or embarrassing to leave?

(A) PTSD

(B) Bipolar disorder

(C) Domestic violence

(D) Agoraphobia

(99) A child is afraid of her mother leaving. This is known as _________disorder.

(A) Separation anxiety

(B) Conduct

(C) Eating

(D) Obsessive-compulsive

(100) In what situation is a person likely to breathe rapidly (gasping, panting) due to a bodily response?

(A) Anxiety

(B) Depression

(C) Stress

(D) Sleeping

(101) Who is most at risk of developing anxiety disorders?

(A) A dancer ready to perform

(B) An individual ready to propose

(C) A job applicant waiting for results

(D) A child after a parent's accidental death

(102) What are the most common medications prescribed for anxiety?

(A) Antidepressants

(B) Antibiotics

(C) Aspirin

(D) Caffeine

(103) What are some long-term consequences of abuse or trauma?

(A) Disturbed sleeping patterns and rage

(B) Physical violence and heroin addiction

(C) Weak eyesight and internet addiction

(D) Eating disorders and self-harm

(104) The effects of trauma are __________.

(A) Unimportant

(B) Poorly studied

(C) Occasionally harmful

(D) Pervasive

Treatment Planning

(105) Which of the following should be a characteristic of a counselor's use of language?

(A) Layman's language

(B) Medical terminology

(C) Condescending tone of voice

(D) Complicated vocabulary

(106) What should be discussed in the first meeting with a client?

(A) Expected outcome of treatment

(B) Whether the client has benefited from therapy

(C) Hidden trauma from the client's past

(D) None of the above

(107) What should a counselor do after listening to a client's input?

(A) Negate the client's opinion of therapy

(B) Include all of the client's suggestions during the course of treatment

(C) Alter the course of treatment appropriately

(D) None of the above

(108) What is a communicative skill that a counselor must use during interactions with patients?

(A) Clarity

(B) Empathy

(C) Humility

(D) All of the above

(109) At the end of a discussion on treatment, a counselor must make sure ________________.

(A) The client is going to go through with the treatment plan

(B) The client knows what to expect at the end of treatment

(C) The client has no say in the treatment plan

(D) All of the above

(110) Which of the following is an advantage of integrating setting goals into client interaction?

(A) It gives the patient a clear idea of how the treatment will proceed.

(B) It helps educate the client.

(C) It motivates the client to follow through to the end of the treatment.

(D) All of the above.

(111) Which part of a basic treatment plan includes information on a client's previous illnesses?

(A) Treatment contract

(B) History and counselor's assessment

(C) Presenting complaint

(D) None of the above

(112) What does the presenting complaint section of the treatment plan include?

(A) The client's current ailments

(B) The client's previous ailments

(C) The goals of the treatment plan

(D) All of the above

(113) What is the main reason the transition stage of group therapy can be difficult?

(A) Group members are reserved about sharing personal information with the group.

(B) Group members are afraid of discrimination from other group members.

(C) A divide could be formed within the group concerning a certain topic.

(D) All of the above.

(114) In what stage of group therapy do clients start to act upon the discussions they have had during the therapeutic sessions?

(A) The working stage

(B) The final stage

(C) The transition stage

(D) The initiation stage

(115) Why do counselors prepare for counselor-initiated interruptions during the course of therapy?

(A) To be considerate toward the client's therapeutic process.

(B) It's legally mandated.

(C) To ensure that they are protected from the consequences of abandoning the client or if they have to leave abruptly.

(D) All of the above

(116) Which section of the treatment plan should a client refer to if he or she is struggling with therapy?

(A) Objectives

(B) Modalities

(C) Strengths

(D) Presenting complaint

(117) Besides the initial stage, when should the mediator of group therapy remind the group members to avoid any breaches in confidentiality?

(A) The final stage

(B) The transition stage

(C) The working stage

(D) None of the above

(118) Which of the following is not typically a concern that needs to be addressed during the initial stage of group therapy?

(A) Concerns due to cultural discrimination

(B) Concerns due to religious discrimination

(C) Concerns related to participation in therapy

(D) Concerns relating to confidentiality of personal information

(119) Why do mediators of group therapy organize ceremonies and more during the final stage of group therapy?

(A) To utilize group therapy funding

(B) To positively enhance clients' milestone achievements

(C) To ensure clients recommend the group therapy to their friends/family

(D) None of the above

(120) Which of the following is not a counselor-initiated interruption?

(A) Ending the sessions because the client is unable to benefit from the counselor's practice

(B) Ending the sessions because the counselor is facing threats from the client

(C) Ending the sessions due to onset of personal illness

(D) Ending the sessions with the client in the middle of therapy because of too much work

(121) What aspect is crucial once a treatment plan has been initiated?

(A) Patient compliance

(B) Patient noncompliance

(C) Patient financial status

(D) None of the above

(122) What kind of care does an emergency case require?

(A) Primary care

(B) Secondary care

(C) Tertiary care

(D) Quaternary care

(123) Which part of the treatment plan includes therapy goals for the client?

(A) Counselor's assessment

(B) Treatment contracts

(C) Treatment goals

(D) None of the above

(124) What is the difference between the four stages of group therapy?

(A) Each stage has a different mediator.

(B) Each stage has different group members.

(C) At each stage, the collective drive and prospects are different.

(D) None of the above.

(125) Which kind of client-initiated interruptions are difficult to prepare for preemptively?

(A) When the client is incapable of benefiting from therapy

(B) When the client loses a job and is suddenly financially unstable

(C) When the client is planning to move to a different area of the country

(D) All of the above

Counseling Skills and Intervention

(126) Which of the following skills must a counselor have to conduct a counseling program properly?

(A) Administrative and supervisory abilities

(B) Tolerance and fortitude

(C) A financial supervisor and secretary

(D) None of the above

(127) Which factors could cause depressive symptoms in adults above the age of 65?

(A) Social status shifts

(B) Decline of physical health

(C) Income decline

(D) All of the above

(128) What is the relationship between socioeconomic status and maturing and wellness?

(A) With a higher income, a person can afford better health care and food.

(B) More money improves the appearance of everything, including aging.

(C) If your income is higher, you can afford a trip or join a gym/spa.

(D) Both A and C.

(129) What is one scenario in which a clinician might violate the strict code of patient confidentiality?

(A) When the therapist has a strong desire to communicate

(B) When the therapist takes a vacation

(C) When the therapist's duty to warn comes into play

(D) All of the above

(130) When people judge others, they tend to favor internal personality traits over external variables. However, when analyzing our own behavior, we tend to attribute our successes to internal personal characteristics and our failures to external environments.

What is this phenomenon called?

(A) Conceitedness

(B) Self-serving bias

(C) Empathy

(D) Love

(131) A counselor could facilitate clients of visibale minority that may experience discrimination and prejudice by recreating culturally sensitive scenes.

This is an example of?

(A) Psychodrama

(B) Existential methodologies

(C) Transactional analysis

(D) Behavior modification therapy

(132) What are some of the benefits of doing community service?

(A) Reaching out to a population that is underserved

(B) Increasing public awareness

(C) Connecting resources with other organizations serving a similar purpose

(D) All of the above

(133) Once behavioral problems have been clearly explained, a starting point can be acquired in behavioral therapy, mirroring the intensity and likelihood of the behaviors prior to treatment.

At this point, what must both the client and the physician decide?

(A) How to assess behavior

(B) Methods for recording behavioral measurement

(C) How the client perceives the behavior

(D) Both A and B

(134) A client says, "My doctor did not call to inform me of the results of my medical tests. She definitely has terrible news and doesn't want to tell me." What kind of distorted thinking does this represent?

(A) Thinking on an all-or-nothing basis

(B) Excessive generalization

(C) Mental filter

(D) Jumping to conclusions

(135) What are two essential aspects of client-centered counseling?

(A) Therapeutic alliances and intervention techniques

(B) Patterns of behavior and thought

(C) Objectives and therapeutic alliance

(D) None of the above

(136) What are two useful techniques associated with multimodal therapy?

(A) Questioning and attention

(B) Imagery and understanding

(C) Bridging and tracking

(D) All of the above

(137) In the acronym BASIC ID, what does the first letter "I" stand for?

(A) Ideas

(B) Idiosyncrasies

(C) Imagery

(D) Illusion

(138) In behavior therapy, what are two terms to describe the changing of someone's behavior?

(A) Understandable and achievable

(B) Specific and quantifiable

(C) Sincere and dependable

(D) Both B and C

(139) What are two main aspects of cognitive therapy that lead to less distorted thinking in clients?

(A) Identifying and mapping

(B) Understanding and concentrating

(C) Replacing and disputing

(D) All of the above

(140) What is the role of a counselor in person-centered therapy?

(A) Assisting clients who have distorted thinking

(B) Developing intervention strategies for the client to practice at home

(C) Interpreting and analyzing dreams, fantasies and visuals

(D) Creating an environment in which people can trust themselves

(141) In multimodal therapy, what do clients respond to best?

(A) Modalities of preference

(B) Personality traits

(C) Strengths

(D) Problem areas

(142) Treatment with multimodal therapy begins with a thorough assessment of seven areas, with questions and scales used to identify both_______ and __________.

(A) Problems and psychological health

(B) Problem areas and areas of strength

(C) Ideologies and convictions

(D) None of the above

(143) Which of the following is a type of descriptive research that requires a 50–57% return rate to be accurate?

(A) Observation

(B) Case study

(C) Analysis

(D) Survey

(144) What is the name of the approach in which a counselor selects a theory and techniques to match a client's characteristics, manpower and situation?

(A) Eccentric

(B) Eclectic

(C) Comprehensive

(D) Casual

(145) According to which of the following theories do therapists believe violence is learned through modeling?

(A) Social dynamism theory

(B) Behavioral theory

(C) Psychodynamic theory

(D) Freudian theory

(146) What is the distinction between suppression and repression?

(A) Suppression is involuntary.

(B) Repression is involuntary.

(C) They are not different.

(D) Repression is voluntary.

(147) Who helped pioneer structured therapeutic sessions?

(A) Joseph Pratt

(B) Carl Rogers

(C) Irv Yalom

(D) Wilfred Bion

(148) According to surveys, the elderly are an underrepresented population in terms of mental health services.

In terms of community outreach, what can a mental health clinic offer to this population?

(A) Psychoeducational classes

(B) Conventional mail services

(C) Brief, solution-focused therapy

(D) All of the above

(149) What are your responsibilities as a member of a multidisciplinary team?

(A) Chairing a committee

(B) Organizing a gathering

(C) Participating in weekly meetings

(D) All of the above

(150) How can a physician gain self-awareness to help him or her find an appropriate therapeutic approach?

(A) Using inventories like the Myers-Briggs Type Indicator (MBTI)

(B) Gaining other people's feedback

(C) Conversing with his or her family

(D) Both A and B

(151) What is a multi-counseling team in the context of therapy?

(A) Professionals from various fields gather in groups for a specific purpose

(B) A group formed to provide disciplinary measures for specific behavioral issues

(C) A meeting of parents and teachers to evaluate student behavior

(D) All of the above

(152) What factors should be considered when developing treatment goals for brief solution-focused therapy?

(A) Goals should be documented.

(B) Clients must find the goals significant and relevant.

(C) Goals should be small and easy to achieve.

(D) All of the above.

(153) Which type of disorder may not benefit from group therapy?

(A) Alcohol abuse

(B) Fear of public speaking

(C) Grief of losing someone close

(D) Autism spectrum disorders

(154) What is the best use for solution-focused therapy?

(A) Problems with adjusting to a new environment

(B) Anxiety and depression

(C) Both A and B

(D) Dissociative identity disorder

(155) Support groups are impactful in which areas of concern?

(A) Divorce

(B) Being a parent of a disabled child

(C) Grief

(D) All of the above

(156) A community is home to a state prison. What kind of community outreach might be required?

(A) Outreach programs for imprisoned spouses

(B) Outreach to children of incarcerated parents

(C) Both A and B

(D) There is no need for community engagement

(157) What kind of therapy would serve as the foundation for a tobacco cessation program?

(A) Adlerian therapy

(B) Dialectical behavior therapy

(C) Cognitive behavior therapy

(D) Interpersonal therapy

(158) Which of the following would most likely have a negative impact on a Hispanic family during therapy?

(A) The belief that individuation from the family is required for healthy functioning

(B) A proclivity for addressing clients by their first names

(C) An aversion to androgynous social conduct

(D) The conviction that truthfulness between people necessitates personal contact

(159) Sarah is a group counselor who creates groups to meet the needs of several clients in her practice. She wants to establish trust easily, have a high sense of consistency and keep group sessions to a certain time frame.

This is most appropriate for:

(A) Non-selective groups

(B) Psychotherapy groups

(C) Closed groups

(D) Transactional examinations

(160) Native Americans retain a historical significance of harmony and balance in their environment, as well as in their interpersonal relationships. Garrett and Garrett referred to this traditional value as?

(A) Ethnic cohesion

(B) Harmony ethic

(C) Ethos of consonance

(D) Unifying ethology

(161) What should a counselor keep in mind while attending to older adults, regardless of the mode of therapy used?

(A) Focus on the clients' past

(B) Focus on the clients' emotions

(C) Focus on the clients' present

(D) Focus on the clients' future

(162) What does it mean to take a culturally sensitive approach to counseling?

(A) To be fluent in the language of the culture

(B) To have knowledge of cultural heritage

(C) To comprehend a culture's understanding of society

(D) Both B and C

(163) In which of the following cases is the influence of social factors on a client's value system least likely?

(A) Xiao Ping, a Chinese student who is depressed because his grades were insufficient to gain admission to law school

(B) David, an 86-year-old who has no idea where he lives

(C) Sophia, who is unemployed due to her poor command of the English language

(D) Julie, a victim of domestic abuse with low self-esteem

(164) This is your first therapy session with a college senior. Because of her failing grades and poor attendance, the senior was referred to you. When you start the interview, she tells you about how her ex-boyfriend mistreated her on a regular basis. She states that they split up when his parents relocated out of state. She also states that she is scared the boyfriend will return and try and take her away.

The greatest thing you can do as a mental health professional at this point in the process is:

(A) Listen empathically without offering advice or suggestions

(B) Demonstrate that you are listening by asking leading questions and eliciting as much information as possible

(C) Provide the student with instances of other victims of sexual assault with whom you have worked so that she knows you comprehend her situation

(D) Interject on a regular basis to provide an explanation of the situation and sympathetic guidance

(165) When providing distance counseling via the internet, therapists should include all of the following items in their explicit consent form except:

(A) A clarification of the benefits and risks of remote counseling

(B) Policies and procedures when the therapist is not reachable

(C) Alternative technique for delivery of services if technical problems occur

(D) A copy of a certificate allowing the counselor to provide remote therapy

(166) Which of the following is attributed to Holland?

(A) He created five developmental stages.

(B) He was the inventor of the field/level categorization.

(C) He introduced six different personality types.

(D) He broadened the concept of developmental roles in life.

(167) Before delegating an assignment, behavioral therapists should keep an eye out for:

(A) Symptoms of resistance to change

(B) Misunderstood directions

(C) Indications that a client doesn't need counseling

(D) Optimism

(168) What are the most major obstacles to reaching out to Native Americans with medical conditions in indigenous societies, aside from rural isolation?

(A) Age

(B) Language

(C) Gender

(D) Career

(169) Which of the following people is regressing?

(A) A child who reads the paper on a daily basis

(B) A teen who weeps when she wants to be noticed

(C) A man in his mid-thirties who wishes to undergo gender reassignment surgery

(D) An elderly man who believes he is reliving World War II

(170) What method might you employ if you genuinely want to get a sense of a group's social order and where you stand in comparison to others?

(A) The genogram

(B) Self-disclosure

(C) Sociometry

(D) Observation of behavior

(171) Which of the following is a reason why you should create a hierarchy for systematic desensitization?

(A) To delegate tasks in a systematic manner

(B) To assist your client in dealing with increasingly stressful stimuli

(C) Because a basic need is associated with Maslow rather than Wolpe

(D) In order to save time during the therapeutic relationship

(172) Which of the following is one of Erik Erikson's outlined psychosocial stages?

(A) Initiative vs guilt

(B) Idiocy vs intelligence

(C) Intimacy vs isolation

(D) Integrity vs despair

(173) Sweeny stated the need to take three additional actions, in addition to intrinsic or extrinsic motivation, to establish a therapeutic relationship.

What was one of those actions?

(A) Concentrate on the client rather than on other people

(B) Concentrate on the humane traits rather than the inhumane

(C) Concentrate on the present rather than the past or the future

(D) None of the above

(174) What does it mean to have a transferential/counter transferential relationship?

(A) A client is projecting a relationship with another person onto the therapist.

(B) The therapist is projecting a relationship with another person onto the client.

(C) Blaming the consequences of one's behavior on someone else.

(D) Both A and B.

(175) A study is being conducted to see if postmodern music improves the ability of police officers to learn new methods of resolving conflicts. Two groups of students study the same content, one group listening to new-age music.

What is the independent variable in this experiment?

(A) The group's composition

(B) Music

(C) Learning

(D) The participants' occupations

(176) Your client calls to tell you that her brother-in-law requires a coroner's evaluation for a judicial matter and has asked you to perform it. You've had training in this area.

How should you proceed?

(A) Once the client has discontinued services, conduct the evaluation.

(B) After both parties have given their informed consent, conduct the evaluation.

(C) Refuse to conduct the evaluation.

(D) Terminate the client.

(177) The primary goal of cognitive information processing-related vocational interference is:

(A) Requiring the client to use cognitive decision-making instead of affective decision-making procedures

(B) Developing innovative methods to implement decision-making processes

(C) Creating situations that will help the client's processing skills grow

(D) Providing a dose of reality on the client's professional decisions

(178) The notions of identity tension line and role asymmetry are most commonly associated with:

(A) Couples with two jobs

(B) Individuals who have retired

(C) Seniors graduating from high school

(D) Avocations

(179) What should a counselor ask him or herself when working with a new patient whose ethnic background differs from the counselor's?

(A) Do I understand the cultural values and beliefs of the client?

(B) Do I have preconceived notions of this client's culture that could impair the healing alliance?

(C) Do I speak the client's native tongue?

(D) Both A and B.

(180) The goal of cognitive therapy is to improve one's ability to reason and come to grips with life's ups and downs.

Is this appropriate for multicultural counseling?

(A) No, because everyone wants to improve their self-awareness.

(B) Yes, because it is more comfortable to share one's thoughts than feelings.

(C) No, studies have shown that cognitive therapy is only effective in Western populations.

(D) Yes, everyone can benefit from cognitive therapy.

Core Counseling Attributes

(181) Who are multicultural psychotherapists?

(A) Those who study and educate clients about multiple cultures

(B) Therapists who belong to multicultural families

(C) Counselors who consider their clients' culture and the ways it affects how they view the world

(D) Therapists who follow the psychodynamic school of thought

(182) Why are therapists' empathy reports considered unreliable?

(A) Therapists may intentionally or unintentionally overrate themselves.

(B) The nature of reports makes it difficult to establish reliability.

(C) All of the above.

(D) None of the above.

(183) What is the focus of counseling?

(A) Diagnosing mental disorders

(B) Researching and reporting the prevalence of mental health issues

(C) Advising people and helping them deal with issues in their lives

(D) All of the above

(184) What is the first thing that a group facilitator needs to discuss at the beginning of a group counseling session?

(A) The duration of the counseling session

(B) The importance of confidentiality

(C) The importance of consent

(D) The ethical guidelines

(185) How can a counselor be effective?

(A) By listening effectively

(B) By asking yes/no questions

(C) By rushing to offer solutions for the client's problems

(D) By being patient and never interrupting or pressuring clients

(186) What should practice counselors and counselors in training do if they experience a conflict between their values and beliefs?

(A) They should end the session and leave without saying anything.

(B) They should report the conflict to their superiors.

(C) They should no longer practice counseling.

(D) None of the above.

(187) How does sincerity in psychotherapy help in counseling?

(A) It develops honesty between the client and counselor.

(B) Being sincere can make the counselor efficient.

(C) It helps form an understanding between the client and counselor.

(D) All of the above.

(188) What should counselors do if they are struggling with individual and professional morals?

(A) Take a break

(B) Open up to clients

(C) Leave practice

(D) Pursue help and training from other mental health experts

(189) What is the importance of consistency in counseling?

(A) It provides faster results and is cost-effective.

(B) It provides a good environment for clients.

(C) It helps counselors be effective.

(D) It helps clients voice their problems faster.

(190) What should counselors always do while listening to clients?

(A) Listen to them quietly

(B) Observe their body language

(C) Put aside their own viewpoints and beliefs

(D) All of the above

(191) What types of questions are usually avoided in therapy sessions?

(A) Yes/no questions

(B) Personal questions

(C) Medical questions

(D) Close-ended questions

(192) What is an affirmation?

(A) A part of educating clients

(B) Helping clients affirm their beliefs

(C) A part of reflecting and reassuring

(D) All of the above

(193) Why is compassion an important healing element?

(A) It helps the counselor sympathize with the client.

(B) It helps the client feel safe.

(C) It helps the client and counselor both be honest.

(D) It makes the client feel understood.

(194) Which of the following things would have a bad impact on the client-counselor relationship?

(A) Building rapport with the client

(B) Learning about the client's history and background

(C) Being sincere and compassionate

(D) Disclosing information about the client and going against the value of confidentiality

(195) What is one of the ways through which counselors can build self-awareness in their clients?

(A) Walking in the park

(B) Journaling

(C) Talking to themselves

(D) All of the above

(196) What makes a client-counselor relationship strong?

(A) Overly empathizing with the client

(B) Restating and rephrasing as a part of reflection

(C) Sympathizing with the clients' problems

(D) All of the above

(197) What is another form of consistency that helps counselors?

(A) Consistency in the duration of sessions

(B) Consistency in counseling techniques

(C) Consistency in beliefs

(D) Consistency in content

(198) What is the major driving force behind multicultural counseling?

(A) Learning about minorities' different perspectives on the world

(B) Learning about the uniqueness of different cultures

(C) Educating clients about different cultures' impact on human lives

(D) All of the above

(199) How does one know if a counselor's empathetic responses were beneficial?

(A) If the client becomes more emotionally closed off

(B) If the client stops attending therapy sessions

(C) If the report by the client is positive

(D) If the client nods or responds verbally

(200) What is the objective of treatment?

(A) To diagnose mental disorders

(B) To help clients realize their irrational beliefs

(C) To help clients no longer have to depend on a therapist

(D) All of the above

Test 1 Answers

Professional Practice and Ethics Answers

(1) (B) Client privilege.

Counseling refers to providing guidance and therapy to patients with mental health issues, whereas privacy refers to the right of clients to choose who has access to data about them. Client privilege protects clients' information from being revealed in judicial proceedings.

(2) (D) All of the above.

The only requirement is that a client open up and share all the essential information about his or her problem. There is no restriction on the medium a person uses to do that.

(3) (A) Dissemination.

After choosing a problem, devising a hypothesis, creating a research design, collecting information and analyzing the results, the final step in the research process is disseminating the results. Researchers then report all of their findings and conclusions.

(4) (B) The counselor did not continuously evaluate the behavior of the patient.

When counselors do not continuously record, evaluate and examine the behaviors of their patients, they draw incorrect conclusions and often fail to help their clients solve their problems.

(5) (A) A few sessions.

A few sessions are required when the problem has just started surfacing or is not very major. However, if a patient has been facing a problem for a long time, it may require extended time with a therapist to resolve the issue.

(6) (D) Five.

The counseling process is usually broken down into five main stages. These include initial disclosure and relationship building, problem assessment and in-depth exploration, goal setting, intervention in counseling and evaluation, and termination or referral.

(7) (B) Empathy, genuineness and unconditional caring.

A patient can only confide in a therapist and a counselor when offered unconditional care, kindness, empathy and genuineness despite anything the patient has to share.

(8) (A) Problem assessment and in-depth exploration.

The second step of the counseling process is the assessment and in-depth exploration of the problem shared by the client.

(9) (B) Entrusted secret.

Anything that a patient shares with a counselor and therapist is confidential and considered an entrusted secret.

(10) (D) All of the above.

Although counselor-client confidentiality is a major component of counseling, there may come a time when the counselor has to breach confidentiality. When the client is facing sexual abuse or having suicidal thoughts, the counselor should immediately contact family members or other authorities.

(11) (A) Tell the parents.

If an emotionally challenged child discloses her plan of running away from home to the counselor, the child's parents should be informed immediately. The child should not be ignored or scolded, as then she will no longer feel safe confiding her concerns.

(12) (B) People feel reluctant seeking therapy and counseling.

If counselors breach client-counselor confidentiality, they can cause severe harm to their profession and their patients as a whole. People will become suspicious and distrustful. They will be less willing to discuss their problems.

(13) (D) All of the above.

To pursue counseling professionally, a counselor should be aware of ethical standards, know the boundaries he or she must practice within and continue consistently learning any new information regarding psychiatric illnesses in order to stay current with the profession.

(14) (A) He should state all the major and minor facts regarding the alleged killer.

The patient holds the privilege of confidentiality; this generally prevents a counselor from revealing any information in court. However, if the situation is serious or if lives depend on the counselor's provision of information, the counselor must then report the pertinent facts to the court.

(15) (D) Both A and C.

When a counselor is dealing with problems in his personal life, it is not wise for him to continue dealing with his patients because he will not be able to give them the correct guidance and might make wrong decisions. Therefore, he should immediately take a break and, with the consent of his clients, should refer his cases to a trusted counselor.

(16) (A) A legally recognized third party.

Counselors cannot make decisions for people who cannot give their consent. They have to seek the permission of a legally recognized third party. The third party doesn't need to be a parent; it can be a family member or guardian.

(17) (D) None of the above.

The Disabilities Act protects the rights of all Americans to access any public building, be it schools, hospitals or parks.

(18) (A) Factual comprehension.

Low IQ and attention deficit disorders affect the factual comprehension of patients. Counselors have to treat such individuals with compassion and build a relationship with them.

(19) (B) As people with the same rights, demands and desires as everyone else.

People with disabilities face emotional trauma because they are not accepted in society. Therefore, counselors need to treat them like normal human beings with the same desires, rights and demands as everyone else.

(20) (C) Both A and B.

Counselors need to be forgiving and compassionate when dealing with patients who have physical or mental disabilities.

(21) (B) Charging exorbitant fees.

Charging unnecessarily high fees in exchange for counseling is undoubtedly unethical.

(22) (A) The conditions and laws regarding confidentiality can change from time to time.

There are specific laws that define confidentiality between the patient and a counselor, and both individuals have to abide by those rules and regulations.

(23) (B) Taking fees on time.

Anything that deals with a patient's problem is part of the counseling process, but taking fees on time has nothing to do with treatment.

(24) (C) Martin Seligman.

Martin Seligman is an American psychologist who stated his belief that an assessment of a patient should recognize a person's significance and uniqueness.

(25) (A) All stages.

Although the counseling process is divided into five major stages, all of them are interconnected and continue even if the client and counselor have moved to the next stage.

Intake, Assessment and Diagnosis Answers

(26) (A) Biopsychosocial.

The BPS, also called the biopsychosocial structure, is a cognitive evolution and functioning method that highlights the importance of an institutional view of the individual and the assimilation of genetic, physiological and cultural forces.

(27) (A) Three.

The BPS is divided into biological, psychological and social components.

(28) (B) Shea.

In 1998, Shea proposed a five-stage universal model for clinical interviewing: introduction, opening, body, closing and termination. Each stage has its own set of relational and technical responsibilities.

(29) (A) Five.

There are five stages to Shea's clinical model for interviewing.

(30) (C) Sixteen.

The CFI is made up of three parts. The first component contains sixteen questions that are asked in an interview that helps counselors understand the cultural context of each question.

(31) (A) When the counselor needs to control the interview situation.

This approach is directive and preferred when the counselor intends to control the interview situation. If an interviewee is going to manage the interview, the nondirective approach is best.

(32) (B) The ability of a screening device to identify accurate cases of a target condition in a population group.

The ability of a mechanism to target people who do not have the disorder is referred to as specificity and not sensitivity.

(33) (D) Only A and B.

Couples therapy is for two people who are facing issues regarding their emotional bond. To solve such problems, counselors usually adopt the cognitive-behavioral technique. The systems technique is usually preferred for family therapy.

(34) (A) Screening.

Clients seeking therapy undergo a screening process that helps counselors identify their weak and strong points. This can make the healing process easier.

(35) (D) All of the above.

Self-reports are self-analyses done by clients about themselves regarding their feelings. These reports help counselors understand their clients better, but it's important to note that clients usually respond diplomatically, overstate their symptoms, face difficulty in evaluating themselves properly and also respond based on what they are feeling at that time. This means the reports may not be truly representative of their original mental state.

(36) (B) Co-occurring diagnoses.

COD stands for co-occurring diagnoses. This refers to the occurrence of multiple disorders in a client.

(37) (A) Adopting a recovery mindset.

There are six main guiding principles for dealing with clients with co-occurring diagnoses: adopting a recovery mindset, taking a multifaceted approach, creating a phased treatment plan, addressing specific real-world issues early on, making plans to accommodate the client's progressive cognitive impairments and using support systems to preserve and broaden treatment efficacy.

(38) (C) Screening, problem analysis and individual evaluation.

In a thorough substance abuse assessment, screening, problem analysis and individual evaluation are the three most important steps.

(39) (A) They can be completed in private.

There are several advantages of writing self-reports for clients. One advantage is that these reports can be completed in private, allowing clients to be open and vulnerable.

(40) (B) Two separate processes.

Although often confused as the same processes, assessment and screening are two separate processes and separate techniques adopted in counseling.

(41) (B) Men underreport problems.

A major dilemma of our society is that it badly stigmatizes men's mental health issues. This is a great concern because it results in men underreporting their problems and trying to cope with them independently.

(42) (A) Biological.

Alcohol abuse can have serious implications on a person's health, and any question regarding it will be asked under the BPS's biological component.

(43) (B) Ingraining hope.

Several objectives should be met before the termination of a session. One of these objectives requires counselors to instill hope in clients so that they can attend future sessions and feel good about seeking therapy.

(44) (C) MSE.

MSE stands for mental status examination. This is an important tool used by doctors to make mental health prognoses. It also helps doctors distinguish between a variety of systemic diseases, as well as neurocognitive and psychiatric disorders.

(45) (A) Body.

The third stage of Shea's 1998 model is the body.

(46) (B) There is dismissiveness and deception.

It is very important to build a relationship with clients before directing direct questions toward them. If this is not done, it leads to dismissiveness and deception, so the purpose of therapy is not achieved.

(47) (D) All of the above.

Culture is an open and highly dynamic term that covers a wide range of areas. It includes language, religion, social structure and more.

(48) (B) Rape.

When a client dealing with trauma approaches a counselor, the counselor should inquire about the situation that led to the trauma unless the client is a rape victim. In that case, the priority should be to make the victim feel safe and ensure his or her mental well-being.

(49) (D) All of the above.

There are several modalities of therapy that are commonly sought these days. They include couples therapy, group therapy and personal therapy.

(50) (B) Identifying people who do not have a disorder as having it.

As the phrase suggests, false positives refer to all those reports that associate a problem or disease with people who do not originally have it.

Areas of Clinical Focus Answers

(51) (C) Terminally ill.

A terminally ill patient usually experiences various emotions, such as loss of hope, regret, sadness, etc.

(52) (A) 2.0 billion.

Keeping in mind the current anticipated life expectancy ratio of citizens in every country—70 years—it is estimated that the total population of people above 60 will be 2.0 billion by 2050.

(53) (B) Depression.

Processing the pain of a loved one's absence is hard and can cause a person to become depressed.

(54) (A) It eases communication.

Therapy is a helpful alternative for those who are seeking to open up about their issues or traumas. It involves mixed sessions with people from diverse ethnicities or family members in order to ease communication and seek clarity.

(55) (A) Initiating treatment, diagnosing and preventing diseases at an older age.

Geriatrics comprises initiating and observing treatment, identifying various problems that arise with aging and assisting in the diagnosis and prevention of various diseases that afflict the human body at an older age.

(56) (C) Sensory loss, improper balance, subconscious loss.

The most common diseases older individuals suffer from are heart and lung disease, improper balance and subconscious loss.

(57) (B) Guilt, lack of physical activity, anger.

Caregivers often feel guilty about forgetting to attend to their own needs and desires. They fully invest themselves in the care of their loved ones and then feel guilty if they take any time for themselves. A total lack of self-care can lead to anger.

(58) (C) Stress, relocation, death of loved ones.

Other than biological changes, stress and grief, moving away from a place filled with memories and the death of loved ones can also speed the process of aging.

(59) (D) Subconscious loss.

Alzheimer's, Parkinson's and dementia do not involve improper balance, sensory loss and dental issues. They are diseases that involve subconscious loss.

(60) (D) A child wants a sibling.

Parents do not normally adopt a child just because their older child wishes for a sibling.

(61) (B) Stress, failed adoption, intrusion of personal space.

Adoption is an expensive process. Stress, failed adoption and intrusion of personal space are all issues parents might go through while adopting.

(62) (D) 55%.

Fifty-five percent of US families have children from an earlier marriage.

(63) (C) Identity crisis.

Identity crisis is a common disruption that children face after adoption or when a parent remarries. Children fail to understand why their parents are not together anymore and begin to resent their new family. Sibling rivalry is a rift between two or more children when another sibling is brought into the house. Conflicts are regular fights and disagreements between a child's parents, and lack of attention is when parents fail to spend enough time with their children.

(64) (A) Bruises on various body parts and distress.

If you are able to see bruises on a child and he or she exhibits clear distress, this could be a sign of physical abuse.

(65) (D) Sexual intercourse and oral-genital contact.

Unsolicited romantic texts, staring inappropriately and sexting are forms of sexual harassment. Examples of sexual abuse are sexual intercourse, oral-genital contact and inappropriate advances and touching of body parts.

(66) (C) Mental torture.

Sexual and physical abuse are all forms of violence that involve harmful physical touch. Ignoring necessities is classified as a form of mental torture.

(67) (A) 30% under 10 years of age; 20% preteens.

It is a fact that 30% of children under the age of 10 are abused.

(68) (D) Failed adoption.

Stress and guilt may be a result of a failed adoption. If adoption happens, intrusion of space may be another outcome. However, when things end before a child is taken home, it is a failed adoption.

(69) (A) Communication.

Strong and effective communication between partners is a basic requirement for a good relationship.

(70) (D) Past experiences and behavioral factors.

A person's upbringing plays a critical role in establishing future relationships. Individuals who grow up in a dysfunctional family are likely to implement the same traits they observed in their parents' relationships. Lack of trust, unnecessary criticism, disrespect and judgment are all reasons that could shift the dynamics of a relationship.

(71) (B) Infidelity.

When one spouse cheats on the other, this is known as infidelity.

(72) (B) Alcoholism and complications at work.

Alcoholism and complications at work are more likely to be a cause of abuse and violence in the family than the other answer options as they trigger anger and stress.

(73) (C) Emotional abuse.

Emotional abuse always takes the longest time to overcome and may have permanent negative impacts. Emotional abuse may involve constant bullying by a family member, being body-shamed, being compared to more successful members of the family or being told one is not good enough.

(74) (A) Domestic violence.

Domestic violence involves emotional, sexual, physical pressure and abuse between spouses.

(75) (A) Litigation.

Contacting legal authorities is the most effective way to tackle domestic violence.

(76) (B) 38%.

Thirty-eight percent of women in the US have reportedly faced rape, physical abuse and mental torture at the hands of a partner.

(77) (B) Technology.

Technology has proven to be one of the biggest hurdles to effective communication. Digital devices and the internet have taken over the private time couples used to have to interact and discuss their problems.

(78) (A) Withdrawal from social events and a morbid fascination with death.

These are a set of indicators that an individual is having trouble with life and contemplating suicide. Fascination with death and a preference for always being alone often leads to severe depression and suicidal ideation. The rest of the factors may indicate other types of mental illnesses.

(79) (D) Identify the client's suicidal feelings and respond appropriately while maintaining trust.

A counselor must always take into account both the client's verbal and nonverbal communication. Responding kindly in a helpful and nonjudgmental manner may motivate the client to trust the practitioner and share his or her intentions of self-harm and suicide. The rest of the answer options are actions a practitioner must never take in this situation.

(80) (C) Fear and anger.

Counselors may be fearful of the client's intentions or angry about the person's thoughts.

(81) (A) Physical exercise, informal support system, a crisis plan.

The combination of these three protective factors is the most helpful out of all the answer choices. Physical exercise clears the mind and provides a distraction. An informal support system helps the individual feel less lonely, and a crisis plan helps the counselor and client during times of emergency.

(82) (B) Talk to the woman about suicide and make the environment safe for suicide risk exploration.

This response will lead to a positive client-counselor relationship and a successful therapy session.

(83) (D) Taking notes to keep track of the client's manners, beliefs, factors of indication.

Taking notes will help the counselor maintain proper records and aid in making future decisions and retaining proof of those decisions where necessary. The rest of the responses break standard therapy protocol.

(84) (A) The client is at high risk of committing suicide.

According to Bond (2009), in a situation where clients are not able to understand the consequences of their actions, the chances of their committing suicide are quite high.

(85) (B) Client-counselor relationship.

For the therapeutic procedure to succeed, a counselor must work efficiently on building a healthy relationship with a client. The rest of the answer choices are a result of a positive client-counselor relationship.

(86) (A) Shame from failure.

Failure to recognize warning signs, involvement of colleagues and retaliation from a client's family are not reasons a counselor would feel stressed in this situation. Shame as a result of failure would be one thing a counselor might feel.

(87) (B) Adjustment disorder.

An adjustment disorder occurs during a change in an individual's life and development. The rest of the answer options are a result of severe trauma or fear.

(88) (A) Sexual abuse by one's partner.

This answer choice is not a reaction to a development in a person's life; hence, it cannot lead to an adjustment disorder.

(89) (C) Adjustment disorder.

Aging, family abuse and suicidal sentiments are not things practitioners would use the DSM-5 to identify. Only an adjustment disorder is.

(90) (A) Nervousness, gloomy mood, behavioral disturbances.

These are symptoms of an adjustment disorder. Headaches, burn marks, harassment, respiratory issues and weak eyesight are other disease/disorder symptoms.

(91) (C) Six months.

The duration of adjustment disorder symptoms can be chronic, which means that they can last up to six months.

(92) (C) Cognitive-behavioral methods.

Cognitive-behavioral methods are used to help an individual build a useful set of interpersonal skills during the therapeutic process.

(93) (B) Alzheimer's.

Alzheimer's is a common disease, but there is a lack of information about its true diagnostic category as no treatment efficacy surveys are available. Thus, psychotropic drugs, such as antidepressants, must be avoided in the treatment of individuals with this condition.

(94) (C) Adolescence.

Identity formation is a crucial stage of adolescence that helps prepare children for becoming adults.

(95) (C) Intellectual property.

IPT is an acronym for intellectual property.

(96) (D) Generalized anxiety disorder.

GAD is a prolonged and exorbitant worry that damages an individual's daily routine. It is a fear that may be heightened by tension, anxiety and body aches, etc.

(97) (A) Choking sensation, chest ache, sweating.

A panic disorder is an overpowering mixture of psychological discomfort, including a sensation of choking, sweating and chest aching that can lead to intense fear.

(98) (D) Agoraphobia.

Agoraphobia is a phobia of being in situations where it is difficult or humiliating to leave. It is a fear out of proportion with the actual situation and may be chronic.

(99) (A) Separation anxiety.

Separation anxiety disorder is the fear or worry of being separated from loved ones. It lasts for at least a month in young kids and six months in adults.

(100) (A) Anxiety.

When people react to danger, they breathe heavily as the lungs are attempting to move more oxygen through the body; in particular instances, a person may feel the need to flee.

(101) (D) A child after a parent's accidental death.

It is hard to process the trauma of a parent's unexpected death, and this can lead to a long-lasting disorder in a child.

(102) (A) Antidepressants.

Antidepressants help relieve symptoms of anxiety and reduce symptoms of depression.

(103) (D) Eating disorders and self-harm.

Trauma occurs as a consequence of events that cause physical and emotional harm. To deal with that, the affected internalize habits that are not good for them, like self-harm and changed eating habits, which can lead to eating disorders.

(104) (D) Pervasive.

Trauma can lead to pervasive effects at many levels. While every person reacts differently, trauma needs to be identified and treated to prevent long-term consequences.

Treatment Planning Answers

(105) (A) Layman's language.

It is important to consider patients' respective levels of education when conversing with them about any matter. It is unfair to assume they will understand difficult medical terminology. Layman's language is a good tool to effectively and respectfully enhance clients' understanding.

(106) (A) Expected outcome of treatment.

It is beneficial for both the client and counselor to establish what they expect when the therapeutic sessions come to an end. This will help clear up any discrepancies between the two parties and also provide inspiration for goal setting.

(107) (C) Alter the course of treatment appropriately.

None of the other options are correct because they provide middle-ground solutions. It is inappropriate for the counselor to completely replace his or her own expertise with the patient's input. At the same time, it is also disrespectful to completely disregard the client's input.

(108) (D) All of the above.

All of the answer options are key components a counselor should employ while interacting with a client. Empathy is needed to encourage patients to speak more freely about themselves; clarity is needed so that there are no misunderstandings between clients and counselors and humility is needed to present a good image of counselors so that clients are more inclined to trust them.

(109) (B) The client knows what to expect at the end of the treatment.

After briefing clients on a treatment plan, it is of utmost importance to ask if they fully understand how the treatment will proceed and what is required. However, it is also beneficial for clients to know the expected outcome of their treatment so that there are no false expectations.

(110) (D) All of the above.

All of the options listed are benefits of goal setting. Counselors are advised to make this a prominent part of their practice because both they and the clients can benefit from it. It helps both parties identify the progress of the patient. Counselors need to do this for record-keeping and future treatment plans. Clients need this because it motivates them to stick to the treatment plan.

(111) (B) History and counselor's assessment.

This part of the treatment plan includes any previous ailments the patient has and a general assessment made by the counselor during the first meeting. This is important because it alerts the counselor to the client's previous conditions and any medications a person may be taking.

(112) (A) The client's current ailments.

The presenting complaint section of the treatment plan is useful for the counselor as it directly states the client's current issues. The counselor will know that these issues are top priority when devising a treatment.

(113) (D) All of the above.

All the options listed are events that occur during the transition stage of group therapy. At this stage, many antagonizing forces form, which gives rise to conflict and its consequences. All of this dies down in the following stages of therapy.

(114) (A) The working stage.

In the working stage of therapy, conflicts and emotions have settled down and a more logical and sensible approach is taken, which is concluded by group members actively listening to constructive criticism and acting upon it in their daily lives.

(115) (D) All of the above.

Counselors prepare for counselor-initiated interruptions during the course of therapy to be considerate toward the client's therapeutic process, to ensure that they are protected from the consequences of abandoning the client or if they have to leave abruptly, and because it is legally mandated. It would be completely inhumane to abandon a client in the middle of the treatment, no matter the reason.

(116) (C) Strengths.

This section is placed in the treatment plan so that it gives clients an extra push when they are feeling low. It is important they acknowledge that not everything is lost and that they still have some qualities or habits that will assist them on their journey toward recovery.

(117) (A) The final stage.

Along with goodbye notes, ceremonies and peer reviews, the mediator must remind all group members of the confidentiality clause they agreed to in the initial stage of their group therapy. The counselor's job is to put into context how harmful it would be if someone were to breach this oath of confidentiality.

(118) (C) Concerns related to participation in therapy.

This is not a topic of discussion during the initial stages of group therapy. The initial stages are for helping the group members become familiar with each other through introductions and informing them of the group's rules and regulations. Participation is most discussed during the transition and working stages of group therapy.

(119) (B) To positively enhance clients' milestone achievements.

Such ceremonies and celebrations are a common part of the final stage of group therapy, and they have a great benefit as they make the group members' milestones memorable. There is also a significant memory attached to their achievement.

(120) (D) Ending the sessions with the client in the middle of therapy because of too much work.

Although not unheard of, a counselor-initiated interruption of a session due to the counselor feeling overwhelmed with too much work is regarded as completely unethical and can be sufficient grounds for legal action. Therefore, counselors must always be aware of the responsibility of the job and the effect it has on the patient. As such, counselors must present a justifiable reason for terminating sessions.

(121) (A) Patient compliance.

Once the therapeutic sessions have acquired a flow, it is important for the counselor to keep track of the client's tangible progress. The counselor must look for any evidence that proves the client has been following through with the counselor's advice. This is done purely for the client's benefit. However, the counselor must not force the client to give in to advice. The counselor must wait for the right time to give the client small pushes towards the goal.

(122) (A) Primary care.

Primary care is responsible for outpatient department visits and also for patients that require immediate care. It is the place where patients stop initially when they need medical care.

(123) (C) Treatment goals.

Treatment goals include short-term and long-term goals. These are included in the client's therapeutic journey.

(124) (C) At each stage, the collective drive and prospects are different.

All stages consist of the same group members and the same mediator. This is important because it helps maintain consistency during the therapeutic process. However, the reason why group members attend the therapy sessions changes at each stage. They become more accepting of the process and may even start to look forward to it.

(125) (B) When the client loses a job and is suddenly financially unstable.

Neither the client nor the counselor can foresee external events such as a client losing a job and becoming financially unstable. Client-counselor interaction is limited to keeping the client's progress at a level that deals with the issues relating to trauma, etc. When this schedule is disrupted, the counselor can only provide the client with a suitable alternative, like a community counselor.

Counseling Skills and Interventions Answers

(126) (A) Administrative and supervisory abilities.

A person with supervisory and administrative skills is required to manage a counseling service effectively. To manage a group of professional and practitioner workers, it may be necessary to be familiar with various approaches to supervision. Management skills, such as the capacity to manage time wisely, collaborate and use interpersonal skills, are all vital.

(127) (D) All of the above.

Life may begin to change after the age of 65. Income loss, the death of a partner or poor physical health can all have an impact on one's social standing. The death of a long-term spouse or partner can result in a wide range of changes, including depression. Fortunately, there are numerous individual and group counseling methods for dealing with grief.

(128) (D) Both A and C.

If more funding is available for better outcomes, better and more abundant food and a wider range of interests and actions, aging will be a better and healthier experience. One of the challenges in developing the correlation between SES, health and growing older is that occupation is the primary status indicator. Because the elderly are mostly retired, they are not included in data collected for economic well-being when the analysis is based on vocation.

(129) (C) When the therapist's duty to warn comes into play.

The duty-to-warn policy is one example of how a therapist may legally violate the nondisclosure code of ethics. If the client expresses a strong desire to commit suicide or harm another person, the therapist will most likely consult with a coworker or superintendent and then act in accordance with the decision reached by the psychiatrist and colleague/supervisor. The therapist's duty is to protect his or her client and anyone else whom the client may harm.

(130) (B) Self-serving bias.

Self-serving bias may be explained using the following example: when we perform well on an exam, we begin to assume, “I am very intelligent” or “I am really good at this subject.” But when we perform poorly on the exam, we usually blame the teacher, the syllabus or the “difficult” questions.

(131) (A) Psychodrama.

Using a psychodrama approach, a therapist can help people evaluate the importance their culture has on them by recreating culturally sensitive scenes. With this strategy, possibilities for developing creativity and originality within the context of the client’s culture may emerge.

(132) (D) All of the above.

There are numerous reasons to provide community outreach, including reaching a disadvantaged population, raising public awareness and linking resources with other organizations serving numerous benefits. Another reason for providing community outreach could be to highlight an event or problem that is marginalized in a particular area.

(133) (D) Both A and B.

The client and physician must agree on how to quantify the behavior and how to record the data. Number and intensity are some of the most popular methods of measuring behavior. Clients are strongly encouraged to record their own behaviors through the use of a checklist, diary or other documentary evidence of the prevalence and magnitude of the unwanted behavior.

(134) (D) Jumping to conclusions.

Jumping to conclusions is a type of dysfunctional behavior that occurs when a person fails to perform one action and immediately believes that something else has occurred.

For example, “Brad and I had a spat this morning, and he is now late for work. I believe he has abandoned me.” Distorted thinking also includes all-or-nothing thinking, oversimplification and mental sorting.

(135) (C) Objectives and therapeutic alliance.

Person-centered counseling relies heavily on objectives and therapeutic alliances. It is more of a way of being with clients and providing them with situations that will influence motivation in this type of counseling than it is designing a specific care plan.

(136) (C) Bridging and tracking.

Bridging and tracking are two multimodal therapy techniques. Bridging involves clinicians intentionally relating to clients first through the client’s dominant modality (thinking, feeling, images, etc.) to establish connection and trust and then branching off into other areas likely to be efficient and improve client skills.

(137) (C) Imagery.

The first “I” in the acronym BASIC ID stands for imagery. Imagery is a preferred modality that refers to daydreams, dreams, recollections, mental pictures and people’s perceptions of themselves, their lifestyles and their prospects.

(138) (B) Specific and quantifiable.

According to behavioral therapists, the first step in altering behavior is to describe it in concrete and clear terms. If possible, specify both the undesirable behavior and the desired change. Helping people change their behavior entails a sequence of relatively structured and easy-to-predict steps.

(139) (C) Replacing and disputing.

After the distorted cognitions have been recognized, addressed and classified, cognitive therapy moves on to refuting and substituting cognitions. Using the refuting and replacing method, the client and clinician collaborate to find alternative cognitive distortions that are more legitimate and likely to be beneficial to the client.

(140) (D) Creating an environment in which people can trust themselves.

A clinician in person-centered therapy creates an environment in which people can trust themselves and maximize their potential. Clinicians do not interpret dreams or develop behavioral interventions for clients. Clients are empowered to change when counselors recognize them, respect their perspectives and actively participate in the treatment process.

(141) (A) Modalities of preference.

People appear to respond best to interventions targeting their preferred modes of communication. A person who concentrates on imagery, for example, is likely to gain from visualization, whereas a person who concentrates on thinking is likely to benefit from the identification and alteration of cognitive distortions.

(142) (B) Problem areas and areas of strength.

A thorough assessment helps to identify both a client's strengths and weaknesses. The seven areas evaluated are behavior, affect, sensation, imagery, cognition, interpersonal factors and drug considerations. The acronym BASIC ID can be used to represent this.

(143) (D) Survey.

Descriptive research is classified into survey, observation and case study. Descriptive research cannot reach inferences, and thus no causal relationships can be determined. For a survey to be accurate, it must receive 50–57% of the responses.

(144) (B) Eclectic.

The eclectic approach can be very effective. Most counselors who use this strategy abide by one or two main counseling theories while drawing techniques from various theories.

When meeting with a client, an effective counselor should consider a person as a whole (body, psyche, feelings, spirit).

(145) (C) Psychodynamic theory.

Albert Bandura's renowned bobo doll experiments demonstrated principles of psychodynamic theory. Children who saw an adult handle a doll aggressively treated the doll much more roughly themselves. Aggression, according to behaviorists, is learned through conditioning. Psychodynamic adherents would explain aggression as a reflex. Unfulfilled needs, according to the humanistic interpretation, cause aggression.

(146) (B) Repression is involuntary.

When disturbing memories are kept out of the rational awareness voluntarily, this is referred to as repression in psychoanalysis. Using individual liberty, psychoanalysts attempt to unearth suppressed memories and feelings during therapy. When a person consciously tries not to think or feel differently, this is referred to as suppression.

(147) (A) Joseph Pratt.

In 1905, Joseph Pratt, a Boston physician, organized a group of tuberculosis patients to teach them. Rogers is known as the "father of counseling psychology." Yalom compiled a list of therapeutic factors for use in group therapy. Bion was a psychoanalyst from the United Kingdom.

(148) (D) All of the above.

Many responses exist in the "how" of community outreach; typically, the focus is on focus, people management and financial concerns. Following the determination of the type of outreach required, those involved must identify a source of funding for the suggested outreach, as well as staffing resources and location.

(149) (D) All of the above.

As a participant of a multidisciplinary team, you may be asked to chair a committee that is investigating the best way to bring assistance to an underserved area of the community, organize an awareness campaign and/or attend regular meetings to fulfill the established goals.

(150) (D) Both A and B.

A physician can gain self-awareness through inventories such as the MBTI and by paying attention to feedback from others. Collecting data on treatment processes can assist a physician in determining a treatment approach by matching the theoretical approach that appears to be most suited to the person at this moment in his or her career.

(151) (D) All of the above.

A multi-disciplinary team is a group of professionals from various fields (or disciplines) who have come together for a common goal. Counselors, criminal justice personnel, domestic abuse shelter staff, state health and well-being workers and other community members engaged in this issue could form a task force to reduce domestic violence.

(152) (D) All of the above.

Treatment goals for brief solution-focused therapy should be significant and relevant to clients, small and achievable rather than large and difficult, and properly documented with a copy given to both the client and physician. Goals should also be realistic and attainable, within the clients' control and quantifiable.

(153) (D) Autism spectrum disorders.

Individuals with autism spectrum disorders may not be suitable for group work. Individuals associated with group work must have clear cognitive skills, the ability to focus on the here and now and the ability to interact communally, offering support and feedback as needed. Autism spectrum disorder patients are more intrinsically motivated, have trouble talking with others and may lack the communication skills required to participate in a group setting.

(154) (C) Both A and B.

Solution-focused brief therapy is particularly suitable for the diagnosis of anxiety and depression and adjustment issues. It does not work well with people who are considering suicide, who are dangerous, have psychosis or antisocial personality disorders or have severe mental illnesses.

(155) (D) All of the above.

Support groups can be an interesting strategy for a variety of issues, including divorce, parenting a disabled child and grieving. Clients receive confidence and guidance from team members through this venue, allowing them to work out issues through the experiences of others. Group work can be especially beneficial because it allows members to try out new skill sets in a safe, nonthreatening environment.

(156) (C) Both A and B.

With a state prison nearby, there may be a population of prisoners' partners and children living in the area who require mental health services. These needs can be met through group therapy, school systems and public awareness campaigns that raise awareness of available services. A multidisciplinary team could be formed to assess the needs of the community and create service ideas.

(157) (C) Cognitive-behavior therapy.

Cognitive-behavior therapy has been shown to be successful in smoking cessation programs, anorexia and psychiatric disorders like depression, anxiety and obsessive-compulsive disorders. Treatment is well-planned and structured, with an emphasis on changing thoughts and actions.

(158) (A) The belief that individuation from the family is required for healthy functioning.

Hispanic families place a high value on communal familial interconnectivity and interconnectedness among relatives.

(159) (C) A closed group.

A closed group is one in which participation is fixed and no new members are admitted for the period of the group's existence. Open groups allow members to be added, which may have an impact on the existing members and interrupt the flow because the early planning phases may need to be addressed again for the group to be restored to a normal working level. The theoretical approach of the group leader can take on a variety of forms, but the issue here is structure.

(160) (B) Harmony ethic.

Traditionally, the harmony ethic guided the native people in their values of communitarian commitment and collaboration to maintain balance both within themselves and in the world around them.

(161) (C) Focus on the clients' present.

Regardless of the therapeutic preference used, the therapist should be focused on the present when counseling older adults. Therapy should be present-oriented and resolve issues such as a death in the family, interpersonal conflicts, role transitions and behavior adjustment to the current environment. The aim of therapy is that of a collaborator and supporter.

(162) (D) Both B and C.

A culturally sensitive approach to counseling relies on current understanding of culture and not necessarily the heritage of the culture.

(163) (B) David, an 86-year-old who has no idea where he lives.

Except for the 86-year-old who can't remember where he lives, the issue of social factors on the value system is significant in all of the answer options. Cultural influences will have little impact on David's worldview because he has no idea where he lives. He most likely has little recollection of his ethnic heritage and identity.

(164) (A) Listen empathically without offering advice or suggestions.

Listening empathically and completely is most important in this situation. The client must be heard. After hearing the entire situation, a counselor is in a position to ask this person, "What can I do to help you get what you need?"

(165) (D) A copy of a certificate allowing the counselor to provide remote therapy.

Remote counseling does not necessitate any special training or certification. Even so, counselors should make every effort to ensure that they are in compliance with state and federal laws regarding technological changes that minimize the breach of confidential data. Counselors should use encryption methods that are compliant with the law. Clients should also be provided with a social media policy.

(166) (C) He introduced six different personality types.

Holland introduced six basic personality types: realistic, investigative, artistic, social, enterprising, conventional (RIASEC).

(167) (A) Symptoms of resistance to change.

When a client is hesitant to change a behavior, it suggests that he or she is not ready to accept responsibility for his or her role, however large or small, in the current dysfunction.

(168) (B) Language.

Many Native Americans do not understand psychological outreach because they do not speak the language of counseling. This is not to say they don't understand English;

rather, they lack the experience with counseling's mental and emotional language to leverage healing initiatives.

(169) (B) A teen who weeps when she wants to be noticed.

Regression denotes a person reverting to a previous point in life. A newborn cries when it needs or wants attention, and a teenager who exhibits this behavior is regressing.

(170) (C) Sociometry.

The science and art of quantifying relationships between social combinations or constructions and mental and emotional well-being is known as sociometry. Self-disclosure refers to both the explicit and implicit act of revealing something about ourselves to others, but it does not assess relationships. Behavioral observation does not quantify relationships; rather, it simply observes them. A genogram is a graphical representation of a client's familial relationships and health information that has nothing to do with sociometry. Sociometry is the only technique that truly examines the social hierarchy of a group and where a person stands in relation to others.

(171) (B) To assist your client in dealing with increasingly stressful stimuli.

Systematic desensitization is a technique for treating phobias (and other anxiety-provoking behaviors) that involves gradually subjecting the client to successively larger anxiety-producing stimuli. The client creates a fear hierarchy, starting with the least anxiety-inducing stimuli and progressing to the most anxiety-inducing stimuli. The client is also taught relaxation techniques.

(172) (B) Idiocy vs. intelligence.

Erikson believed that personality develops sequentially through eight stages of psychosocial development, from birth to adulthood. During each stage, the person goes through a developmental disorder, which can positively or negatively impact his or her personal growth. According to the theory, completing each stage successfully results in a balanced lifestyle and the acquirement of basic virtues. Basic qualities are distinguishing characteristics that the ego can employ to resolve subsequent crises.

(173) (C) Concentrate on the present rather than the past or the future.

Sweeny believed that concentrating on the present rather than the past or the future would aid in the formation of a therapeutic relationship with the client.

(174) (D) Both A and B.

A transferential relationship occurs when clients realize something about the therapist that reminds them of their mother (for example) and begin overlaying their mother's relationship's traits and potential fears onto their therapist. A counter-transferential relationship is the inverse of a transferential connection. Therapists notice characteristics in clients that remind them of another important person in their lives and transfer their feelings toward that individual onto the client.

(175) (B) Music.

A variable that induces or impacts another variable is referred to as an independent variable. In this case, that is music.

(176) (C) Refuse to conduct the evaluation.

Counselors executing forensic assessments cannot assess current or former clients, clients' relatives or clients' intimate relationships, per the ACA's Code of Ethics.

(177) (B) Developing innovative methods to implement decision-making processes.

According to Peterson, Sampson, Reardon and Lenz's cognitive information processing model, the primary goal of career psychotherapy is to enhance clients' problem-solving and decision-making knowledge and skills related to career paths.

(178) (A) Couples with two jobs.

Dual-career couples frequently experience a great deal of conflict between family and occupational roles, as well as gender roles. Identity tension lines appear when a couple approaches a boundary that one of the individuals has ascertained to be his or her relationship's limit of transformation. Asymmetry refers to the degree of equality between married couples and can include occurrences of increased opportunity for women and a decline in chauvinistic roles.

(179) (D) Both A and B.

Clinicians can assess whether or not they have a thorough understanding of their clients' cultural norms and values. This knowledge can help to avoid misconceptions and guide the clinician in aiding clients in potential therapeutic beneficial ways. Being aware of our own worldview, acknowledging that we may have stereotyped details about certain societies and examining this before beginning work with a client ensures that these thoughts/beliefs do not cause misinterpretation and obstacles to therapy.

(180) (B) Yes, because it is more comfortable to share one's thoughts than feelings.

In many cultures, individuals are more comfortable sharing their thoughts on certain subjects than talking about their feelings. Because this kind of therapy is not very intrusive and most people do not have to talk about traumatic experiences they are unwilling to share, it works well across all cultures.

Core Counseling Attributes Answers

(181) (C) Counselors who consider their clients' culture and the ways it affects how they view the world.

As multicultural therapists, counselors do not conduct therapy in a void. They are cognizant of their clients' backgrounds and how this impacts their understanding of the world. Counselors should adapt their roles to meet the needs of these individuals. Cultural diversity constitutes various perspectives, taking into account the diverse challenges faced by ethnic, racial and other types of minorities, including historically oppressed communities and their impact on society.

(182) (A) Therapists may intentionally or unintentionally overrate themselves.

Methods for measuring a therapist's empathy exist in several forms—first, the self-report rating. In the therapy session, the therapist rates his or her own empathetic skills. Reports from therapists are known to be inaccurate, as therapists may intentionally or unintentionally overrate their performance compared with ratings from their clients.

The second way to measure a therapist's empathy is through client reports. Clients are asked to rate their therapists; typically, therapist behavior involving nurturing and self-disclosure is interpreted as being empathic by clients, reflecting behaviors that are related to empathy but do not necessarily belong to it.

Thirdly, empathy can be measured through written assessments of therapists. This measure is also less favored as an alternative to direct observational assessment because of its inability to relate strongly with straight measures of empathic reflections in therapy sessions.

(183) (C) Advising people and helping them deal with issues in their lives.

In contrast to guidance that focuses on helping individuals choose the right path for themselves, counseling focuses on helping people make changes and address issues in their lives. Counselors serve as advisors.

(184) (B) The importance of confidentiality.

A confidentiality agreement during therapy sessions can help members feel free to share their ideas, emotions and experiences. During group counseling, the facilitator should emphasize the importance of confidentiality to all members and ensure their compliance.

(185) (D) By being patient and never interrupting or pressuring clients.

Counselors need to be patient in order to be effective. Oftentimes, clients take a while to explain their circumstances clearly. To be effective, counselors need to always wait for clients, never pressure or interrupt them, tolerate clients' anger, ask them what the problem is, understand nonverbal communication, interpret it and create a welcoming, trusting environment by smiling.

(186) (C) They should no longer practice counseling.

When counselors in the field of practice and those in counseling training find themselves in conflict with their values and beliefs and the demands of ethical guidelines, they are faced with three ethically acceptable options. It is possible for them not to engage in counseling or to practice in an environment that does not require a license and adherence to a code of ethics. There is also the option to take a "both/and" perspective. During therapy sessions, counselors can maintain their beliefs, adhere to ethical guidelines and perform the role and function of a professional counselor, depending on their preference.

(187) (C) It forms an understanding between the client and counselor.

When advising clients, counselors should always be sincere as clients will likely act on the advice. True sincerity in psychotherapy can be soothing because understanding is achieved and it restores lost hope of sincerity in the patient.

(188) (D) Pursue help and training from other mental health experts.

It is not the aim of the American Counseling Association to change a person's beliefs. There will always be clients with whom counselors disagree for whatever reason, which can lead to counselors feeling frustrated and distressed. A counselor in pain or confused about individual and professional values must seek out mental health experts for help and training. Whenever clients push counselors outside of their comfort zones, counselors are provided with growth opportunities.

(189) (A) It provides faster results and is cost-effective.

It has been proven that consistency in counseling will lead to better results faster and at a lower cost. It takes an effective counselor fewer appointments to achieve maximum results. Appointments that are far apart can delay both the process and the results. Delays make it more difficult for clients to attend appointments, and they often lead to a communication gap between counselor and client. By achieving goals during counseling sessions, a motivated client saves money by making health care a priority.

(190) (C) Put aside their own viewpoints and beliefs.

To listen to and understand a client, counselors must always set aside their views. The best thing to do is to remain silent and to listen to the client without interrupting. Rather than critiquing or judging clients, the aim is simply to listen to what they are saying.

(191) (D) Close-ended questions.

Asking questions is supportive in a therapeutic environment because this allows counselors to learn more about their clients. Questioning allows counselors to gain more insight into their clients in a therapeutic environment. Counselors can easily set the tone and flow of a session by asking particular questions. As a result, the whole process will be calmer. As closed questions do not promote exploration of the problem more deeply, they are avoided most of the time.

(192) (C) A part of reflecting and reassuring.

The process of reflecting also involves affirmation and reassurance. Clients feel empowered when their progress is acknowledged. To be genuine and congruent with their words, counselors must be honest. Since every therapist's approach to therapy varies, it is important to stay honest with both verbal and nonverbal signals in all counseling techniques.

(193) (D) It makes the client feel understood.

Compassion helps the client feel understood. It contributes significantly to concepts of acceptance, empathy and unconditional positive regard in therapeutic practice. In other words, it means connecting with the client's grief and acting to promote change. The definition of compassion is broader and deeper than empathy because it is about understanding the clients beyond their symptoms.

(194) (D) Disclosing information about the client and going against the value of confidentiality.

Confidentiality in health matters can differ depending on the situation. However, counselors must maintain confidentiality on every issue they confront. It will damage the counselor-client relationship if the counselor ends up disclosing any information about the client to others.

(195) (B) Journaling.

Four guiding principles can be used to build self-awareness for counselors: increasing self-care, practicing mindfulness and meditation, journaling and seeking social support.

(196) (B) Restating and rephrasing as a part of reflection.

During a counseling session, reflections accurately describe the clients' condition from their verbal or nonverbal signals. When clients reflect, their sentiments are heard, but sometimes counselors must dig deeper to describe their feelings within their statements. Reflecting helps counselors build a more solid client-counselor relationship through restating and rephrasing what is said. Using a client's statement in a new way can provide further clarity on what is being understood incorrectly and helps a counselor to gain an in-depth understanding of a client.

(197) (D) Consistency in content.

Consistency in content is also an important aspect for counselors. Taking notes manually or arranging sessions on a digital device helps therapists cut down on notating each session, helping them stay on schedule and avoiding frustration. With a template, counselors can efficiently and accurately take notes.

(198) (A) Learning about minorities' different perspectives on the world.

Counselors, therapists and psychologists must be subtle and sensitive to the unique situations and needs of minorities as the driving force for multicultural counseling. In the multicultural counseling field, counselors possess empathy and care for their patients since they recognize how their life situation is different from the patient's situation. Different approaches to multiculturalism revolve around the exploration of the circumstances and challenges that impact ethnic, racial and other minorities, including historical oppression and its consequences.

(199) (D) If the client nods or responds verbally.

If the counselor's empathy has been helpful, it is easy to recognize. Counselors' responses were helpful if the client nods or responds verbally. When clients become frustrated or indicate nonverbally that they want to stop, the counselor has failed to provide a valid response.

(200) (C) To help clients no longer have to depend on a therapist.

Clients may be highly emotional when they visit a counselor. As a result, the client may perceive the counselor as being very supportive and giving during the session. When a client opens up, the relationship will inevitably progress toward genuine familiarity. Though counselors study compassion and empathy, they may become too close with their clients in the course of their work. During therapy, an effective therapist assures the client that the objective of treatment is to enable the client to become an independent individual who does not become emotionally dependent on the counselor or therapist.

Test 2

Professional Practice and Ethics

(1) In which of the following contexts can therapy be performed?

(A) Personal

(B) Professional

(C) Both personal and professional

(D) None of the above

(2) Which of the following people can benefit from therapy?

(A) Children

(B) Adults

(C) Only A

(D) Both A and B

(3) "Goal setting" is the ________________ stage of counseling.

(A) First

(B) Third

(C) Last

(D) It is not a part of counseling

(4) Which of the following is a Seligman reason for assessing a client?

(A) Allowing counselors to make a precise diagnosis

(B) Making goal-setting more manageable

(C) Charging exorbitant fees

(D) Only A and B

(5) How long should a counseling session ideally last?

(A) 5 hours

(B) 30–50 minutes

(C) 10 minutes

(D) 24 hours

(6) Which of the following is/are the benefit(s) of seeking psychotherapy?

(A) Boosts well-being

(B) Heals troubling symptoms

(C) Improves the affected person's normal level of function

(D) All of the above

(7) Which of the following is the first step taken when a counselor decides to research a certain psychotherapy case?

(A) Choosing a problem

(B) Collecting information

(C) Making a research design

(D) Devising a hypothesis

(8) Dissemination of the results is the final step in the research process. Which of the following is a mode adopted by researchers to report their findings?

(A) Research paper

(B) Presentation

(C) Both A and B

(D) None of the above

(9) According to Thompson and Rudolph, which of the following is the best definition of privacy?

(A) The right that protects the client's private information from being revealed in judicial proceedings

(B) The right to choose who has access to data about them

(C) The right that allows them to pay according to their financial ability

(D) The right that allows them to choose a therapist of their own choice

(10) In recent times, there has been a sharp rise in the number of children who are seeking therapy. Which of the following is a prominent issue faced by counselors when dealing with children?

(A) The amount of detail to be shared with the parents

(B) The irregularity and non-serious attitude of children

(C) The noise the children make in the office

(D) The difficulty in convincing the children to open up about their issues

(11) A child informs his counselor about his suicidal thoughts and mentions how he often looks for chances to commit suicide. What should the counselor do?

(A) Scold the child

(B) Immediately inform his parents

(C) Seek help from a fellow counselor

(D) Consider it an emotional speech and ignore it

(12) A counselor is approached by a child who is dealing with anxiety. Although the counselor has no expert knowledge about anxiety in children, he takes the case and tries to give the child the same advice he provides to his other clients. Which of the following terms best describes this behavior?

(A) A necessity

(B) Normal behavior

(C) Unethical conduct

(D) Ethical behavior

(13) Who developed the term "entrusted secret"?

(A) Martin Seligman

(B) Victor Basili

(C) Gerd Huber

(D) Kurt Schneider

(14) A husband is suffering from AIDS, and he only conveys this information to his psychotherapist. What should the psychotherapist do?

(A) Terminate the case

(B) Refer the man to a doctor

(C) Inform the man's wife about his illness

(D) Keep the information secret

(15) When a counselor is working in a group, who should he choose as his group members?

(A) His friends

(B) Counselors who have similar needs and goals

(C) Counselors who take completely different cases than him

(D) It is not wise for a counselor to work in a group

(16) How can a counselor assess his effectiveness?

(A) Request peer monitoring

(B) Compare how many patients he has compared to his fellow counselors

(C) Both A and B

(D) None of the above

(17) During a case, a counselor faces a breakup that is taking an emotional toll on his mental well-being. He is unable to give his best expertise to the client. What should the counselor do?

(A) He should continue until the case ends.

(B) He should seek therapy simultaneously.

(C) He should immediately take a break.

(D) None of the above.

(18) Charging exorbitant charges is a/an ________.

(A) Unethical practice

(B) Counselor's demand

(C) Drawback of seeking therapy

(D) Normal behavior

(19) What is the role of personnel in private buildings, day rehab centers and workshops toward the differently-abled people of society?

(A) Help them find jobs and homes

(B) They have no role

(C) Treat them differently

(D) None of the above

(20) Which of the following acts safeguards the rights of people with intellectual or other disabilities in America?

(A) The Canadian Human Rights Act

(B) The Disabilities Act

(C) Both A and B

(D) None of the above

(21) Which of the following information is expressed numerically by a client seeking therapy?

(A) Age

(B) Test scores

(C) Both A and B

(D) None of the above

(22) Identify the process that is continuous throughout therapy.

(A) Assessment

(B) Research

(C) Dissemination

(D) Classification

(23) __________ is an important step in the counseling process.

(A) Allowing the client to speak

(B) Charging exorbitant fees

(C) Breaching confidentiality

(D) Involving other counselors

(24) According to Martin Seligman, which of the following processes should help a counselor recognize the client's significance and uniqueness?

(A) Diagnosis

(B) Assessment

(C) Goal setting

(D) Exploration

(25) Identify the person who can be consulted when a client is unable to give consent.

(A) The client's parents

(B) Only the client can give consent

(C) A legally recognized party

(D) The client's closest friend

Intake, Assessment and Diagnosis

(26) "What adjectives would you use to describe yourself?"

The above question is asked under which of the following components of the BPS?

(A) Social

(B) Psychological

(C) Biological

(D) All of the above

(27) When a counselor is approached by a rape victim experiencing trauma, what should be the counselor's priority in dealing with the client's trauma?

(A) Make him or her feel safe and protected.

(B) Inquire about the incident in detail.

(C) Do not take cases of rape victims.

(D) None of the above.

(28) Shea proposed a popular method for clinical interviewing. How many stages make up this model?

(A) Six

(B) Four

(C) Nine

(D) Five

(29) ________ refers to learned and passed-down systems of awareness, concepts, rules and processes from one generation to the next.

(A) Religion

(B) Culture

(C) Language

(D) Spirituality

(30) The CFI is made up of three components. How many supplementary modules make up the third component?

(A) Twelve

(B) Sixteen

(C) Three

(D) Ten

(31) Which of the following is a danger that a client might face while seeking therapy?

(A) Society shaming

(B) Exposing a long-buried and forgotten trauma

(C) Financial crisis

(D) None of the above

(32) Counselors should take a client-centered approach. They should respond to clients in which of the following two ways?

(A) Strongly directive or extremely nondirective

(B) Pragmatic or prescriptive

(C) Assisting or accepting

(D) Assessing or comforting

(33) What is the number of steps the first component of CFI can be broken down into?

(A) Four

(B) Three

(C) Ten

(D) Two

(34) What does MSE stand for in counseling?

(A) Mental status examination

(B) Mental score examination

(C) Mental sanity examination

(D) Mental sobriety examination

(35) What is another name for personal therapy?

(A) Group therapy

(B) Individual therapy

(C) Family therapy

(D) All of the above

(36) Which of the following is a commonly followed approach by counselors to deal with family therapy cases?

(A) Behavioral

(B) Cognitive

(C) System

(D) All of the above

(37) Counselors either adopt a nondirective approach or a directive approach to deal with their clients' interviews. In which of the following cases is a nondirective framework ideal?

(A) When the interviewee wants to manage the interview

(B) When the counselor wants to manage the interview

(C) Both A and B

(D) None of the above

(38) Which of the following is an advantage of seeking therapy in groups?

(A) It saves time.

(B) It makes the environment more accepting.

(C) Therapy should never be sought in groups.

(D) None of the above.

(39) Which of the following is the most important reason why men underreport their problems compared to women?

(A) Men are generally introverted.

(B) Society has attached a severe stigma around the mental health of men.

(C) Men do not have problems that require therapy because of their dominance in society.

(D) All of the above.

(40) What is a drawback of self-reports?

(A) Lack of self-awareness

(B) Simplicity

(C) Price

(D) Privacy

(41) What does MMPI stand for in counseling?

(A) Minnesota Multiphasic Personality Inventory

(B) Multiphasic Minnesota Personality Inventory

(C) Multipurpose Mini Personality IQ

(D) None of the above

(42) Which of the following is a therapeutical concept for evaluation?

(A) Reliability

(B) Validity

(C) Both A and B

(D) None of the above

(43) Which of the following measures can be contributed by the community members by the end of the psychotherapy?

(A) Work-related measures

(B) Customer records on criminal incarceration rates

(C) Both A and B

(D) None of the above

(44) Screening and assessment are often confused as being _________.

(A) Similar processes

(B) Different processes

(C) Incorrect approaches to deal with psychiatric patients

(D) Correct approaches to deal with psychiatric patients

(45) Which of the following is/are one of the six key components that comprise the ideal delivery of addiction counseling for COD clients?

(A) Getting access

(B) Completing a comprehensive evaluation

(C) Maintaining patient care

(D) All of the above

(46) The universal model for clinical interviewing proposed by Shea in 1998 comprises five stages. The first stage is introduction.

In which of the following ways can the introduction take place?

(A) In a phone call

(B) Online

(C) When clients read about counselors online

(D) All of the above

(47) A doctor wants to differentiate between delirium and dementia. Which of the following tools can assist him in doing so?

(A) Mental status examination

(B) Co-occurring diagnoses

(C) Both A and B

(D) None of the above

(48) The ability of a mechanism to target people who do not have a disorder is referred to as __________.

(A) Sensitivity

(B) Specificity

(C) Administration

(D) Assessment

(49) What is the difference between screening and assessment?

(A) They are both synonymous.

(B) Screening checks for the existence of an issue but does not diagnose its severity.

(C) Assessment checks for the existence of an issue but does not diagnose its severity.

(D) None of the above.

(50) What is an ideal time frame for a therapy session?

(A) About an hour

(B) A minimum of 15 hours

(C) Not more than 10 minutes

(D) At least 24 hours

Areas of Clinical Focus

(51) Why does a person who nears death lose appetite and face extreme weight loss?

(A) Mood swings

(B) Loss of interest and energy to function

(C) Lack of love and support

(D) Change in taste

(52) What are some ways through which a person can move on?

(A) Accepting and understanding the loss

(B) Sleeping continuously and forcing oneself to forget

(C) Overeating and spending time alone

(D) Ignoring the pain and finding new hobbies

(53) What does an individual experience while grieving?

(A) Validation, sadness, guilt, refusal

(B) Rejection, shame, withdrawal, fear

(C) Confirmation, happiness, sorrow, regret

(D) Denial, anger, bargaining, depression, acceptance

(54) What are some risks that may come along with retirement?

(A) Health concerns, childbirth, relying on social security

(B) Market collapse, depression, fear of heights

(C) Increased savings, high investments, medical support

(D) Life security, sudden illness, death of a spouse

(55) How do sudden illnesses threaten a person's quality of life after retirement?

(A) Paying for daily medication can eat into a person's savings.

(B) Children may stop being supportive if a parent falls suddenly ill.

(C) A sudden surgery could severely impact a person's finances.

(D) A sudden illness can have a severe spiritual impact.

(56) What aspects of human behavior does geriatrics study?

(A) Mental, educational and romantic changes

(B) Physical, emotional and psychological changes

(C) Personality, stereotypical and body changes

(D) Social, interpersonal and spiritual changes

(57) Issues that arise when an individual crosses the age of 60 are called?

(A) Thalassemia

(B) Down syndrome

(C) Cystic fibrosis

(D) Geriatric syndrome

(58) By how much has the average lifespan of people above 65 years increased in the US?

(A) 5%

(B) 10%

(C) 15%

(D) 20%

(59) As clusters of cellular and molecular damage occur, what happens to the human body?

(A) Metabolizing

(B) Aging

(C) Reproducing

(D) Organizing

(60) What sort of a personality will a strict household produce?

(A) One which harbors bitterness

(B) One which spreads love

(C) One which initiates positive relationships

(D) One which is organized

(61) What issue does a child face if he has difficulty when trying to roll over and walk for the first time?

(A) Lack of cognitive skills

(B) Language issues

(C) Anxiety

(D) Motor delays

(62) What are some examples of neurobehavioral disorders?

(A) Depression and anxiety

(B) Hyperactivity and autism

(C) Hormonal imbalance

(D) Slowed speech development

(63) What is a child experiencing if she has trouble comprehending and thinking about what is being said?

(A) Developmental delays

(B) Social delays

(C) Emotional delays

(D) Psychological delays

(64) What happens to a child when his parents are not in sync and the child has to resolve problems?

(A) He becomes confident and feels grown up.

(B) He becomes an introvert and spends time alone.

(C) He feels hatred and depression.

(D) He studies harder and improves his focus.

(65) What is the biggest hurdle in co-parenting?

(A) Communication gaps

(B) Financial barriers

(C) Different schools of thoughts

(D) Emotional instability

(66) Is using children to hurt others, especially an ex-spouse, acceptable?

(A) Yes

(B) No

(C) In some situations

(D) Depends on the child

(67) What sort of parenting methods must be discussed before co-parenting a child?

(A) Clothing

(B) Cartoons and movies

(C) Religious beliefs

(D) Food brands

(68) Why do private organizations have a stronger hold on parents in terms of providing services?

(A) Efficient coordination

(B) Improved marketing

(C) Better counselors

(D) Affordable options

(69) People are more likely to have a specific attachment style depending on?

(A) The relationships they watched in their favorite movie

(B) The relationships they observed as children

(C) The relationships they fantasize about with their partner

(D) The relationships they had with their pets while growing up

(70) What are the red flags that represent a communication barrier in a relationship?

(A) Love, distance, curiosity

(B) Trust, teamwork, time apart

(C) Lightheartedness, respect, independence

(D) Disrespect, criticism and judgment

(71) What is an important factor in determining if two people stay together?

(A) Financial status

(B) Number of children

(C) Compatibility

(D) Physical appearance

(72) If a person has to remarry to provide her children with love and support, which were missing in the previous marriage, what is such a situation called?

(A) Financial dependability

(B) Emotional abuse

(C) Forced marriage

(D) Arranged marriage

(73) What are some of the reasons that lead to failed communication between couples?

(A) Discussing problems and taking time to resolve issues

(B) Avoiding talking about a disagreement, having high expectations of each other and not communicating

(C) Listening without being defensive and avoiding mind-reading

(D) Being specific and freely expressing all sentiments

(74) What are the four types of sexual dysfunction?

(A) PTSD, depression, an endocrine disorder, autonomic dysfunction

(B) Neuromuscular disorder, anorexia nervosa, pica, rumination disorder

(C) Desire disorder, arousal disorder, orgasm disorder, pain disorder

(D) Bulimia nervosa, binge-eating disorder, Addison's disease, diabetes mellitus

(75) Is getting married again always the right step to move on from an ex?

(A) Yes

(B) No

(C) Depends on the situation

(D) That's up to the couple

(76) What is it called when a man finds it difficult to get physically aroused?

(A) Orgasm disorder

(B) Pain disorder

(C) Arousal dysfunction

(D) Autonomic dysfunction

(77) Who can cause abuse?

(A) Family

(B) Friends

(C) Medical experts

(D) Anyone

(78) What is the most difficult situation for a counselor to work with?

(A) A client affected by sexual abuse

(B) A client affected by physical violence

(C) A client with suicidal thoughts

(D) A client with a lack of communication skills

(79) What does it suggest when a person who is experiencing major personal loss withdraws from social events and talks about death?

(A) The person is suffering from anxiety.

(B) The person is suicidal.

(C) The person is about to call an abusive ex-spouse.

(D) The person regrets past behavior.

(80) How can protective factors help clients in finding a way forward?

(A) By aiding them in taking responsibility for their safety

(B) By aiding them to improve their communication skills

(C) By aiding them in silencing a victim of abuse

(D) . By aiding them to record their crimes

(81) Is prompting clients to think about suicide always an effective way to know if they are thinking about it?

(A) Yes

(B) No

(C) Depends on how the client processes the prompt

(D) Depends on how the counselor presents the prompt

(82) What is an effective way for therapists to discuss suicide with a client?

(A) Rating on a scale of 0–10

(B) Forcing the client to talk about it

(C) Making the client write his or her thoughts down

(D) Discussing someone's death with the client

(83) How is a client likely to behave in the future if she is skeptical about her psychological condition?

(A) She is going to commit suicide.

(B) She is not going to commit suicide.

(C) She may harm herself or someone else.

(D) She might kill someone.

(84) Why is the formation of a crisis plan advantageous for a client?

(A) It helps a person to regularly attend sessions and take therapy seriously.

(B) It helps a person to open up and communicate sentiments without any fear.

(C) It helps a person to acknowledge the intensity of the situation and highlights protective factors.

(D) It helps a person to understand the nonjudgmental nature of the practitioner.

(85) If the client insists on suicide, should the practitioner go against the client's wishes of isolation?

(A) Yes.

(B) No.

(C) The practitioner must discuss it with the client.

(D) The practitioner must discuss it with senior therapists and managers.

(86) What can have an impact on a counselor's reaction to suicide?

(A) Personal opinions influenced by religious and social beliefs

(B) Fear of suicide or losing the client

(C) The current mental state of the client

(D) The resources and history of the client

(87) What is commonly used to detect adjustment disorders?

(A) Medicines and their impact on the health of the client

(B) Anesthesia and injections

(C) Suggesting prompts to talk about issues

(D) Symptoms and how they affect a person's ability to behave properly

(88) What is it called when a person is feeling tearful, helpless and doesn't enjoy things that previously were fun?

(A) Depression combined with anxiety

(B) Downbeat mood

(C) Disturbed behavior

(D) Unspecified

(89) What are two examples of adjustment disorders?

(A) Acute and diabetes

(B) Acute and tenacious

(C) Tenacious and paranoia

(D) Tenacious and asthma

(90) What is the treatment for adjustment disorders based on?

(A) Age, the severity of signs, tolerance

(B) Religious beliefs and social opinions

(C) Antibiotics and injections

(D) Personal preference and antidepressants

(91) What is the most common treatment for adjustment disorders?

(A) Medication

(B) Cognitive-behavioral therapy

(C) Family/couples therapy

(D) Therapy

(92) What sort of therapy focuses on the development and application of interpersonal and social skills?

(A) Hypnotherapy

(B) Interpersonal psychotherapy

(C) Behavioral therapy

(D) Peer-to-peer therapy

(93) What is a process that is dynamic, immersive and changes dramatically during adolescence?

(A) Ethnic identity

(B) Identity formation

(C) Religious formation

(D) Political identity

(94) What are the everyday social settings of a healthy person?

(A) Hospital, research lab, colleagues, doctors

(B) Forest, roads, hotels, bars

(C) Books, television, apartment, toys

(D) Home, school/work, friends, community members

(95) Does the accepted centralized racial framework in the United States disregard rights and opportunities through ethnic, social and class isolation?

(A) Yes

(B) No

(C) Varies from state to state

(D) Varies from community to community

(96) What sort of physical symptoms can anxiety result in?

(A) Clammy hands and shaking legs

(B) Jumping around and pacing

(C) Sleeping too little and having bad dreams

(D) Picking physical fights with strangers

(97) Can anxiety be experienced daily?

(A) Yes

(B) No

(C) Varies from person to person

(D) Varies from medicine to medicine

(98) Due to the serious nature of the symptoms, what is a panic attack often perceived as being?

(A) Asthma

(B) Kidney failure

(C) Liver cirrhosis

(D) Heart attack

(99) What is an abnormal fear of a certain objective, activity and situation that is not inherently dangerous?

(A) Phobia

(B) Violence

(C) Disorder

(D) Depression

(100) If an individual is going to great lengths to avoid a certain situation, requires company or suffers from intense anxiety, what sort of phobia is the person experiencing?

(A) Acrophobia

(B) Aerophobia

(C) Agoraphobia

(D) Autophobia

(101) What are the two most common methods to treat anxiety?

(A) Talk therapy and prescription drugs

(B) Antibiotics and social events

(C) Book reading and sleeping

(D) Loneliness and painkillers

(102) What is the process of discussing a client's sentiments and behavior to narrow down a diagnosis and rule out potential complications?

(A) Emotional evaluation

(B) Physical evaluation

(C) Cardiac evaluation

(D) Psychological evaluation

(103) What are the consequences of depression-related fatigue?

(A) A sudden surge in energy levels and cheerfulness

(B) Difficulty concentrating and moodiness

(C) Apathy and empathy

(D) Exhaustion and nausea

(104) Can depression and pain coexist?

(A) Yes

(B) No

(C) Varies from medicine to medicine

(D) Varies from client to client

Treatment Planning

(105) Which of the following is known to have a positive effect on the yield of treatment?

(A) Setting goals in sequential order

(B) Setting goals randomly

(C) Setting goals without a time frame

(D) All of the above

(106) Which of the following is not an advantage of adding a progress and outcomes clause to a treatment plan?

(A) It can be used when updating clients about their progress.

(B) It can be used to assist a client in developing future goals.

(C) It can help a client achieve the goal faster.

(D) It helps cancel out superfluous parts of the therapy.

(107) Which of the following types of care can include experimental medicine?

(A) Quaternary care

(B) Tertiary care

(C) Secondary care

(D) Primary care

(108) What must counselors do in a situation where they are being threatened by clients' family members or friends?

(A) Keep the therapeutic process going

(B) Terminate the therapeutic process

(C) Inform the clients about the threats

(D) None of the above

(109) What kinds of clients does a counselor usually meet in rural areas?

(A) Clients who are illiterate

(B) Highly educated clients

(C) Shy clients

(D) All of the above

(110) What causes a divide to form during the transition stage of group therapy?

(A) Alpha members of the group influence the beta members and impose their opinions strongly.

(B) Members of the group learn to accept critiques from others.

(C) A member of the group decides to share a personal traumatic incident.

(D) All of the above.

(111) In most cases, when a patient gets primary care, this means?

(A) The person's condition has been ongoing for a few years.

(B) The illness is mild to moderate.

(C) The patient is unable to treat him or herself at home.

(D) All of the above.

(112) What does the term follow-up care refer to?

(A) A normal session in the middle of the therapeutic process

(B) A session after a break with the client

(C) Checking up on the client's general situation after termination or discharge

(D) All of the above

(113) When forming a treatment plan, what aspects relating to the client should come into special focus?

(A) Age, gender, nationality

(B) Religious beliefs, ethnicity, cultural tendencies

(C) Education level and work experience

(D) None of the above

(114) What is the first topic of discussion in the initial stage of group therapy?

(A) Exploration of personal traumas

(B) Critiquing group members on their issues

(C) Introductions between different group members and the mediator

(D) None of the above

(115) What is the major difference between tertiary and secondary care?

(A) Patients are unable to care for themselves in their home environment.

(B) Patients are concerned about the genetic factor of their condition in regards to their offspring.

(C) Patients are presented with a new condition in addition to their previous one.

(D) Patients are unsure of which prescriptions to use.

(116) What is a strategy a mediator can use during the transition stage of group therapy to guide the group in the right direction?

(A) The mediator can use an authoritative tone of voice when needed.

(B) The mediator can identify minor issues and address them appropriately.

(C) The mediator can identify hidden strains and solve them with input from the group members.

(D) All of the above.

(117) What is it called when a client is well versed in the language of communication but is unable to understand some words due to certain pronunciations?

(A) A dialect barrier

(B) A language barrier

(C) A speech/hearing disability

(D) None of the above

(118) What is expected from a client if her treatment is altered to include pharmaceutical methods?

(A) The client must stop taking all her previous medications.

(B) The client must inform the counselor of any previous or current illnesses and medications.

(C) The client must alter the medication according to her own preference.

(D) None of the above.

(119) Why is follow-up care after discharge from a hospital facility more complicated?

(A) The client might decide to abandon the treatment once home.

(B) The client is in a fragile state emotionally and physically after leaving a very structured, supportive environment.

(C) The client might develop suicidal tendencies without a support system.

(D) All of the above.

(120) Which kinds of goals are repetitive in nature?

(A) Short-term goals

(B) Intermediate goals

(C) Long-term goals

(D) All of the above

(121) What does the term modality refer to in the context of a treatment plan?

(A) It refers to the means used to assist with the accomplishment of a target.

(B) It refers to the kind of transport a client uses.

(C) It refers to the education level of the counselor.

(D) None of the above.

(122) Which of the following is an example of a tertiary care setting?

(A) Renal dialysis unit

(B) Specialized surgery

(C) 24/7 laboratory facilities

(D) All of the above

(123) Concerning group therapy, what must the mediator do if some members of the group feel like their therapeutic journey has not come to an end during the final stage?

(A) The mediator must convince those members that there is no alternate solution after group therapy.

(B) The mediator must guide those group members toward alternative medicinal practices.

(C) The mediator must provide those group members with resources to an alternate group setting or take them on in their own new group.

(D) All of the above.

(124) What effect does setting goals have on the client?

(A) It slows the client's progress.

(B) It involves the client's family members.

(C) It increases the client's sense of independence.

(D) None of the above.

(125) During what stage of group therapy does the environment of the group become most amicable?

(A) The working stage

(B) The transition stage

(C) The final stage

(D) None of the above

Counseling Skills and Interventions

(126) Sexual harassment is chiefly an outward manifestation of ______________, not of sexual attraction.

(A) An animalistic act

(B) A primitive deed

(C) An idiotic act

(D) An assertion of authority and an abuse of power

(127) Managers are classified into two types based on their assumptions about human nature. What is one theory or theories managers might have about their employees?

(A) Theory A: All employees spend an inordinate amount of time visiting.

(B) Theory X: All employees despise their jobs and are slackers.

(C) Theory Y: All employees enjoy their jobs and want to be in charge.

(D) Both B and C.

(128) The theory that the individuals involved in executing a decision are also involved in making it is a primary technique of Theory Y management.

This is known as:

(A) Decision-making through participation

(B) Choosing a combination approach

(C) Making management decisions

(D) Making employee decisions

(129) Which of the following is not a barrier to minorities seeking mental health care?

(A) Treatment apprehension and mistrust

(B) Reliance on mental health services

(C) Variations in language and communication

(D) Prejudice and racism

(130) You are attending a wedding when you notice a current client sitting a few tables away from you.

What should you do?

(A) Request a meeting with the client.

(B) Greet the client warmly.

(C) Do not acknowledge the patient unless he or she acknowledges you first.

(D) Terminate the client the following week.

(131) Which of the following is a true statement about sexual harassment?

(A) Older women who report sexual harassment are frequently ignored or mocked.

(B) Young, attractive women who report such incidents are frequently said to be "asking for it."

(C) If they fight back or report the sexual harassment, victims frequently face dismissal.

(D) All of the above.

(132) Sarah is a therapist who has recently opened her own practice. She would like to promote her practice through her personal social media profile.

Is this appropriate?

(A) Counselors are not allowed to use social networking sites.

(B) Yes, as long as her posts adhere to the ACA's directives.

(C) No, her personal and professional pages must be kept separate.

(D) There are no restrictions on how a counselor promotes a practice.

(133) Your client, David, is a homosexual and has notified you that he believes he is the victim of sexual orientation workplace discrimination.

David's rights are protected by which of the following laws?

(A) Workplace law

(B) Americans with Disabilities Act (ADA)

(C) Equal Employment Opportunity Commission (EEOC)

(D) Affirmative action

(134) What can a company learn from an employee performance evaluation?

(A) Both B and D are correct.

(B) Any reservations the employee may have

(C) How much time do you spend in the 'break room'

(D) Identifies training requirements and employee skillset

(135) Which of the following best describes the concept of transference?

(A) A patient fantasizes about marrying her therapist.

(B) A client wishes for her mother to accompany her to therapy sessions.

(C) A client regards her therapist as unattractive.

(D) A client sobs when her therapist interrogates her about her mother.

(136) When one person meets another, instant impressions are formed. These initial impressions are frequently hard to change.

What word or words are used to describe this situation?

(A) First meeting syndrome

(B) Subjectivity

(C) First impression syndrome

(D) None of the above

(137) A career counselor meeting with a client might ___________.

(A) Request that the client complete an interest inventory

(B) Assist the patient with self-exploration in order to establish goals

(C) Teach decision-making abilities

(D) All of the above

(138) Typically, staff training begins with a training course. What is the primary unspoken goal of orientation?

(A) Spreading organizational culture

(B) Increasing technical knowledge

(C) Determining the location of the break room

(D) None of the above

(139) Which of the following techniques can explain why a group decision will be less conservative than an informed choice?

(A) Apathy among bystanders

(B) Risky shift phenomenon

(C) Cynicism

(D) Conditioning

(140) What does self-worth mean in Bandura's social cognitive theory?

(A) It is a person's belief in his or her ability to manage and carry out the actions necessary to achieve a desired result.

(B) It is a person's belief that all the actions he or she takes will benefit him or her.

(C) It is a widely held belief that everyone thinks the best of themselves.

(D) None of the above.

(141) Which of the following is most closely associated with incompetent practice?

(A) Practicing in areas where education or training is lacking

(B) Working while suffering from a physical disability

(C) Understanding a client's ethnicity

(D) All of the above

(142) What are the clients' rights in relation to the testing process?

(A) There are no special rights.

(B) They must be aware of when a test is being administered and the results.

(C) They require informed consent and a signed release for any information provided to others.

(D) None of the above.

(143) What ethical concerns arise as a result of the research process?

(A) Plagiarism, taking accurate notes

(B) Humane animal care

(C) Institutional endorsement

(D) All of the above

(144) What does the term "life roles" mean in the context of career counseling?

(A) As we get older, we take on more roles in life, which influences our career choices.

(B) Life roles define how a person sees himself or herself.

(C) There are no "life roles" in the context of career counseling.

(D) Both A and B.

(145) Amanda is the leader of a four-week-old therapy group. A painful topic was brought up at the start of today's session, and an immediate conflict arose. Within a few minutes, the conversation had shifted to a more pleasant subject. Amanda was relieved to see the group quickly resolve the problem.

What happened in this situation?

(A) Conflict avoidance, as well as Amanda's failure to provide sufficient structure to instruct members how to express their feelings, thoughts and responses.

(B) Amanda witnessed effective transference and counter-transference among group members in dealing with a painful issue.

(C) There was effective conflict resolution and group agreement on how to deal with difficult feelings.

(D) Group members exhibited a fear response that Amanda did not address.

(146) A predesigned mental health care model does not usually address complex issues facing Native Americans.

Which would not be one of these issues?

(A) Feeling a lack of belonging in society

(B) Traumatic historical events

(C) Poor work conditions

(D) Continuing attack on Native American sovereignty

(147) Which of the following describes the concept of dysfunctional thinking?

(A) A client is fixated on one explanation for a negative occurrence.

(B) A client cannot logically move from point A to point B.

(C) A client lacks the ability to reflect on past events.

(D) A client is not able to communicate.

(148) Almost every company conducts staff appraisals annually. During the assessment, a phenomenon known as the "halo effect" occurs.

What does this mean?

(A) The proclivity to identify one individual as better than all the others

(B) The proclivity to question people's religion

(C) The proclivity to evaluate people based on a single outstanding characteristic

(D) The proclivity to overestimate people

(149) According to social cognitive career theory, individuals sometimes don't consider certain career paths because __________.

(A) They have extremely specific interests.

(B) They have erroneous beliefs in their own capabilities

(C) They are following in their parents' path.

(D) None of the above.

(150) How can a social cognitive career counselor help clients change incorrect self-efficacy beliefs?

(A) Change their mindsets and get new results

(B) Create new ideas about their capabilities and reexamine past experiences

(C) Restructure their résumés and rearrange their skills

(D) None of the above

(151) Kohlberg's theory shows that morality develops in...

(A) Five stages

(B) Six stages

(C) Seven stages

(D) None of the above

(152) Your client is in the fourth grade. Your client's parents sign a release form allowing you to interact with the child's school, with only the name of the school listed on the form.

Is it okay for you to talk to the instructor and the school counselor?

(A) Yes. You do not require a separate release because both the teacher and the school counselor are part of the school.

(B) You are permitted to speak with the teachers but not with the school counselor.

(C) Speaking with school personnel would be inappropriate because it would violate confidentiality.

(D) The names of the teacher and school counselor must be included on the release in order for you to interact with them.

(153) What topics might be taught in diversity or cultural sensitivity training?

(A) Food preferences of each culture

(B) Belief structures of various cultures

(C) Geographical locations of cultures of origin

(D) None of the above

(154) A Hispanic counselor agrees to work with a client of Asian descent. What does this therapist not require to effectively assist her client?

(A) Diversity education

(B) A diploma in Asian culture

(C) A referral from another therapist

(D) A desire to help the client

(155) What does the client need to know about the framework when a counselor is seeing clients under guidance?

(A) The client needs to know how frequently the counselor meets with his or her supervisor.

(B) The client needs to know that the counselor is being overseen and will consult with a licensed clinician about the client's situation.

(C) The client does not need to be aware that the counselor is under guidance.

(D) Both A and B.

(156) Who is Victor Frankl?

(A) The founder of psychotherapy

(B) A behavioral theorist

(C) A movie star

(D) An early existentialist therapist

(157) ____________involves increasing job satisfaction by matching people's personalities to the type of work they do.

(A) Theorem Y

(B) The Hawthorne Hypothesis

(C) The Theory of Personality-Job Fit

(D) None of the above

(158) Structuralism was one of the first schools of thought. What was the school's focus or hypothesis?

(A) It centered on the fundamental sensations and emotions of experiences.

(B) It was dedicated to the investigation of mental processes.

(C) It was concerned with sensitive issues.

(D) Both A and B.

(159) A counselor's professional ethics require him or her to avoid dual relationships.

What is a "dual relationship"?

(A) A client relationship that is ongoing

(B) Seeing multiple clients from the same family

(C) Seeing a client who also happens to be the counselor's accountant

(D) Both A and C

(160) Miranda's client admitted to binge drinking at a party. Which of the following questions is most likely to irritate the client?

(A) How did you feel about that?

(B) What happened?

(C) What would you change the next time?

(D) Why did you consume so much alcohol?

(161) When should clinicians refer patients to other professionals?

(A) When a client is incarcerated

(B) When additional issues are discovered that are not within the clinician's area of expertise

(C) When the clinician is having a terrible day

(D) When a client makes the decision to marry

(162) What is one aspect of role induction?

(A) Paying attention to the client

(B) Educating the client on the nature of counseling

(C) Making certain that the room is set up right

(D) None of the above

(163) Self-talk is a technique in which people repeat to themselves supportive and optimistic phrases throughout the day.

Which of the following therapies employs this method?

(A) Psychodynamic therapy

(B) Cognitive behavioral therapy

(C) Analytical therapy based on Jungian concepts

(D) This is not a therapy technique.

(164) What is one thing that all effective treatments have in common?

(A) Being invited to the patient's residence

(B) Creating new perceptions or perspectives on a person's stress factors or problems

(C) Having fun with the counseling process

(D) A sense of accomplishment

(165) According to Carter and McGoldrick, one of a new couple's first tasks is?

(A) Increasing each partner's personal autonomy

(B) Learning how to share with a partner

(C) Creating a support group

(D) Adjusting to lower energy levels

(166) In object-relation therapy, what is meant by the "object"?

(A) Inanimate objects around the client

(B) Traumatic events in the client's life

(C) The client's parents or siblings

(D) The client's financial standing

(167) What is the phenomenon of conforming to group pressure in order to gain acceptance and approval known as?

(A) Normal fruition

(B) Conformity to norm

(C) Normative social influence

(D) Normalization

(168) What is the focus of Bowenian therapy?

(A) Finding early symptoms of bipolar disease

(B) Alleviating chronic anxiety

(C) Assessing a war veteran for signs of PTSD

(D) Tracking the development of an adolescent

(169) Who theorized the attachment theory in 1960?

(A) Sigmund Freud

(B) John Bowlby

(C) B.F. Skinner

(D) Marie Curie

(170) Which of the following is not a valid cause for a counselor to end a relationship with a client?

(A) Client resistance

(B) Failure of the client to pay for services

(C) Client no longer requires therapy

(D) Client makes no progress

(171) What is a "norm" when it comes to group behavior?

(A) The person who has the most outbursts

(B) A typical occurrence

(C) The overall behavior of the group

(D) A person's unusual behavior

(172) What is an amicable termination?

(A) A friendly departure from one's home country

(B) A friendly departure from one's place of practice

(C) A mutual decision by the client and counselor to terminate their counseling sessions

(D) A mutual decision made by superiors to terminate a fellow counselor

(173) What is the aim of strategic therapy?

(A) Developing competencies and skills in a client

(B) Developing strategies to overcome the pain of divorce

(C) Helping grieving spouses meet individuals in the same boat

(D) Focusing on issues with retirement

(174) What is the most effective way to reduce destructive forms of obedience?

(A) Acceptance

(B) Adaptation

(C) Conformity

(D) Responsibility

(175) What are the two most common types of social influence?

(A) Approval and imitation

(B) Acceptance and subjectiveness

(C) Obedience and conformity

(D) Information and accountability

(176) You've just begun working with the Chung family, who moved to the United States a few years ago. As a culturally diverse counselor, you are cognizant that child-rearing is a priority in Asian-American families. This includes:

(A) Internal locus of control and progression

(B) Social abilities and career advancement

(C) Respect for authority and schooling

(D) Acknowledgment

(177) According to Freud, the psychosexual advancement of a person's personality occurs primarily during which three main stages?

(A) Anal, phallic and latency

(B) Oral, anal and phallic

(C) Phallic, maturity and genital

(D) Genital, oropharyngeal and anal

(178) Attribution is afflicted with a saliency bias. Which of the following statements best describes what this means?

(A) Some people's personalities/behaviors stand out more than others.

(B) Some people simply appear/act guilty.

(C) It's a type of cause-and-effect behavior.

(D) There isn't such a thing.

(179) What is the goal of family therapy?

(A) To have a good time with family

(B) To reestablish family bonds

(C) To bring out all of the dysfunctional family dynamics

(D) To lessen family arguments

(180) What is the most serious potential issue with group therapy?

(A) A person might dislike the group.

(B) The group leader may be insufficiently trained or experienced.

(C) There might not be enough breaks.

(D) None of the above.

Core Counseling Attributes

(181) When clients are hesitant to talk in therapy, they tend to:

(A) Leave the session and never come back

(B) Start getting annoyed in the session

(C) Judge the personality of the counselor

(D) All of the above

(182) What is a vital factor in psychotherapy?

(A) Asking good questions of the client

(B) Listening to the client

(C) Sympathizing with the client

(D) Empathizing with the client

(183) How can delays in therapy appointments have a bad effect on the outcome of therapy?

(A) It has a bad impact on the counselor.

(B) It makes the client feel unwanted.

(C) It demotivates the client to visit and causes a communication gap.

(D) None of the above.

(184) Which of the following is an unreliable therapist empathy assessment?

(A) Summative assessment

(B) Confirmative assessment

(C) Self-reporting

(D) Client-reporting

(185) Why is it important for counselors to feel compassion toward their clients?

(A) It helps counselors understand why clients are emotional.

(B) It helps make clients talk.

(C) It helps the counselor form a positive response.

(D) All of the above.

(186) Why is it important for clients to feel acknowledged in a group therapy session?

(A) It provides clients with a sense of belonging.

(B) Clients feel that they are equally entitled to participate in the group and have a chance to contribute positively.

(C) Clients feel like a part of a bigger group, and it makes them feel validated.

(D) It helps clients realize that they have something worthwhile to say.

(187) What is one of the most important counseling skills?

(A) Talking

(B) Asking questions

(C) Keeping everything confidential

(D) Listening

(188) What is nonjudgmental listening?

(A) Listening to the client without discriminating

(B) Trying to understand the client's perspective

(C) Not judging the client's background

(D) All of the above

(189) What is an essential part of developing multicultural counseling expertise?

(A) Understanding people's differences

(B) Taking account of people's experiences

(C) Examining one's own biases and privilege

(D) All of the above

(190) How can counselors take notes efficiently and effectively?

(A) By writing them in a notebook

(B) By recording them

(C) By utilizing a template for notes

(D) All of the above

(191) What should counselors consider when they treat patients who grew up in extreme wealth, as well as those who lived well below the poverty line?

(A) Environmental circumstances

(B) Economic circumstances

(C) Political circumstances

(D) Socioeconomic circumstances

(192) What is one of the American Counseling Association Code of Ethics' laws?

(A) "It is unethical to provide treatment to minors with parental consent."

(B) "Refrain from giving treatment to terminally ill patients."

(C) "Counselors act to avoid harming their clients, trainees and research participants and to minimize or to remedy unavoidable or unanticipated harm."

(D) None of the above.

(193) What are mistakes counselors might make while empathizing that could lead to a gap between client and counselor?

(A) Showing respect and tolerance toward the client

(B) Showing inappropriate levels of intensity to the client's expressed feelings, not considering the client's history in context and responding selectively to the client's responses

(C) Empathizing with the client's issues and problems

(D) All of the above

(194) Which of the following should counselors incorporate into their practice?

(A) The act of listening

(B) The act of talking

(C) The act of self-awareness

(D) All of the above

(195) Rather than bringing insight on issues, a member is wondering how sharing would help?

(A) It helps them process their problems.

(B) It helps them figure out their feelings and thoughts.

(C) It helps boost their self-esteem.

(D) All of the above.

(196) What should a counselor do if a patient is angry?

(A) Leave the session.

(B) Take a break.

(C) Refer the client to another counselor.

(D) Ask the reason the person is angry.

(197) What are the two most important components of the client-counselor relationship?

(A) Patience and unconditional positive regard

(B) Listening and advising

(C) Honesty and trust

(D) Respect and tolerance

(198) How can a counselor set the flow and tone of the session?

(A) By comforting the client

(B) By talking to the client

(C) By asking questions

(D) None of the above

(199) What should the leader of a group therapy session pay attention to?

(A) The content of the session

(B) The motivation of the members

(C) The participation level of each group member

(D) The nonverbal movements of the members, as well as the changes in their verbalizations

(200) What is "empathy" defined as?

(A) The skill of encouraging others

(B) The skill of showing compassion

(C) The skill of listening to others

(D) The skill of being understanding

Test 2 Answers

Professional Practice and Ethics Answers

(1) (C) Both personal and professional.

The privilege of seeking therapy is not limited to certain individuals. It can be sought professionally, in groups, as a couple and as a family.

(2) (D) Both A and B.

Like every other disease, mental illness can affect any age group. Therefore, there is no age limit on people who can access treatment. Even children, who cannot give consent, are eligible for seeking therapy along with adults.

(3) (B) Third.

The process of counseling is usually divided into five major steps. The third step is goal setting.

(4) (D) Both A and B.

Martin Seligman is an American psychologist who placed great emphasis on assessing a client. He believed that assessment allows counselors to make a precise diagnosis and makes goal-setting more manageable.

(5) (B) 30–50 minutes.

A counseling session should not last for more than an hour. If the problem is serious and the client might need a lot of visits, the counselor can increase the number of sessions, but increasing the duration of a session is not advised because it can become draining for both the counselor and the client.

(6) (D) All of the above.

Psychotherapy deals with psychiatric issues. It significantly reduces the symptoms of clients, helps them function normally in their daily lives and contributes greatly to their mental and physical well-being.

(7) (A) Choosing a problem.

Before anything, a counselor needs to choose a problem to research. This should then be followed by a hypothesis, a research design and then collecting as much information as possible to solve the problem.

(8) (C) Both A and B.

Although it is better to report the findings of the research through a presentation as it allows people to ask questions, a research paper is also a mode adopted by researchers to report their findings.

(9) (B) A right to choose who has access to data about them.

Privacy is people's right to decide who can access data about them. The right that protects that information from being revealed in courts is the client's privilege.

(10) (A) The amount of detail to be shared with the parents.

No matter how difficult children may be, it is the responsibility of counselors to deal with them patiently. The only problem counselors usually face while dealing with children is the difficulty in deciding the amount of information about a child they should share with the parents.

(11) (B) Immediately inform his parents.

The parents should be aware of any suicidal thoughts their child is entertaining. Ignoring the child and considering his problems as merely emotional can be regarded as negligent behavior. But if the parents do pay attention and scold the child, they will only make the child feel his emotions more strongly. A counselor should know how to deal with such a situation rather than seeking help from a fellow counselor.

(12) (C) Unethical conduct.

Dealing with someone's mental illness is a very sensitive matter. Counselors are expected to only practice within their area of expertise. They should certainly not advise any patient regarding something they are not aware of. That is unethical.

(13) (D) Kurt Schneider.

It was Kurt Schneider, a well-known German psychologist, who referred to the information revealed by a client to a counselor as an entrusted secret.

(14) (C) Inform the man's wife about his illness.

Terminating the case will only further stigmatize the issue. Keeping it secret can cause severe implications on people who are close to the afflicted person, especially the man's wife. Before referring the client to a doctor, the counselor should inform the client's wife so she can take the necessary precautions.

(15) (B) Counselors who have similar needs and goals.

Collaborative work is always better. Counselors should work in groups with people who have similar needs and goals. This way people will be able to seek expert advice when they are stuck and discuss important issues with each other.

(16) (A) Request peer monitoring.

The most reliable way a counselor can assess his effectiveness as a therapist is to request that his peers and fellow counselors monitor his work and give their honest opinions and reviews.

(17) (C) He should immediately take a break.

If a counselor is facing problems in his personal life that are affecting his mental well-being and ability to make correct decisions, he should prioritize his mental health and take a break immediately. This is in the best interests of both the counselor and the client.

(18) (A) Unethical practice.

It is the responsibility of counselors to make therapy affordable for people. Charging exorbitant fees is, therefore, an unethical practice.

(19) (A) Help them find jobs and homes.

Society treats disabled people as less than human, which is a major reason why these people face mental issues.

(20) (B) The Disabilities Act.

The Disabilities Act ensures the fair treatment of disabled individuals in America.

(21) (C) Both A and B.

Both age and test scores are collected in numerical forms to make the data easy to comprehend.

(22) (A) Assessment.

Research needs to be carried out before a case is taken up. An assessment should be carried out continuously, so any progress is regularly monitored.

(23) (A) Allowing the client to speak.

A counselor can only fully understand a problem when the client opens up about it. Charging exorbitant fees and breaching confidentiality are unethical practices. Consulting another counselor should only be done when there are complications and is thus not an important part of the counseling process.

(24) (B) Assessment.

According to American psychologist Martin Seligman, assessment strives to recognize the significance and uniqueness of the client.

(25) (C) A legally recognized party.

There are several instances when a client is not able to give consent. In these circumstances, the counselor should seek the permission of a legally recognized party to start treatment. This party can be anyone and is not always the parents.

Intake, Assessment and Diagnosis Answers

(26) (B) Psychological.

The BPS (biopsychosocial structure) looks for the social, psychological and biological contributions behind the problem a client is facing. Asking clients to describe themselves often falls under the psychological aspect of the structure.

(27) (A) Make him or her feel safe and protected.

When a traumatized patient approaches a counselor, he or she is asked to describe in detail the reason behind the trauma. However, in the case of rape victims, the mental well-being of the patient is prioritized over anything.

(28) (D) Five.

In 1998, Shea proposed a comprehensive model for clinical interviewing. It has five stages: introduction, opening, body, closing and termination.

(29) (B) Culture.

Culture is the term used to refer to the passed-down systems of awareness, concepts, rules and more from one generation to the next. Language, religion and spirituality are all parts of culture.

(30) (A) Twelve.

The third component of the CFI consists of 12 modules that expand on the dimensions of the core and informant CFIs and can result in a more complex project assessment.

(31) (B) Exposing a long-buried and forgotten trauma.

One of the major risks a person seeking therapy can face is that he or she might unwillingly be reminded of forgotten or repressed trauma. This can make it more difficult for the suffering person to heal.

(32) (A) Strongly directive or extremely nondirective.

Counselors should either be straightforward and direct or purely nondirective. Anything in between might make things complicated for clients.

(33) (B) Three.

The CFI can be broken down into three parts. The first part consists of 16 questions and can be further divided into three more parts.

(34) (A) Mental status examination.

MSE helps doctors in making reliable mental health prognoses. It also helps them differentiate between various psychiatric illnesses.

(35) (B) Individual therapy.

As the phrase itself suggests, personal therapy is another name for individual therapy—one-on-one sessions between a client and a counselor.

(36) (C) System.

Behavioral and cognitive approaches are adopted by counselors to treat couples seeking therapy. However, in family therapy cases, the system is the preferable approach. The family as a whole is considered a system, and each member depends on the other.

(37) (A) When the interviewee wants to manage the interview.

When a directive approach is adopted, the counselor manages the interview. However, in a nondirective approach, it is the interviewee who manages the interview.

(38) (B) It makes the environment more accepting.

Some people dismiss their feelings and consider themselves unintelligent for feeling a certain way. When people faced with similar issues seek therapy in groups, a major advantage is that it helps them open up and feel more accepting toward their own problems.

(39) (B) Society has attached a severe stigma around the mental health of men.

During screening and assessment, men respond differently than women. They are not very open about their problems. This is because society has severely stigmatized men's mental health, which makes it difficult for them to open up as they fear being mocked.

(40) (A) Lack of self-awareness.

Although self-reports are simple, can be completed in private and are reasonably priced, they may not present facts due to a lack of self-awareness from clients.

(41) (A) Minnesota Multiphasic Personality Inventory.

MMPI stands for Minnesota Multiphasic Personality Inventory. It is a personality quiz and psychometric survey.

(42) (D) None of the above.

Neither reliability nor validity are theoretical concepts. They are established by evaluating the measurement equipment.

(43) (C) Both A and B.

The community or organization members can contribute to the measures, including customer records on criminal incarceration rates, work-related measures or therapeutic medical measures.

(44) (A) Similar processes.

Screening and assessment are often confused as similar processes, but in reality are two different processes and techniques used in psychotherapy.

(45) (D) All of the above.

Six key components comprise the ideal delivery of addiction counseling for COD clients: getting access, completing a comprehensive evaluation, providing a sufficient level of care, achieving integrated care, providing all-inclusive services and maintaining patient care.

(46) (D) All of the above.

The introduction usually just involves getting to know the basics about the counselor and the client. It can be done over a phone call, an online video call or even through written letters.

(47) (A) Mental status examination.

MSE is an important tool for doctors because it helps them make mental health prognoses. It also helps them differentiate between psychiatric disorders such as delirium and dementia.

(48) (B) Specificity.

Specificity is the term used to refer to the ability of a mechanism to target people who do not have a disorder. On the other hand, sensitivity is the ability of a screening device to accurately identify cases of a target condition in a group.

(49) (B) Screening checks for the existence of an issue but does not diagnose its severity.

Screening and assessment are often confused, but they are entirely different processes and techniques. Screening helps in the identification of an issue, but a thorough assessment of that issue helps in getting information regarding its severity.

(50) (A) About an hour.

An ideal therapy session should last for around 45 minutes and at most an hour. Anything beyond that can get draining and tiring for both the client and counselor.

Areas of Clinical Focus Answers

(51) (B) Loss of interest and energy to function.

As people reach old age, they eventually lose interest in the world and lose their appetite as they don't do a lot of activity that requires a great deal of energy.

(52) (A) Accepting and understanding the loss.

Acceptance and comprehension of a loss are the only way forward. The rest of the choices might lead to depression and loneliness, which could trigger guilt and overthinking.

(53) (D) Denial, anger, bargaining, depression, acceptance.

Denial, anger, bargaining, depression and acceptance are the stages an individual experiences when grieving.

(54) (D) Life security, sudden illness, death of a spouse.

At the age of retirement, a sudden illness or the death of a spouse could cause risk to an individual's life security.

(55) (C) A sudden surgery could severely impact a person's finances.

Normally, retirement plans only include cost of living. No one can predict the necessity for a sudden surgery that could severely impact a person's finances.

(56) (B) Physical, emotional and psychological changes.

Geriatrics studies the physical, emotional and psychological changes in older adults.

(57) (D) Geriatric syndrome.

Geriatric syndrome arises specifically in the latter part of life, whereas the rest of the issues can originate in any part of life.

(58) (D) 20%.

The average lifespan of people above 65 years in the US changed from 30% to 50%. That is an increase of 20 %.

(59) (B) Aging.

As cellular and molecular damage occur within the body, it is an indication of aging.

(60) (A) One which harbors bitterness.

As children grow up observing and experiencing emotional abuse, they may start to resent their surroundings. Overly strict households can damage a child's ability to function later in life.

(61) (D) Motor delays.

Motor delays occur when children's ability to control their muscles is affected. This impacts their ability to roll over and walk.

(62) (B) Hyperactivity and autism.

Neurobehavioral disorders consist of a vast group of behavioral impairments found in association with brain disease.

(63) (A) Developmental delays.

Developmental delays refer to a situation where a child has not gained the developmental skills expected of him or her compared to others of the same age. Examples include initiating a conversation and comprehending what the other person says.

(64) (C) He feels hatred and depression.

Frequent fights between parents in front of their children never lead to a positive outcome. It causes anger and hatred in children, along with depression. The rest of the answers are the positive outcomes of living in a healthy household.

(65) (A) Communication gap.

The biggest hurdle is a lack of communication or a communication gap between parents.

(66) (B) No.

Hurting your ex-spouse or anyone else is never a healthy or normal thing. Children should never be made a part of a couple's disagreements.

(67) (C) Religious beliefs.

Before coming together to parent a child, a couple must discuss important decisions, such as which parent's religion they are going to follow as a family or if they are going to follow one or not. This can help prevent problems later on.

(68) (A) Efficient coordination.

Private organizations are better at providing services to clients because of their ability to coordinate efficiently and understand things clearly, which makes their counselors effective. However, these private organizations are out of financial reach of many people.

(69) (B) The relationships they observed as children.

People tend to become what they saw growing up. Even after reaching adulthood, the majority of people are likely to treat their spouses the way they observed their parents/guardians treat each other. They may take inspiration from other sources but are most likely to practice what they saw as children.

(70) (D) Disrespect, criticism and judgment.

Disrespect, criticism and judgment are three communication barriers that can end a relationship. These factors promote negativity and discourage partners from communicating efficiently. The rest of the choices are factors of a healthy relationship that promotes effective communication between partners.

(71) (C) Compatibility.

Compatibility is a significant factor that helps to determine if people can stay in a relationship and make it work.

(72) (A) Financial dependability.

There are situations in which remarriage is the only option for some people. These people include being victims of abuse who have no other choice but to find someone they can depend on. In cases where children are involved, individuals usually look for a father or mother figure for their children.

(73) (B) Avoiding talking about a disagreement, having high expectations of each other and not communicating.

When spouses avoid talking to each other about disagreements and ignore their problems, it leads to a gap between them and makes the situation worse. Having high expectations and assuming that one partner should know about the needs and desires of the other without communicating with them also leads to failed communication.

(74) (C) Desire disorder, arousal disorder, orgasm disorder, pain disorder.

This is the right answer choice as none of the other dysfunctions/diseases mentioned are sexual. Sexual dysfunction is present in both men and women and can have a negative impact on a relationship.

(75) (B) No.

Remarriage is not always the right step to move on. The solution must depend on the reason for divorce. If the previous marriage ended because the partner was dominant and lacked communication skills, it is possible that the person's next marriage will also end on a negative note. The person should take a break from serious relationships and reflect on him or herself.

(76) (C) Arousal dysfunction.

This occurs when a man is unable to feel physical arousal. It happens when a man doesn't feel intimacy or attraction toward a partner. Arousal dysfunction often leads to failed relationships.

(77) (D) Anyone.

Anyone can cause abuse and violence, be it family, friends, medical experts, teachers, strangers, etc.

(78) (C) A client with suicidal thoughts.

It is not easy for a counselor to determine if a client is contemplating suicide if the person does not talk about it but gives off all signs and symptoms. Determining if a client is suicidal is harder than communicating with a client who has a lack of communication skills or with someone who has gone through sexual or physical abuse.

(79) (B) The person is suicidal.

If a person talks about death and fantasizes about it while going through the trauma of losing a loved one, these are major signals that the person is having suicidal thoughts and needs effective and quick therapy.

(80) (A) By aiding them in taking responsibility for their safety.

Protective factors provide a path forward for clients. They help clients consider how they can keep taking responsibility for their safety and health and how they might provide themselves with support.

(81) (B) No.

Prompting the client about suicide is not always an effective way to initiate a conversation as it might get a negative reaction.

(82) (A) Rating on a scale of 0–10.

This is the most effective way for a therapist to discuss suicide with a client. Forcing the client to talk or write about it will make the person uncomfortable and damage the client-counselor relationship. Discussing someone's death might trigger trauma and/or an unexpected reaction from the client.

(83) (C) She may harm herself or someone else.

If a client is skeptical about her psychological condition, she will also be skeptical about her behavior. This may lead her to harm her peers or herself.

(84) (C) It helps to acknowledge the intensity of the situation and highlights protective factors.

A crisis plan helps clients understand the danger they are in. It aids in clarifying their mental situation and informs them about the availability of protective factors around them.

(85) (D) The practitioner must discuss it with senior therapists and managers.

The decision of involving a third party in a therapeutic procedure must not be made without the consent of senior therapists and managers, as their experience in dealing with clients helps the counselor in making the final decision. Whatever the counselor thinks is best for clients must be discussed with them before implementation.

(86) (A) Personal opinions influenced by religious and social beliefs.

Therapists must control their personal opinions when performing their job as it makes clients feel judged and uncomfortable when these intrude on a therapy session.

(87) (D) The symptoms and how they affect a person's ability to behave properly.

The most effective way to detect adjustment disorders is to recognize the symptoms and their ability to affect a person's behavior. The rest of the choices are ways that can be adopted to find a solution for an adjustment disorder after its diagnosis.

(88) (B) Downbeat mood.

People are going through a downbeat mood when they are extremely sad and break down from time to time, feeling helpless. They are confused, too, as they don't enjoy the things they used to have fun doing.

(89) (B) Acute and tenacious.

These are examples of adjustment disorders. The rest of the answer options are different diseases. For acute adjustment disorders, the symptoms last for six months or less. They lessen or disappear as the source of stress is reduced. For tenacious adjustment disorders, the symptoms can last up to six months.

(90) (A) Age, the severity of signs, tolerance.

These are the right factors for determining the appropriate treatment for adjustment disorders. The rest of the choices may be the causes of an adjustment disorder or the treatment itself.

(91) (D) Therapy.

If a person is diagnosed with an adjustment disorder, a mental health professional may be recommended by the health-care provider.

(92) (D) Peer-to-peer therapy.

Peer-to-peer therapy focuses on the development and application of an effective interpersonal and social skillset.

(93) (B) Identity formation.

Identity formation is a decisive stage of adolescence. Identity is a person's personality traits, and identity formation is the process that develops those traits.

(94) (D) Home, school/work, friends, community members.

These are the most normal social settings for a healthy individual as they involve family, friends and education/work.

(95) (B) No.

The answer is no for United States on a legal level. However, according to Abrafdo-Lanza, Florenz, Armbrister and Aguirre, 2006; Grewal, 2003; and Portes & Rumbaut, 1996, all racial minorities are denied access to resources of mental health improvement due to the accepted centralized racial framework in the country that disregards rights and opportunities through ethnic, societal and class isolation.

(96) (A) Clammy hands and shaking legs.

Anxiety leads to nervousness, which can cause clammy hands and shaky legs.

(97) (A) Yes.

A person suffering from anxiety can face it every day, even more than once a day.

(98) (D) Heart attack.

The symptoms of a heart attack and panic attack are often the same. These symptoms include having difficulty breathing, feeling a tickling sensation in some areas of the body, muscle pain, shivering and feeling lightheaded.

(99) (A) Phobia.

Phobias are extreme fears that cause distress to the individuals suffering from them. Violence, disorders and depression are all dangerous situations as they can lead to harmful outcomes.

(100) (C) Agoraphobia.

Agoraphobia is the fear of being in situations where leaving is difficult or humiliating or where aid is unavailable.

(101) (A) Talk therapy and prescription drugs.

This is the only correct choice as the rest of the methods aren't suitable for dealing with anxiety.

(102) (D) Psychological evaluation.

Psychological evaluation is the process of discussing a client's sentiments and behavior to narrow down a diagnosis and rule out potential complications.

(103) (B) Difficulty concentrating and moodiness.

Depression-related fatigue is caused by trauma; hence, it can cause difficulty in concentrating and moodiness, apart from just pain and tiredness.

(104) (A) Yes.

Depression and pain can coexist as depression causes fatigue that can lead to pain.

Treatment Planning Answers

(105) (A) Setting goals in sequential order.

This is beneficial because it enhances the tracking process and makes it easier for the counselor to look back at previously used techniques when updating the treatment plan.

(106) (C) It can help a client achieve the goal faster.

There is no specific time frame in which goals are achieved. This is because time should not be a priority; setting time goals may cause the patient to act irrationally due to the pressure.

(107) (A) Quaternary care.

This kind of care is usually the last resort of patients dealing with critical illnesses. This care includes highly specialized equipment that is not ordinarily available at hospital facilities. Furthermore, this care is usually provided by laboratories performing trial phases of research.

(108) (B) Terminate the therapeutic process.

It is common for counselors to disengage themselves from a situation that may put them in harm's way. There are no rules or regulations that bind them to the client in such a situation. In such circumstances, counselors are allowed to terminate the process for their own safety.

(109) (A) Clients who are illiterate.

It is common for counselors to come across such individuals when visiting rural areas. Counselors who take part in such outreach programs must know alternative methods of communication.

(110) (A) Alpha members of the group influence the beta members and impose their opinions strongly.

This is common ground for conflict during the transition stage of group therapy. Influencing members can have a detrimental effect on other members' participation and expression. It is important that the counselor stop the conflict if it is taking a turn for the worse.

(111) (B) The illness is mild to moderate.

Primary care settings are usually run by general physicians who are only equipped to deal with outpatient services. This means they can only treat patients with mild illnesses through prescribed tests and medicines. If patients have a long-term disease, they might come to a primary care facility to seek a referral to an appropriate specialist.

(112) (C) Checking up on the client's general situation after termination or discharge.

Follow-up care is a crucial part of the recovery process. It is especially beneficial for patients who have been released from rehabilitation centers. Therefore, it is provided at the time of discharge to ease patients' transition into an unstructured environment. Counselors provide follow-up care to their clients after the therapeutic sessions have been terminated. This is done to provide the clients with any alternate resources if needed.

(113) (B) Religious beliefs, ethnicity, cultural tendencies.

A counselor is obligated to tend to these aspects as they normally have a great influence over a client's life and decisions. They can also be an underlying root cause of some problems.

(114) (C) Introductions between different group members and the mediator.

It is only logical to make sure all group members have been properly introduced to each other and the mediator. After introductions have been made, the mediator briefs everyone on the rules and regulations. The mediator might choose to tell the clients about what to expect at the end of the group sessions too.

(115) (A) Patients are unable to care for themselves in their home environment.

Although there exist many differences between tertiary and secondary care, the main difference is that patients who require tertiary care are in a somewhat critical state and are unable to sustain themselves without a hospital's facilities. These facilities include specialized staff, 24/7 care, special intravenous drugs and 24/7 lab facilities, etc.

(116) (D) All of the above.

All the answer options listed are beneficial strategies a mediator can apply according to the situation at hand. During the transition state, the group tends to be difficult to handle, which is why it is okay for the mediator to intervene as many times as needed to guide people toward recovery.

(117) (A) A dialect barrier.

A dialect barrier is not all that different from a language barrier, as they both pertain to a conversation between the client and counselor. A client can be a fluent English speaker, but his or her pronunciation might prove difficult to understand.

(118) (B) The client must inform the counselor of any previous or current illnesses and medications.

It is inappropriate for clients to alter their medications themselves, and discontinuing medications abruptly without a physician's order can also lead to problems. Therefore, adjusting medication should be up to the counselor. The client should inform the counselor about any previous or current medication and illnesses.

(119) (D) All of the above.

Follow-up care is mandatory for patients who have been discharged from a rehabilitation facility. During their time at the facility, they were under close watch and protection. The sudden loss of this structured atmosphere might lead to erratic behavior.

(120) (A) Short-term goals.

These goals are repetitive so that it is easier to achieve them. This enhances patients' motivation, which causes them to adhere to the treatment plan with more enthusiasm.

(121) (A) It refers to the means used to assist in the accomplishment of a target.

Modality, frequency and targets are part of a treatment plan. This category includes information on goals and their characteristics. Modality and frequency are both terms used in relation to the targets.

(122) (D) All of the above.

A renal dialysis unit, specialized surgery facility and a 24/7 laboratory are all examples of facilities that are available in any hospital. The facilities are examples of tertiary care.

(123) (C) The mediator must provide those group members with resources to an alternate group setting or take them on in their own new group.

It is crucial for the counselor to support the decision of group members if they feel like their therapeutic journey has not come to an end when group therapy has been terminated. Keeping this in mind, the counselor should provide the clients with alternatives to continue their therapy.

(124) (C) It increases the client's sense of independence.

This is not the sole purpose of setting targets; however, it is definitely of great benefit to the patient as the feeling of increased control over treatment motivates an individual to stick to it.

(125) (A) The working stage.

At this stage, group members have come to civil understandings with each other and their mediator. They understand each other better because they can relate to shared trauma.

Counseling Skills and Interventions Answers

(126) (D) An assertion of authority and an abuse of power.

Many people mistakenly think that sexual harassment is primarily motivated by sexual attraction. Instead, it is an assertion and display of abuse and authority over another person.

(127) (D) Both B and C.

There are two main types of managers: those who are derogatory toward their employees, always searching for their mistakes, and those who are pleasant toward their staff, looking for the best in each employee.

(128) (A) Decision-making through participation.

Participatory decision-making is a model in which the people involved in executing a decision also participate in its creation. It encourages teamwork and helps to avoid disputes between managers and employees.

(129) (B) Reliance on mental health services.

Minorities face numerous barriers to receiving mental health care. Many of these obstacles apply to all Americans (e.g., cost, unavailability, treatment taboo), but others that may deter minority communities include deep distrust and fear of therapy, speech and language differences, prejudice and racism.

(130) (C) Do not acknowledge the patient unless he or she acknowledges you first.

It is critical for counselors not to have dual relationships with their clients; however, some intersections in society circles cannot be prevented. It is best to clarify to your clients during the intake session how you will act if you see them out in public. If they acknowledge you, it is suitable to respond with a polite hello; however, it is not recommended that you initiate a greeting with the client. To protect the client's secrecy and retain your professional boundaries, keep conversation to a reasonable level.

(131) (D) All of the above.

Unfortunately, sexual assault is still prevalent in many workplaces. One of the common misconceptions is that it is frequently reported. But according to a survey, 75% of harassed women ignored the abuse, while only 18% reported it. Men can be victims of sexual abuse as well, but it appears to be less prevalent.

(132) (B) Yes, as long as her posts adhere to the ACA's directives.

According to the ACA Code of Ethics, counselors must maintain separate social media profiles for their private and organizational virtual presences.

(133) (C) Equal Employment Opportunity Commission (EEOC).

Homosexuality was removed from the DSM-II in 1973 and is no longer considered an impairment. Discrimination in the workplace against sexual orientation, as well as race, kids, nationality, religion, gender, age, impairment, sexual preference, gender expression and genetic information, is prohibited by the Equal Employment Opportunity Commission (EEOC) and Title VII of the Civil Rights Act in some states.

(134) (A) Both B and D.

An employee performance evaluation can span a wide variety of topics. One-on-one time with a superintendent can be a bonding experience for all types of concerns, job contexts, praise and future training requirements. Of course, how it is managed is a major factor.

(135) (A) A patient fantasizes about marrying her therapist.

Transference occurs when clients project major problems from past interactions with important people in their lives onto the therapist.

(136) (B) Subjectivity.

When two people meet for the first time, clothing or facial appearance can help form a first impression. Subjectivity describes these first impressions.

(137) (D) All of the above.

Career counseling entails using various inventories developed to evaluate the client's interests, talents and values to help the client identify career goals. The counselor may also assist the patient in self-exploration and value clarification to increase the probability of setting successful goals. The counselor may also teach skills like decision-making, effective action planning and personal development.

(138) (A) Spreading organizational culture.

The primary unspoken goal of orientation is to convey organizational culture. Each organization has its own culture, complete with stigmas, traditions, assumptions and so on. To gain insight into corporate culture, a new employee should look beyond what is said and read between the lines.

(139) (B) Risky shift phenomenon.

Risky shift is a social psychology phenomenon and a type of group polarization. This is related to the diffusion of responsibility, which occurs when a member of a group gives up some self-identity, resulting in a loss of self-control and self-awareness. Another term from social psychology is bystander apathy, which occurs when people presume that someone else has already taken measures to help because there are other people around.

(140) (A) It is a person's belief in his or her ability to manage and carry out the actions necessary to achieve the desired result.

Self-efficacy is an individual's belief in planning and carrying out the actions necessary to achieve the desired result. According to Bandura's theory, self-efficacy is based on personal performance, vicarious experiences, social reinforcement and emotional and physiological factors. Motivation is heavily reliant on self-efficacy. People who believe they can do something will try and try again until they achieve their goal.

(141) (A) Practicing in areas where education or training is lacking.

Working with a client in an area where a counselor has not been properly trained is inappropriate and unethical.

(142) (C) They require informed consent and a signed release for any information provided to others.

In addition to the right to an interpreter, if necessary, the client must give informed consent, and if any knowledge about the test results is to be shared with anyone, the client must give written consent. Of course, there may be mitigating factors that necessitate special consideration.

(143) (D) All of the above.

All of the factors mentioned are directly related to the research process. Plagiarism, or the use of another person's work, is completely unethical. Great care is taken to ensure that any animals used in research receive the best possible health care and treatment. Because institutional approval is frequently required, accurate and valid note-taking is essential. Material fabrication is strictly prohibited.

(144) (D) Both A and B.

One's life roles are considered in career counseling. At one point in life, a person may be regarded as a "student," with an emphasis on education. Or a person may be viewed as a "primary caregiver," with the emphasis on earning a living to support a family. To achieve the best possible outcome, future roles may need to be evaluated in career counseling. At a future date, one's role could be both "physician" and "mother." How well these roles fit together may depend on taking a precautionary look at the prospect of taking on both positions prior to entering into professional development to become a clinician, particularly if the woman values the role of "mother" for later in life.

(145) (A) Conflict avoidance, as well as Amanda's failure to provide sufficient structure to instruct members how to express their feelings, thoughts and responses.

When a group is starting out, the group leadership must be active in the early stages, providing a framework to help the group members work effectively because this is not a skill they have perfected on their own. Group leadership is required until the group members are ready to face conflict and identify their own and the group's feelings, thoughts and reactions.

(146) (C) Poor work conditions.

Issues relating to Native American individuals are complex and linked to historical events and current experiences. Because of the historic trauma suffered by Native Americans, subtle messages that indicate a lack of belonging in contemporary society and a continuing attack on Indian sovereignty, mental health problems within this population are perpetuated.

(147) (A) A client is fixated on one explanation for a negative occurrence.

Dysfunctional thinking refers to a client's inability to think of alternative explanations for negative occurences. The client remains fixated with only one explanation.

(148) (C) The proclivity to evaluate people based on a single outstanding characteristic.

The halo effect is the proclivity to overestimate or underestimate individuals based on a single outstanding trait. This effect is a common flaw in rating scales.

(149) (B) They have erroneous beliefs in their own capabilities.

According to this theory, many people do not consider a variety of jobs because they do not feel capable of thriving in those fields. People who lack confidence in math or science may rule out engineering or medical professions because they believe they will struggle academically.

(150) (B) Create new ideas about their capabilities and reexamine past experiences.

A social cognitive career counselor can help clients change incorrect notions about self-worth by assisting them in developing new capabilities.

(151) (B) Six stages.

Kohlberg's theory shows the development of morality in kids, as well as moral reasoning.

(152) (A) Yes. You do not require a separate release because both the teacher and the school counselor are part of the school.

You may speak with any school staff if a parent includes the name of the school on a release of documents. If the parent gives you a specific person's name, you are only permitted to speak with that person.

(153) (B) Belief structures of various cultures.

Culture awareness training includes cultural beliefs and practices, conversational skills, worldview of the culture (how life is viewed as a whole) and other areas required for effective interaction, understanding and connection with a person from a specific culture.

(154) (B) A diploma in Asian culture.

Diversity training provides knowledge of various cultures, as well as insight into the cultural norms of a specific community. Diversity training includes realizing the meaning of family, differences in point of reference and how mental health concerns are presented in a specific culture. A degree in Asian culture or a suggestion from another therapist is not required. A willingness to help the client would also be beneficial, but diversity training is what is required.

(155) (B) The client needs to know that the counselor is being overseen and will consult with a licensed clinician about the client's situation.

In most states, the counselor will need to obtain the client's right to share information before meeting with the supervisor to discuss consultation progress. Clients must understand that the counselor is being supervised by a licensed clinician and what this means for them. Although the client may inquire, the counselor does not have to disclose how frequently he or she is meeting with a supervisor.

(156) (D) An early existentialist therapist.

Victor Frankl is one of the foremost therapists related to the development of existentialism. He was born in Vienna, Austria, in 1905 and spent much of WWII in a Nazi prison camp.

(157) (C) The Theory of Personality-Job Fit.

According to the personality-job fit theory, job security results from a match between temperament and occupation. It is also important to have supportive coworkers, supportive workplace conditions, intellectually demanding work and equal and fair rewards.

(158) (B) It was dedicated to the investigation of mental processes.

Structuralism emphasized the importance of investigating mental processes by focusing on the sensations and feelings of conscious awareness.

(159) (D) Both A and C.

For counselors, an asynchronous or dual relationship is normally regarded as being unethical. Counselors, for example, should not participate in intimate relations with patients, nor should they share leisure events, financial dealings or other nontherapeutic relations.

(160) (D) Why did you consume so much alcohol?

The question "why did you consume so much alcohol?" has a derisive ring to it and can put the client on the defensive, effectively shutting down further communication between the client and physician. "How did you feel about that?" elicits the client's feelings about her behavior in a nonjudgmental manner, likely leading to a discovery of her emotions behind the action of alcohol abuse. "What happened?" is a broad question that elicits additional context and leads to further discussion. "What would you change the next time?" allows the client to see binge drinking as an action she can choose or not choose, leading to further discussion and depth of understanding into her actions.

(161) (B) When additional issues are discovered that are not within the clinician's area of expertise.

When a client raises a concern in this area, clinicians must refer the person to a medical practitioner for medical evaluation. Also, if an inherent substance abuse problem has been revealed and the client would benefit from participating in a support network, a referral to a relevant authority or community group may be made.

(162) (B) Educating the client on the nature of counseling.

Role induction is the process of acquainting clients with the basics of counseling, their duties in this participatory partnership and the kinds of changes that can logically be anticipated from treatment. It can assist both the client and the counselor in seeing themselves as partners in a common undertaking that is likely to succeed.

(163) (B) Cognitive-behavioral therapy.

If a person has low self-esteem or is used to hearing a lot of negative messages, either externally or internally, a cognitive therapist may ask the individual to self-talk. Affirmations, which are positive and reinforcing slogans, are closely related to self-talk. People can put these affirmations anywhere they will see them frequently, such as on the fridge door or the bathroom wall.

(164) (B) Creating new perceptions or perspectives on a person's stress factors or problems.

Acquiring new knowledge and understanding of oneself and developing new perceptions or perspectives on one's troubles are both commonalities in successful therapy. Another factor associated with client change is a belief that change is required, as well as warmth and assistance from another person. Enjoyment of the treatment plan is not a predictor or factor in successful therapy.

(165) (B) Learning how to share with a partner.

One of the most important early tasks for a new couple is learning to share with a partner. Personal autonomy is typically learned when a person leaves home for good, perhaps to attend college or to get his or her first apartment, and developing a support group should be discussed whenever the person moves. Getting used to having less energy is usually a challenge specific to new parents.

(166) (C) The client's parents or siblings.

Objects in object-relation theory are typically people, parts of people or symbols of one of these. The way a person has or acquires an object is referred to as portrayal. An internal object is a person's portrayal of another, such as a child's relationship with his or her mother.

(167) (C) Normative social influence.

Normative social influence is the adherence to group pressure due to a need for respect and recognition. This can range from asking what everyone is wearing to a social occasion to engaging in destructive or unethical activities in order to maintain approval and acceptance.

(168) (B) Alleviating chronic anxiety.

Bowen's theory is based on the interaction of two forces. The first is a sense of community, and the second is a sense of individuality. Too much connectedness leads to fusion and inhibits individuality and the development of one's own sense of self. Individualism leads to a distant and detached family. Bowen was the first to recognize that people's personal past creates a template that influences each generation's value systems, thoughts and perspectives.

(169) (B) John Bowlby.

The first attachment theorist was British psychologist John Bowlby, who defined attachment as "a profound emotion known to human beings." Bowlby was fascinated by the detachment anxiety and depression children experience when separated from their parents.

(170) (A) Client resistance.

During treatment, counselors should make every attempt to address clients' resistance. If a client's opposition cannot be countered, the counselor may ask if the person wants to proceed or seek a referral to another therapist.

(171) (C) The overall behavior of the group.

A norm is a usual outcome that members of a group follow. Norms are society's expectations of how we "should" act. These norms vary from one culture to the next and from one group to the next within each culture.

(172) (C) A mutual decision by the client and counselor to terminate their counseling sessions.

An amicable termination happens when both the client and the counselor decide to terminate the counseling process mutually.

(173) (A) Developing competencies and skills in a client.

Strategic therapy is a type of interactional therapy in that it does not address the underlying causes of the patient's problem but rather aims to increase aptitude and cultivate problem-solving skills in the client.

This expansive term includes solution-focused therapy, which is unquestionably interactional. Despite its close relationship to strategic methods, not all therapists regard solution-focused therapy as "strategic."

(174) (D) Responsibility.

According to research, when participants are made aware that they will be held accountable for an outcome, destructive obedience drops dramatically. Sessions to remind individuals that they are responsible for their actions play a big part in negating the "group-think" factor and the deindividuation that can be a consequence of it.

(175) (C) Obedience and conformity.

The two most powerful forms of social influence are conformity and obedience. When people recognize all of the variables in a situation, they can use that understanding to determine when obedience and/or conformity are suitable and morally correct.

(176) (C) Respect for authority and schooling.

Respect for authority and schooling are important values in Asian-American households.

(177) (B) Oral, anal and phallic.

Freud intended to convey that sexual fuel accumulates and is released as we mature biologically when he described individual human behavior as psychosexual. (Note: Freud used the term "sexual" in a broad sense to refer to all pleasurable feelings and actions.)

Freud emphasized the importance of the first five years of life in the development of adult personality. To fulfill societal needs, the id must be governed; this creates a conflict between confused wishes and cultural standards.

(178) (A) Some people's personalities/behaviors stand out more than others.

When explaining the causes of behavior, bias is a tendency to concentrate on evocative (salient) or more visible factors. The fact that the more visible factors highlight the situational factors allows us to make faster decisions. This leads to a second factor known as "blaming the victim."

(179) (B) To reestablish family bonds.

Family therapy can encourage the growth of family members, as well as the family as a whole. It is capable of completing a family intervention and restoring family relations.

(180) (B) The group leader may be insufficiently trained or experienced.

The group leader has significant responsibilities; if he or she is not well educated and prepared, the interactions may become emotionally damaging.

Core Counseling Attributes Answers

(181) (C) Judge the personality of the counselor.

In the beginning, clients are often hesitant and shy to open to their counselors. To feel comfortable around a counselor, they try to judge and understand their counselor's personality. Hence, the counselor needs to be sympathetic and understanding toward clients and provide a safe environment where clients can talk easily.

(182) (D) Empathizing with the client.

Research has discovered that therapist empathy functions as a fundamental element of treatment and exerts a medium-sized but variable presence on client outcomes across psychotherapeutic lines. Channeling empathy into a counseling session is a complex process involving many factors, including, but not limited to, working toward a common understanding of client sentiments, demonstrating warmth and esteem to the client and responding with similar sentiments.

(183) (C) It demotivates the client to visit and causes a communication gap.

A consistent approach in counseling has been shown to improve results, and it has also been found to be cost-effective. Most counselors make the most of the smallest number of appointments. Appointments in which there are long gaps can prolong the process and cause results to be delayed. Delayed sessions often discourage clients from attending sessions and make it more difficult for them to communicate effectively with the counselor, which further worsens the clients' difficulties.

(184) (C) Self-reporting.

Therapist empathy can be assessed using several methods. The first is self-reporting. Therapists evaluate themselves on their empathetic abilities during a session. It is known that therapists typically overrate themselves in comparison with the ratings given by their clients, both intentionally and unintentionally.

(185) (A) It helps counselors understand why clients are emotional.

A therapeutic concept of unconditional positive regard, awareness and acceptance can be healing through compassion. Through connecting with the client's grief, the counselor promotes change by taking action. Compassion extends beyond empathy and allows clients to feel understood.

(186) (B) Clients feel that they are equally entitled to participate in the group and have a chance to contribute positively.

A client experiencing a sense of acknowledgment in a group setting feels a sense of relief and validation, including feeling that he or she has the same rights and opportunity to contribute as other group members. This gives group members a chance to learn that they must accept and respect those around them. In turn, the acceptance from the group gives participants the confidence to contribute to the discussion of other members' issues.

(187) (D) Listening.

An important skill in a therapeutic relationship is listening. By being attentive to a client, a counselor can reflect understanding, mirror the person's body language and make eye contact as needed. It may seem minor to the counselor, but it means a lot to the client. This will help people voice their problems more easily.

(188) (B) Trying to understand the client's perspective.

The goal of nonjudgmental listening is to understand the perspective of the client. In essence, it goes beyond simply hearing what the client is saying and involves understanding what the client is trying to convey. Professionals working in mental health and counseling are trained to listen nonjudgmentally.

(189) (C) Examining one's own biases and privilege.

It is challenging yet essential to examine one's own biases and privileges to build multicultural counseling expertise. A multicultural counselor must be conscious of how his or her childhood and background have shaped the way he or she treats clients.

(190) (C) By utilizing a template for notes.

Counselors can use consistency in content to aid in their work. If the therapist formats the sessions on a digital device or takes notes manually, this helps reduce the time spent notating each session and prevents counselors from feeling frustrated if they fall behind schedule. If counselors use templates for notes, this is a much more effective and efficient way to stay up to date with clients' information.

(191) (D) Socioeconomic circumstances.

Racial, geographic and ethnic differences are integral elements of how people are perceived by family, friends and colleagues and how they express themselves in social situations. A wide range of socioeconomic circumstances must be considered by counselors.

(192) (C) "Counselors act to avoid harming their clients, trainees and research participants and to minimize or to remedy unavoidable or unanticipated harm."

This is taken straight from the American Counseling Association Code of Ethics (2014).

(193) (B) Showing inappropriate levels of intensity to the client's expressed feelings, not considering the client's history in context and responding selectively to the client's responses.

Counselors must consider the following problems that may cause them to be insensitive: intensity, context and selective responses. Taking an appropriate level of intensity into consideration when responding to feelings expressed by a client is essential. When the process of reflecting on emotions is not done correctly, there will be a rift between the counselor and the client.

(194) (C) The act of self-awareness.

Counseling is considered a unique profession. A practitioner must use interventions that extend beyond learned skills and knowledge. To be effective, counselors must incorporate self-awareness.

(195) (B) It helps them figure out their feelings and thoughts.

It is also the group members' responsibility to inspire the group. A member's participation encourages shy or demotivated members to speak up. Through sharing, members gain insight into the issues they are facing, but most importantly, it is through sharing that they determine their feelings and form their opinions. When therapeutic values are present, group members feel relieved, gain self-confidence and insight and feel appreciated.

(196) (D) Ask the reason the person is angry.

Good counseling requires patience. Often, clients are hesitant to open about their problems until they have a clear understanding of them. Effective counselors always wait for their clients, never interrupting or pressing them into action. Upon seeing an angry client, ask what is making the person angry and listen to the individual's feelings. Keep an eye out for nonverbal communication signals and interpret them accordingly. A smile demonstrates warmth and establishes a sense of trust and acceptance.

(197) (D) Respect and tolerance.

Respect and tolerance are essential elements of any successful relationship; these components are also reflected in the client-counselor relationship. A respectful gesture indicates acceptance, admiration, consent and loyalty. Counselors are required to respect all clients regardless of their personality, background or behavior because clients have sought assistance from them and deserve to be treated as individuals of value and worth. A counselor who is effective shows respect for clients by recognizing their good qualities and by acknowledging and valuing a person's spirit when a client comes to therapy with low self-esteem.

(198) (C) By asking questions.

Asking questions allows counselors to learn more about their clients. When counselors ask questions about clients, they gain a deeper understanding. An effective counselor can establish the flow and tone of a session simply by asking a set of specific questions. Having a clear understanding of the process will make it more efficient. The goal is to avoid closed questions, as they do not facilitate deeper exploration. It is recommended to ask open-ended questions so that clients can explore their responses.

(199) (D) The nonverbal movements of the members, as well as the changes in their verbalizations.

A facilitator is essential for group therapy and is responsible for ensuring the sessions run smoothly. For groups to be effective, the group leader must assess whether they are successful. A member should be empathetic and pay attention to subtly changing behavior and changes in the words of other group members.

(200) (D) The skill of being understanding.

Understanding, awareness and sensitivity are traits of empathy. Being able to experience thoughts, experiences and feelings among a group of people without ever being told the sentiments in a direct manner is the definition of empathy. When communicating with a client, exercising empathy is a critical part of being an effective counselor. Empathetic counseling ensures clients that their concerns will be heard and makes them feel comfortable.

Test 3

Professional Practice and Ethics

(1) Researchers carry out investigations on topics to better educate themselves. They first choose a problem and then devise a hypothesis regarding it.

What is their prediction usually based on?

(A) A theory

(B) Prior studies regarding the topic

(C) Their random conclusions

(D) A and B

(2) Client privilege is a legal right that protects the client's private information from being revealed in judicial proceedings. Who determines the people that will be granted this privilege?

(A) The state law

(B) The counselor

(C) The patient

(D) None of the above

(3) Which of the following responsibilities assigned by the law to counselors necessitates the breaching of confidentiality?

(A) They are required to act as agents of social control.

(B) They cannot keep anything secret.

(C) They have to reveal every detail to the state.

(D) None of the above.

(4) A child who is suffering from depression approaches a counselor. What should the counselor ask the child about?

(A) His age

(B) His school life

(C) If he has any plans of self-harming

(D) His relationship with his parents

(5) A counselor is faced with an issue he is not able to deal with on his own. He seeks his fellow group counselors' help but fails to get any satisfactory answer.

Which of the following could be a reason for that?

(A) He should not work in a group.

(B) People in his group have dissimilar interests.

(C) He is not learned enough.

(D) His colleagues lack basic knowledge.

(6) Which of the following types of information revealed by a client to a counselor can be counted?

(A) The number of times a student experiences test anxiety in a day

(B) The regularity of positive statements conveyed in a romantic relationship

(C) Both A and B

(D) None of the above

(7) Who should be most engaged in a psychotherapy session?

(A) The counselor

(B) The client

(C) Both A and B

(D) None of the above

(8) Which of the following is the fourth stage of the counseling process?

(A) Goal setting

(B) Intervention in counseling

(C) Initial disclosure

(D) Relationship building

(9) According to ________, empathy, genuineness and unconditional caring are the three key conditions for establishing an effective counselor-client relationship.

(A) Carl Rogers

(B) Martin Seligman

(C) Kurt Schneider

(D) Albert Einstein

(10) Which of the following problems faced by people can be solved through psychotherapy?

(A) The loss of a loved one

(B) Depression

(C) The effects of trauma

(D) All of the above

(11) When is unethical behavior most likely to occur in psychotherapy?

(A) When the patient tests the temper of the counselor

(B) When the counselor sets standards and acts completely in contradiction to them

(C) When the counselor is dealing with problems in his or her personal life

(D) When the patient finds it difficult to open up to the therapist

(12) Which of the following is/are the basic right(s) of a client seeking psychotherapy?

(A) Confidentiality

(B) Privilege

(C) Privacy

(D) All of the above

(13) According to Kurt Schneider, what is an entrusted secret in counseling?

(A) The secrets shared by the counselor

(B) The age of the client

(C) The information revealed by the client to the counselor

(D) None of the above

(14) Psychotherapists are supposed to maintain records of all the major and minor details regarding their clients. Which of the following is an important responsibility of the counselor pertaining to those records?

(A) Ensuring transparency of transfer

(B) Maintaining those records

(C) Providing access to the clients upon request

(D) Both A and C

(15) Which of the following is a major limitation faced by counselors in maintaining the confidentiality of extremely young clients' personal information?

(A) Sexual abuse

(B) Parental pressure

(C) Difficulty in maintaining secrecy

(D) All of the above

(16) According to Wubbolding, which of the following could help in the identification of suicidal people?

(A) Their hopelessness

(B) They cannot be identified unless they openly reveal their thoughts.

(C) Their social life

(D) All of the above

(17) According to Fujimura et al., how can the majority of suicides be avoided?

(A) By scolding suicidal people

(B) By making an example of people who try to commit suicide but survive

(C) By recognizing, assessing and effectively intervening in crisis situations

(D) By making suicide a punishable offense

(18) Which of the following issues may arise when a client's right to privacy is violated?

(A) Client dependence

(B) Low income for counselors

(C) Prejudice

(D) Both A and C

(19) Which of the following conditions can impair the factual comprehension of a person?

(A) Dementia

(B) Financial problems

(C) The weather

(D) None of the above

(20) Who is considered a legally recognized third party in the case of clients who are unable to give their consent?

(A) The client's parents

(B) The client's caregiver

(C) The client's guardian

(D) Any individual involved

(21) What is the basis of the Disabilities Act of America?

(A) To discriminate against people dealing with disabilities

(B) To ensure fair and equal treatment for people regardless of their disabilities

(C) To restrict the movement of disabled people in public buildings

(D) To prevent disabled people from accessing jobs that normally functioning people are employed in

(22) Which of the following is widely discussed as a critical skill for living well with an impairment or disability?

(A) Self-hate

(B) Staying silent

(C) Self-compassion

(D) Adjustment

(23) Losing physical or emotional abilities is referred to as a disability. If not treated with kindness and empathy, what are a disability's effects on the sufferer?

(A) Panic attacks

(B) Fear

(C) Trauma

(D) All of the above

(24) Psychotherapy is a treatment for several kinds of mental issues. If the problem is urgent and has just surfaced, how long should therapy ideally last?

(A) For a year

(B) A few sessions

(C) A few minutes

(D) Six months

(25) Where should all the information regarding a research problem be gathered?

(A) In a database

(B) In the researcher's mind

(C) In a cell phone

(D) In a notebook

Intake, Assessment and Diagnosis

(26) What is the best time to carry out a biopsychosocial evaluation (BPS)?

(A) The start of therapy

(B) The middle of therapy

(C) Toward the end of therapy

(D) A few months after therapy is completed

(27) "How much of your stress is caused by your job and working environment?"

Questions like these are asked under which of the following components of the BPS evaluation?

(A) Biological

(B) Psychological

(C) Social

(D) All of the above

(28) Which of the following terms best describe(s) the statements made by a counselor-case manager about the latent interpretations of a client's statements, actions, behavioral patterns, perceptions, interactions and feelings?

(A) Objective facts

(B) Subjective impressions

(C) Both A and B

(D) All of the above

(29) What year did Shea propose his popular method for clinical interviewing?

(A) 1995

(B) 2001

(C) 1678

(D) 1998

(30) The CFI comprises three components. Which component evokes the perspectives of people nearest to the patient, such as family members, acquaintances and care providers?

(A) First

(B) Second

(C) Third

(D) All of the above

(31) Identify the fourth stage of Shea's model.

(A) Closing

(B) Termination

(C) Body

(D) Introduction

(32) What does a mental status examination include?

(A) The patient's previous medical history

(B) Data collected by the counselor throughout the patient's clinical visit

(C) Both A and B

(D) None of the above

(33) Which of the following terms best describes the first meeting between a client and therapist?

(A) Outtake

(B) Intake

(C) Introduction

(D) Initial meeting

(34) System is a therapeutic approach used to treat cases of __________.

(A) Couples therapy

(B) Individual therapy

(C) Family therapy

(D) Group therapy

(35) Identify a drawback of group therapy

(A) A lot of people find it difficult to open up in front of crowds.

(B) It wastes a lot of time.

(C) Both A and B.

(D) None of the above.

(36) In which of the following cases of therapy is it appropriate to begin with a trauma history?

(A) Rape

(B) Loss of a loved one

(C) Accident-causing disability

(D) Both B and C

(37) ___________ rise(s) as specificity rises.

(A) False positives

(B) False negatives

(C) Sensitivity

(D) Assessment

(38) Which of the following is a computerized version of authenticated paper questionnaires?

(A) CAGE

(B) CFI

(C) MSE

(D) MPPI

(39) Which of the following processes is/are typically performed at the start of therapy?

(A) BPS

(B) Screening

(C) Assessment

(D) All of the above

(40) A substance abuse assessment is for patients who are addicted to drugs. The process usually comprises three major steps.

Identify one of the steps from the following options.

(A) Individual evaluation

(B) Pragmatism

(C) Termination

(D) Closing

(41) Self-reports have several advantages and disadvantages. A major issue with self-reports is that they are usually inaccurate.

Which of the following makes self-reports inaccurate?

(A) The clients may understate their problems.

(B) The clients may give diplomatic responses.

(C) The clients may overexaggerate their condition.

(D) All of the above.

(42) Which of the following most accurately describes the term “reliability”?

(A) It indicates that the measure yields the same result over multiple applications.

(B) It implies that the measure evaluates the outcomes it intends to represent and provides data that is generally applicable.

(C) It is the ability of a mechanism to target people who do not have a disorder.

(D) It is the ability of a screening device to identify accurate cases of a target condition in a population group.

(43) Which of the following is not a common modality of psychiatric treatment?

(A) Individual therapy

(B) Group therapy

(C) Family therapy

(D) None of the above

(44) Which of the following is a technique that is not used on people seeking couples therapy?

(A) Cognitive

(B) Behavioral

(C) System

(D) Both A and B

(45) Which of the following is a general protocol followed by counselors for assessing trauma exposure?

(A) Posing questions empathically and nonjudgmentally

(B) Inquiring about a rape victim's trauma history

(C) Asking direct questions without first developing rapport

(D) All of the above

(46) Simply bringing up the topic of substance abuse with patients ____________.

(A) Is a wrong practice

(B) Can be beneficial

(C) Is useless

(D) None of the above

(47) What best describes the word "termination" in therapy?

(A) Closing of a session

(B) Termination of therapy

(C) Both A and B

(D) None of the above

(48) What is the difference between the directive and nondirective approach during the clinical interviewing of a client?

(A) The directive approach is adopted when counselors want to manage the interview, and the nondirective approach is adopted when interviewees want to manage the interview.

(B) The directive approach is adopted when interviewees want to manage the interview, and the nondirective approach is adopted when counselors want to manage the interview.

(C) They are both similar approaches.

(D) None of the above.

(49) Which of the following is/are the advantage(s) of labor force participation for addicts recovering from mental disorders?

(A) Helps in improving self-efficacy

(B) Helps in improving self-identity

(C) Offers a sense of belonging to society in general

(D) All of the above

(50) Culture refers to learned and passed-down systems of ____________ from one generation to the next.

(A) Concepts

(B) Awareness

(C) Rules

(D) All of the above

Areas of Clinical Focus

(51) Aging is a natural process. Is it possible to stop it?

(A) Yes

(B) No

(C) Sometimes

(D) Depends on a person's financial resources

(52) What symptom is common between Alzheimer's, Parkinson's and dementia?

(A) High cholesterol levels

(B) Low insulin levels

(C) Sensory loss

(D) Subconscious loss

(53) Specialists who are trained through various courses and hired through agencies or hospitals for long-term guidance and support are called?

(A) Professional caregivers

(B) Professional counselors

(C) Family caregiver

(D) Family trainer

(54) Why is it important to talk about death in a healthy manner?

(A) To emotionally blackmail the family

(B) To understand a person and be able to implement his or her decisions at a later stage

(C) To help a person figure out his or her thoughts and sentiments

(D) To give an idea to a person about suicide

(55) What are some factors due to which a person cannot get over grief?

(A) Acceptance and depression

(B) Detachment and lack of trust

(C) Non-satisfactory investments

(D) Outliving one's savings

(56) If someone is not able to process the hurt he or she is going through, what might the pain lead to?

(A) Anxiety

(B) Depression

(C) Bipolar disorder

(D) Coronary disease

(57) How can a person avoid not having enough money for retirement?

(A) By investing in better opportunities

(B) By dividing money among children

(C) By saving up more

(D) By spending less

(58) What is an end-of-life issue that is usually overlooked?

(A) Solid retirement plans

(B) Communication

(C) Depression

(D) Lack of emotional support

(59) Why is it difficult to move on for some individuals?

(A) Loneliness

(B) Detachment

(C) Holding onto feelings

(D) Acceptance

(60) What are the signs of an inability to let go of a previous relationship?

(A) Marrying another person and co-parenting children

(B) Changing cities and getting a new job to support oneself

(C) Encouraging children to hate the other parent and shout at him or her

(D) Spreading hatred about the ex-spouse and blaming him or her for the separation

(61) What should happen if a person starts to miss his or her child and wonders what the child might be doing with an ex-spouse?

(A) The person must keep texting his or her ex-spouse.

(B) The person must file a complaint against his or her ex-spouse.

(C) The child must be filled with hatred against the other parent.

(D) The child should be given the freedom to be with the other parent.

(62) What does adoption of a child mean to families?

(A) Financial burden

(B) Emotional fulfillment

(C) Physical violence

(D) Social embarrassment

(63) How can parents stop their children from practicing bad habits they might have observed and learned from someone?

(A) By beating them

(B) By looking them up in a room

(C) By explaining how those behaviors are wrong

(D) By making them apologize

(64) What is something important that must be assessed about a child during the process of adoption?

(A) Ethnicity

(B) Religious beliefs

(C) Parents

(D) Health

(65) When a child has the capability to comprehend information and talk about it confidently, develop ideas and put them into practice, what kind of skill is this?

(A) Interpersonal skill

(B) Cognitive skill

(C) Communication skill

(D) Social skill

(66) What steps must be taken to improve a primary care provider's work?

(A) Strategies for an individual-focused approach and advocating for health-care services

(B) Investing funds for marketing and training practitioners

(C) Reducing prices for health care and giving citizens discounts

(D) Employing better counselors and terminating the existing ones

(67) Should legal professionals be consulted to resolve a conflict between two parents?

(A) Yes

(B) No

(C) Depends on the situation

(D) Legal professionals don't work on these issues

(68) What happens when a conflict is left unresolved between parents?

(A) Children help to resolve it.

(B) Spouses take a break from parenting.

(C) Issues of trust and dependency arise.

(D) Parents immediately separate.

(69) What are couples who surround themselves with positive friends and coworkers likely to do?

(A) Cheat on each other

(B) Stay married

(C) Waste money with friends

(D) Not spend time with family

(70) What sort of major changes can have a negative impact on a couple after a relationship is built?

(A) Change in career, change in the family vehicle, etc.

(B) Studies of children, friends of the couple, etc.

(C) Dividing finances, having a child, etc.

(D) Change in income, change in climate, etc.

(71) Why is divorce a good option for a couple wanting to part ways?

(A) They are able to bond with their children.

(B) They are able to enjoy freedom.

(C) They are able to cook for themselves.

(D) They are able to divide the property.

(72) What is a leading cause of divorce?

(A) Abuse

(B) Finances

(C) Infidelity

(D) Lack of communication

(73) Why has there been a decline in divorce rates in the United States?

(A) Positive impact of romantic movies

(B) Career-oriented youth

(C) Fear of harassment from partner

(D) Compromise from a spouse

(74) What is the main cause for a person developing angry tendencies?

(A) Spouse

(B) Job

(C) Friends

(D) Stress

(75) What is it called when a woman faces a delay in orgasm?

(A) Arousal disorder

(B) Pain disorder

(C) Orgasm disorder

(D) Desire disorder

(76) In which age group is remarriage most common?

(A) 30+

(B) 40+

(C) 50+

(D) 60+

(77) How does renewing vows and getting remarried to the same person help?

(A) It strengthens the relationship and enables a fresh start.

(B) It helps partners to move on from traumatic events of their previous relationship.

(C) It creates a good impact on children and the home environment.

(D) It renews love and makes more room for financial dependability.

(78) Is having difficulty eating or sleeping, coupled with a visible change in appearance, a sign of a suicidal individual?

(A) Yes

(B) No

(C) Varies from situation to situation

(D) Varies from person to person

(79) What are some protective factors in suicide prevention?

(A) Eating and sleeping erratically

(B) Spending time alone and disassociating with friends

(C) Feeling love from parents and getting a divorce

(D) Effective coping mechanisms and counseling

(80) Why is it essential for counselors to provide a safe environment to clients?

(A) So they can develop romantic feelings for the counselor

(B) So they can express their true feelings about suicide, depression, etc.

(C) So they feel safe in telling their plans of harming someone

(D) So they take the therapeutic procedure lightly

(81) Should a counselor be worried if a suicidal client is able to make her own treatment decisions and takes control of whether or not she lives or dies?

(A) Be very worried

(B) Not at all

(C) Not worried, but should work on it

(D) Put them on the red list

(82) Are therapists supposed to conduct a thorough examination of a person's mental state or capacity?

(A) Yes

(B) No

(C) Depends on the situation

(D) Depends on the therapist

(83) What should a counselor do if a client gets a high rating on a suicide scale?

(A) Immediately involve the family and inform the manager and senior therapists

(B) Ask the client if he or she intends to end his or her life and find out where the risk comes from

(C) Be afraid of the client and provide the individual with all necessary helplines

(D) Prescribe antidepressants and sleeping pills to divert the client's attention

(84) Can a therapist predict the future events of clients' lives by counseling them regularly?

(A) Yes

(B) No

(C) Depends on how much a client is comfortable with the therapist

(D) Depends on the history of the client's illness

(85) What is a crisis plan intended to do?

(A) Concentrate on the risk factors associated with a client's illness

(B) Concentrate on a client's appearance

(C) Concentrate on a client's verbal and nonverbal actions

(D) Concentrate on a client's history

(86) Who is better positioned to work with clients after having thought about safety and well-being by debating their thoughts and reactions?

(A) Therapists

(B) Physicians

(C) Both

(D) None

(87) What plays a significant role in identity formation issues during adolescence?

(A) Ethnic identity

(B) Religious identity

(C) Educational identity

(D) Family identity

(88) What is a way to examine the results of evolving identities?

(A) Using constant surveys

(B) Using medicines

(C) Using peer-to-peer counseling

(D) Using status-based identity structure

(89) How should an emergency psychological situation be dealt with?

(A) Medication

(B) Therapy

(C) Intervention

(D) Tolerance

(90) When a person has behavioral issues such as rash driving and picking on children, what kind of disorder is this?

(A) Adjustment disorder

(B) Bipolar disorder

(C) Schizophrenia

(D) PTSD

(91) In what sort of individuals are adjustment disorders commonly diagnosed?

(A) People of older age

(B) Children and young adults

(C) Newborn children

(D) Women and transwomen

(92) If a person's inherent abilities to cope are not sufficient to make the individual feel at ease in new surroundings in a short amount of time, this may lead to?

(A) Bipolar disorder

(B) Stress

(C) Illness

(D) Adjustment disorder

(93) What factors can impact the inherited effects passed onto the next generations?

(A) Racial and ethnic identity

(B) Sexual identity

(C) Spiritual and religious identity

(D) Academic identity

(94) Who faces great isolation in the US due to its culture?

(A) Politicians

(B) Doctors

(C) Students

(D) Migrants

(95) “Adolescents who have a well-defined ethnic identity have better psychological adjustment than those who have a limited ethnic identity.”

Is this statement true?

(A) Yes

(B) No

(C) To some extent

(D) It is a biased approach

(96) What can be classified as complementary mind-body therapies?

(A) Watching TV and resting

(B) Sleeping for longer hours and showering

(C) Mindfulness and yoga

(D) Buying books and exercising

(97) In which of the following situations is a person more likely to be deeply affected by a tragic experience?

(A) Under pressure or stress

(B) Living alone

(C) Feeling a very close attachment

(D) Adjustment disorder

(98) What can occur as a result of anything that interrupts a child's sense of safety?

(A) Physical violence

(B) Fights with friends

(C) Traumatic experiences

(D) Phobias

(99) What sort of illnesses are people who have experienced trauma likely to develop?

(A) Borderline personality disorder and depression

(B) Post-traumatic stress disorder and brain hemorrhage

(C) Diabetes mellitus and liver cirrhosis

(D) Pancreatic cancer and hepatitis

(100) What must counselors respect while clients are going through a tragedy and trying to overcome it?

(A) Their intentions to die

(B) Their coping strategies

(C) Their eating patterns

(D) Their abusive natures

(101) What sort of traumatic experiences can negatively affect a child's sense of safety?

(A) Horror movies and shows

(B) Theft at home

(C) Abuse and neglect

(D) A pet's illness

(102) Can childhood abuse lay the foundations for future trauma?

(A) Yes

(B) No

(C) Varies from child to child

(D) Depends on the extent of abuse

(103) What type of medication is commonly used in mental therapy procedures?

(A) Antibiotics

(B) Antidepressants

(C) Multivitamins

(D) Cannabis

(104) Is it important for every survivor to discuss and express trauma-related emotions?

(A) Yes

(B) No

(C) Depends on the client

(D) Depends on the trauma

Treatment Planning

(105) Which kinds of goals are achieved at the end of the treatment?

(A) Short-term goals

(B) Intermediate goals

(C) Long-term goals

(D) None of the above

(106) Why is measurability important when setting goals during a treatment plan?

(A) It ensures the client adheres to the goals.

(B) It aids the client in seeking help from family members.

(C) It helps the client keep track of his or her own progress.

(D) None of the above.

(107) Which of the following is an obstacle in communication during interactions with clients?

(A) A general inability to communicate in the same language efficiently.

(B) The client's inability to convey emotions properly.

(C) The counselor's inability to relate to the client's problem.

(D) All of the above.

(108) Which of the following is the most challenging stage of group therapy?

(A) The transition stage

(B) The final stage

(C) The initial stage

(D) The working stage

(109) What extra advantage does a tertiary care setting have over a secondary care setting?

(A) Availability of specialized doctors

(B) Availability of specialized equipment and testing facilities

(C) Authority to prescribe medicine

(D) All of the above

(110) What is the term used to describe the subdivision of goals, and what kind of effect does it have on clients' treatment?

(A) Additions – these help clients create a sustainable support group.

(B) Delays – these give clients more time to achieve their goals.

(C) Objectives – these tend to have a positive effect on clients' motivation to achieve these goals.

(D) Rank – this helps clients compare their progress with other clients.

(111) What is the solution to language barriers during patient interaction?

(A) Refusing to treat the client

(B) The counselor attempting to translate the unfamiliar language

(C) Providing a skilled translator who ensures confidentiality

(D) None of the above

(112) Concerning group therapy, what is an important strategy the mediator of the group must apply in order to yield the best results?

(A) The mediator must be able to pick up on unvoiced cues.

(B) The mediator must give commands instead of suggestions.

(C) The mediator must repeatedly single out members who refuse to participate.

(D) All of the above.

(113) How should a counselor approach a client who has a negative opinion of the counseling practice?

(A) The counselor must refuse to provide treatment.

(B) The counselor must explain to the client that the current visit will yield different results as compared to the person's previous experiences.

(C) The counselor should take advice from the client's previous counselor to find out the problem.

(D) None of the above.

(114) At what stage of group therapy are clients able to accept self-critiques from the mediator?

(A) The transition stage

(B) The initial stage

(C) The final stage

(D) The working stage

(115) What should counselors do if clients are unwilling to follow their advice on a certain problem due to religious beliefs?

(A) Force the clients to ignore their religious beliefs

(B) Provide adequate alternate options

(C) Assure the clients that their religious beliefs are false

(D) All of the above

(116) What is the difference between "abandonment" and "termination"?

(A) Abandonment means to withdraw from a client on amicable terms.

(B) In abandonment, the client is satisfied with the counselor's work.

(C) Abandonment is used to describe the time when a relationship between a client and counselor is ended on unsuitable terms.

(D) All of the above.

(117) A patient who has been receiving treatment for a lifelong illness resides in a tertiary care setting.

What must the physician in charge of the patient do to ensure that the modified treatment is updated and continued?

(A) Take over the patient's secondary care.

(B) Debrief the secondary care physician about the client's hospital stay and change prescriptions if needed.

(C) Set the patient up in a quaternary care facility.

(D) None of the above.

(118) What is the top priority related to a client's personal information?

(A) Reliability

(B) Accountability

(C) Confidentiality

(D) None of the above

(119) What is usually the first stage of care in which a specialist doctor becomes involved?

(A) Secondary care

(B) Tertiary care

(C) Primary care

(D) Quaternary care

(120) Why do counselors set standards for completion during the initial stages of the therapeutic process?

(A) To make sure that the patient has a support system in place

(B) To slow down the therapeutic process

(C) To ensure that the client and counselor are on the same page about the goals of the treatment

(D) To ensure that the client and counselor know each other well enough to proceed

(121) What should a counselor do if a client is unsure about a treatment plan?

(A) Force the patient to follow the plan anyway.

(B) Take the time to properly brief the client about every aspect of the treatment plan.

(C) Tell the client that everyone who seeks therapy for the first time is unsure before they see their treatment plan.

(D) None of the above.

(122) Why is it necessary to mention the approximate time frame for the therapeutic process when obtaining informed consent?

(A) To ensure the client books the future sessions in advance

(B) To allow the client to be prepared when the time for termination arrives

(C) To allow the patient to plan a vacation

(D) None of the above

(123) Patients with which kinds of conditions usually go to secondary care settings?

(A) Patients in need of emergency care

(B) Patients with chronic, lifelong illnesses that refuse to heal from OPD treatment

(C) As a last resort, since no other treatment has been effective

(D) Patients with a minor cold or flu

(124) Which of the following is not a part of the informed consent process?

(A) Getting permission from the client to start the therapeutic process

(B) Devising an appropriate treatment plan

(C) Informing the client about all applicable information regarding the counseling interaction

(D) Telling the client the approximate time the therapy might last for

(125) If a patient outright refuses certain aspects of the treatment plan or even the treatment plan as a whole, what must a counselor do?

(A) The counselor must refuse treatment.

(B) The counselor must not force the patient to make decisions based on his or her advice.

(C) The counselor must refer the patient to a colleague.

(D) None of the above.

Counseling Skills and Interventions

(126) A counselor has difficulty working with a client to achieve the goals set out in the treatment regimen. What are some options for resolving this issue?

(A) Consult with other counselors.

(B) Stop working with the client.

(C) Request that another counselor sit in on a session (with client permission).

(D) Both A and C.

(127) What is diversity training?

(A) Instruction on how to use various types of therapeutic interventions

(B) Instruction on how to work with people of different ages

(C) Training in various cultures, ethnicities and experiences

(D) Both B and C

(128) In the Adlerian therapeutic journey, what does the stage "reorientation" represent?

(A) When the counselor establishes a strong bond with the client

(B) When the counselor helps the client build perspective on his or her own life

(C) When the client achieves a milestone in group therapy

(D) When the client is encouraged to apply the newly developed perspective to his or her current situation

(129) Sigmund Freud's theory is still debated and heavily criticized. Why?

(A) Much of his theory had no basis.

(B) Its foundation is an individual test case without a control group of "normal" people.

(C) His methods and principles are difficult to scientifically investigate.

(D) All of the above.

(130) Often, the lead clinician decides which counselors see new clients. What factors influence placement?

(A) Area of expertise of the counselor

(B) Client's age and gender

(C) Counselor workload

(D) All of the above

(131) Why are new editions of the DSM published?

(A) To include new information

(B) To incorporate changes in the perception of abnormal behaviors

(C) To alter descriptions and categories

(D) All of the above

(132) The therapeutic relationship relies heavily on confidentiality. Why?

(A) It makes patients feel more secure during treatment.

(B) It encourages clients to share potentially painful or embarrassing information.

(C) It increases clinicians' trust in the client.

(D) Both A and B.

(133) The duty to warn is an essential component of professional ethics in therapy.

What is a part of the duty to warn?

(A) The obligation to protect others who are threatened by a client.

(B) Protecting clients who threaten suicide or other types of bodily harm.

(C) When confronted with a potential breach of confidentiality, it is incumbent upon the employee to seek advice from a colleague or supervisor.

(D) It is key to warn the client when the therapist won't be available in the office.

(134) Clients suffering from which of the following disorders are most likely to be incapable of engaging in the self-examination prescribed by Adlerian therapy?

(A) Disorders of impulse control

(B) Disorders of the mind

(C) Personality flaws

(D) Anxiety problems

(135) What is the goal of a strengths-based assessment?

(A) Concentrating on the client's strengths in all parts of life

(B) Giving meaning to one's struggle

(C) Raising awareness of the difficulties that clients have faced

(D) Aiding in the selection of a treatment method

(136) What is the purpose of the ego's defense mechanism in psychoanalytic theory?

(A) To bring about harmony within a person

(B) To keep people from becoming anxious

(C) To keep people safe from robbers

(D) None of the above

(137) Which theory is brief solution-based therapy based on?

(A) The ego's inability to repress modest drives creates problems.

(B) Acceptance and unconditional positive regard fosters self-esteem and client growth.

(C) Small changes in behavior lead to increased changes, which affect the entire system.

(D) People are autonomous and have complete control over their emotions, actions and emotional responses.

(138) What should a counselor always do when analyzing the progress of the client?

(A) Inquire about the client's well-being

(B) Consult the treatment plan

(C) Seek the help of other peers at the therapy center

(D) Not be concerned about measuring progress

(139) Which of the following is a source of concern for elderly couples?

(A) Finances

(B) Physical fitness

(C) Memory lapses

(D) All of the above

(140) What is the benefit of joining a support group?

(A) Meeting a future spouse

(B) Getting out of the house

(C) Limiting self-destructive behaviors

(D) All of the above

(141) Every culture has its own set of "norms." One that appears to apply to all cultures is maintaining an acceptable distance between people.

This distance is known as:

(A) Physical area

(B) Interpersonal disconnection

(C) Appropriate space

(D) Personal space

(142) Which psychotherapist proposed the object-relations theory?

(A) B.F. Skinner

(B) Sigmund Freud

(C) John Bowlby

(D) Carl Rogers

(143) The process of suspending talk therapy or counseling with a client normally happens in one of three ways: at the clinic's discretion, at the client's discretion or by mutual consent.

A counselor can stop working with a client if:

(A) The counselor is sick of dealing with the client.

(B) The counselor is going through life changes.

(C) The counselor is retiring form practice.

(D) All of the above.

(144) What is the main focus of systemic therapy?

(A) It focuses on exploring the relationship dynamics of the client.

(B) It focuses on altering behavior patterns in adolescents.

(C) It focuses on increasing abstinence in teenagers.

(D) It focuses on a child's overview of the world.

(145) What is conformity?

(A) Following the lead of the group

(B) Changing one's behavior as a result of real or imagined peer pressure

(C) Doing what is fashionable at the time

(D) All of the above

(146) Advertisers pay attractive celebrities and popular sports stars large sums of money to endorse specific products because they know normal people want to be as popular as they are.

What is the name of this major factor in conformity?

(A) Genuine talent groups

(B) Groups of reference

(C) Groups at the pinnacle of success

(D) Factors of attractiveness

(147) Individuals appear to be influenced by groups in a variety of ways, one of which stems from a desire for direction and information, as well as the belief that the group has more understanding than the individual.

This is known as:

(A) Social informational influence

(B) Influence of individual need

(C) Group influence

(D) None of the above

(148) Cognitive therapy is predicated on the discovery that changes in thinking result in changes in:

(A) Stress levels and sleeping ability

(B) Thoughts and hormones

(C) Consideration, emotion and action

(D) Believing and acting

(149) Displaced aggression occurs when lower-class groups criticize each other rather than the wealthy elite or the class structure itself.

What is the source of this misplaced aggression?

(A) The source is too powerful to be defeated.

(B) The source has the ability to retaliate.

(C) People frequently direct their rage at a nonthreatening target.

(D) All of the above.

(150) Which of the following best describes family systems therapy?

(A) The family is viewed as an interconnected system, with each member playing an important role.

(B) Each member usually has problems that are similar to one another.

(C) People gain knowledge by playing and observing various roles in relationships.

(D) Some families face more difficulties than others.

(151) There are three types of group therapy: family therapy, support groups and ________.

(A) Groups for mental health

(B) Groups for evaluation

(C) Encounter group

(D) None of the above

(152) What other particular loss groups might there be, aside from those that support spousal loss?

(A) For those who have lost a pet

(B) For those who are recovering from a significant financial loss

(C) For those who have suffered the loss of a child

(D) All of the above

(153) What are some of the benefits of group counseling during the grieving process?

(A) People recognizing that they are not alone and getting the chance to learn from others

(B) Socializing and meeting new people

(C) Thinking about anything else and planning activities

(D) Giving people something to do other than cry

(154) In general, group polarization occurs when a decision process becomes__________________.

(A) More exaggerated

(B) Inconsistent

(C) More dependable

(D) More conservative

(155) What is the most beneficial aspect of group therapy?

(A) Hearing about other people's problems

(B) Observing how others react to dilemmas

(C) Hearing similar remarks about one's problem/behavior from many group members

(D) There are no beneficial aspects

(156) What is “deindividuation”?

(A) Getting rid of one’s rage

(B) Creating a new identity

(C) Putting one’s normal identity on hold for the time being

(D) Going completely insane

(157) In Lawrence Kohlberg’s moral phases of development, the ability to identify good and bad intentions in oneself is seen:

(A) From the standpoint of social systems

(B) From a contractual standpoint

(C) From the standpoint of social relationships

(D) As blind egoism

(158) Which theorist posited that the stage of development known as identity vs. role confusion begins in adolescence?

(A) Skinner

(B) Erikson

(C) Kohlberg

(D) Bandura

(159) Are there any concerns pertaining to the effectiveness of group psychotherapy?

(A) It is beneficial to everyone.

(B) There are some issues, but nothing to be concerned about.

(C) In some cases, group members' symptoms have worsened, or new symptoms have appeared.

(D) There are numerous concerns.

(160) What are two of group psychotherapy's goals?

(A) To assist patients in identifying disruptive behavior and to provide clients with a supportive structure

(B) To meet new people and improve one's social skills

(C) To alleviate stress and lessen rage

(D) None of the above

(161) What should a counselor be mindful of when providing group counseling?

(A) Finding a suitable venue for the group's meeting

(B) Being aware of group member choices, as well as group member and leadership roles

(C) Being comfortable with group counseling approaches and processes

(D) Both B and C

(162) What tools can a counselor employ to accelerate the awareness and empowerment of a group in session?

(A) Interaction and focus

(B) Feedback and assistance

(C) Humor and understanding

(D) Love and solace

(163) Some groups are led by a trained professional, while others are made up of:

(A) Eligible peers

(B) Four or five advisors

(C) Funeral directors

(D) Anyone who is willing to do it

(164) Why do some adults have a disconnection between their current situation and their childhood experiences?

(A) The selective manner in which people recall personal experiences

(B) The complexity people have in viewing themselves in the same light as they do young children

(C) Memory loss is a key factor

(D) Previous experiences are less significant than present experiences

(165) According to Erikson, older people go through a crisis. What is this crisis?

(A) Mistrust vs. trust

(B) Despair vs. ego integrity

(C) Approval vs. rejection on emotional grounds

(D) Superiority vs. industry

(166) Which of the following factors contributes to the importance of caring for others in development?

(A) Piaget's

(B) Erik Erikson's theory

(C) Theoretical psychoanalysis

(D) Psychosocial theory

(167) Early memories help to define the coherent and distinctive pattern of social and emotional conduct and qualities that define an individual.

This is known as_______________.

(A) Personality

(B) Self-actualization

(C) The nature of man

(D) Memorization

(168) Which of the following did Jung believe in?

(A) In the second half of adulthood, men's and women's personalities become more similar.

(B) It is possible to reach an ideally mature state after age 50.

(C) The second half of a person's life is more valuable than the first.

(D) Our personalities change as we age.

(169) Common grief symptoms include all of the following except?

(A) Sleeping problems and appetite loss

(B) A strong desire to engage in physical activity

(C) A feeling of emptiness in the stomach

(D) A feeling of throat stiffness

(170) Adults devote a significant amount of time to problem solving. What becomes most important to the adult thinker?

(A) Context

(B) Problem

(C) Information

(D) Solution

(171) Chloe is two years old. Her favorite word, according to her parents, is "no." Which of the following theories best describes the child's developmental stage?

(A) Piaget's concrete operational stage

(B) Freud's oral stage of development

(C) Kohlberg's viewpoint on social systems

(D) Erikson's theory of autonomy vs. shame and doubt

(172) In some instances, well-meaning individuals advise parents to "let the baby cry, or you will spoil him/her by picking him/her up too much." According to early childhood development specialists, a newborn under the age of six months cannot be "spoiled" by reacting to his or her cries, and it is essential to act in a responsible manner to ensure adequate bonding.

Which theory and stage of development would back up the experts' position?

(A) Sigmund Freud's oral stage of development

(B) Erikson's stage of development of trust versus mistrust

(C) Sensorimotor development as defined by Piaget

(D) This stance is not supported by any theory.

(173) Prejudice and discrimination in groups have long been a part of society. What do the terms "in-group favoritism" and "out-group negativity" mean?

(A) An in-group considers itself to be more attractive, whereas an out-group considers itself to be less attractive.

(B) The in-group is the one to which you belong, while the out-group is everyone who is not a member of the in-group.

(C) People form in-groups and out-groups by preferring one type of person over another.

(D) All of the above.

(174) Rational emotive behavior therapy (REBT) is especially well-suited for group treatment.

What does it allow participants to do?

(A) Keep an eye on and listen to others

(B) Observe and experiment with different behaviors

(C) Role-play and lead others

(D) Demonstrate abilities and express emotions

(175) Which of the following are examples of culture-specific symptoms?

(A) Headache, memory problems and breathlessness

(B) Body pains, headaches and stomach upset

(C) Insomnia, nervous and tenseness

(D) All of the above

(176) Is there a "cultural" difference between male or female clients?

(A) Yes. Males and females use different terms to describe the same type of ailment.

(B) No. Culture does not apply to this.

(C) No. Males and females have no differences aside from biology.

(D) Yes. They are very different in terms of physical, hormonal and interpersonal makeup.

(177) Which of the following socioeconomic factors might have an impact on the performance of restorative counseling?

(A) Utility bills

(B) Inadequate positive social conventions for entering therapy

(C) Inadequate intrinsic motivation

(D) None of the above

(178) All but one of the following are key fundamentals in Albert Bandura's social cognitive theory.

Which of the following does not fit into his theory?

(A) Learning through observation

(B) Self-efficacy

(C) Symbolic expression

(D) Determinism based on reciprocity

(179) There are three main approaches to reducing cultural divide. Which of the following is not one of them?

(A) Investigating one's mental processes

(B) Adapting one's behavior to fit another person's culture

(C) Just carrying on as usual; others will adjust

(D) Recognizing that cultural differences can be emotionally draining.

(180) What describes the acknowledgment of shared feelings and bad encounters among members of a group that validates encounters, eliminates isolation and increases self-esteem?

(A) Imitative behavior

(B) Uniformity

(C) Universality

(D) Catharsis

Core Counseling Attributes

(181) How does compliance with confidentiality help the members of group therapy?

(A) Members feel that their ideas will be accepted and appreciated without judgment.

(B) Members feel valued.

(C) Members feel free to express their ideas and sentiments.

(D) All of the above.

(182) During group therapy sessions, who leads and ensures that the sessions run smoothly?

(A) Psychologists

(B) Facilitators

(C) Nurse

(D) Doctors

(183) What is counseling defined as?

(A) Advising clients about various issues and life challenges

(B) Diagnosing mental disorders

(C) Solving mental health and human development problems via a cognitive, behavioral or systemic approach

(D) None of the above

(184) What can counselors do to cultivate empathy?

(A) Practice mindfulness meditation

(B) Exercise daily

(C) Engage in breathing exercises before therapy sessions

(D) All of the above

(185) Counselors must:

(A) Impose their personal beliefs on clients

(B) Rush into providing various solutions to clients' problems

(C) Respect and accept clients as they are

(D) All of the above

(186) What is a complex process comprised of several components in a therapy session?

(A) Channeling sympathy

(B) Channeling compassion

(C) Channeling respect

(D) Channeling empathy

(187) What does it mean when counselors choose to be nonjudgmental?

(A) They are choosing to be understanding and accept clients as they are.

(B) They are choosing to interpret clients' behavior in various ways.

(C) They are choosing to separate clients' behavior from who they are as people.

(D) None of the above.

(188) What does active listening mean?

(A) Listening with all your senses

(B) Listening without discriminating

(C) Listening with all your heart

(D) All of the above

(189) What makes a client feel empowered?

(A) Encouragement

(B) Acknowledgment

(C) Being listened to

(D) Affirmation

(190) What does a counselor's duty depend on?

(A) Personality

(B) Specialty

(C) Values

(D) Morality

(191) Why is it important to know the client's personality and thoughts?

(A) It helps the therapist to learn more about the client.

(B) Learning about the client's personality can help with treatment.

(C) This makes it easier for a therapist to stay present with the client while dealing with internal reactions.

(D) All of the above.

(192) What are the factors that usually facilitate compassion in therapy?

(A) Understanding clients and their family history

(B) Sympathizing with clients' pain and understanding client dynamics

(C) Talking and listening to clients discussing their problems

(D) None of the above

(193) Who are professional counselors?

(A) During difficult moments of life, they help clients process their emotions and manage their pain.

(B) They help solve workplace problems.

(C) They cultivate various values and personality traits in clients to help them lead a balanced life.

(D) They focus on resolving past traumas.

(194) What is one of the therapist's empathy assessment methods?

(A) Empathy by doctors

(B) Empathy by coworkers

(C) Empathy by facilitators

(D) Empathy by clients

(195) Why should counselors be sincere with their advice?

(A) To get a good review and a positive result.

(B) Their reputation depends on it.

(C) Clients are most likely to act upon it.

(D) None of the above.

(196) What does it mean when a client becomes frustrated or sends nonverbal indications of stopping?

(A) The counselor failed to send a valid response.

(B) The client is having a breakdown.

(C) The client has a mental health disorder.

(D) All of the above.

(197) What should counselors practice to cultivate empathy?

(A) Meditation

(B) Assessments

(C) Exercise

(D) Yoga

(198) What builds an early connection and rapport when deliberating problematic subjects during a therapy session?

(A) Sympathy

(B) Listening

(C) Empathy

(D) Talking

(199) In what types of settings do counselors perform their duties?

(A) In a diverse community setting

(B) In an environmentally friendly setting

(C) In a hospital setting

(D) None of the above

(200) What leads to the development of self-confidence, insight, feelings of appreciation among group members and relief?

(A) Being open

(B) Psychotherapy

(C) Voicing problems

(D) Therapeutic values

Test 3 Answers

Professional Practice and Ethics Answers

(1) (D) A and B.

The hypothesis is based on all the theories and previous studies related to that topic.

(2) (A) The state law.

Client privilege is not granted to each person seeking therapy. The state law determines what people can access to this right. The counselors and the patients have to abide by the boundaries and legislations set by the state.

(3) (A) They are required to act as agents of social control.

Confidentiality is the basic right of every client seeking therapy. However, the state demands that counselors be agents of social control, so they have to breach confidentiality in certain cases.

(4) (C) If he has any plans of self-harming.

The counselor should first inquire about any plans the child has of harming himself. If the child indicates that self-harm is on the table, the counselor should then inform the child's parents about the situation immediately.

(5) (B) People in his group have dissimilar interests.

Counselors are often encouraged to work in groups as it helps them get answers to any problems they face and get expert advice as well. However, if the group members do not have similar interests and goals, they may not be able to reap the benefits of collaborative working.

(6) (C) Both A and B.

There are preferable methods of recording each type of information. Counting is advised for evaluating the number of times a child faces test anxiety in a day or expresses positive statements in an emotional relationship.

(7) (C) Both A and B.

Psychotherapy can only be beneficial and fruitful when both the client and the counselor are equally engaged and involved.

(8) (B) Intervention in counseling.

The fourth stage is intervention.

(9) (A) Carl Rogers.

According to American psychologist Carl Rogers, genuineness, empathy and unconditional caring are the three key conditions of developing a healthy client-counselor relationship.

(10) (D) All of the above.

Psychotherapy is a treatment for people suffering from illnesses that affect their mental health and well-being. These illnesses can be trauma or a mental disorder, such as depression or the loss of a loved one.

(11) (B) When the counselor sets some standards and acts completely in contradiction to them.

It is the responsibility of the counselor to patiently bear with the client even if a person is acting out of bounds or is finding it difficult to open up. A responsible psychotherapist also makes sure to take a break when he or she is dealing with something personal. The only reason why unethical behavior arises is when a counselor sets some standards and does not follow them.

(12) (D) All of the above.

When seeking therapy, the client has the rights of privacy, confidentiality and privilege.

(13) (C) The information revealed by the client to the counselor.

It is not easy to open up about your personal problems and be vulnerable in front of a stranger. Therefore, any personal information that a client reveals to a counselor is considered an entrusted secret.

(14) (D) Both A and C.

The counselor should ensure a transparent transfer of those records if clients are seeking a different counselor and/or provide access to the requests upon request.

(15) (A) Sexual abuse.

If a child is facing sexual abuse and reveals to his counselor what he is going through, the counselor should immediately breach confidentiality and bring this to the knowledge of the parents.

(16) (A) Their hopelessness.

It is quite easy to recognize people dealing with suicidal thoughts. They appear hopeless and closed-off. However, social life cannot indicate who is suicidal and who isn't because a lot of people are not social by nature.

(17) (C) By recognizing, assessing and effectively intervening in crisis situations.

Making suicide an offense, making an example out of people who commit it and scolding them will further stigmatize the issue. The only way is to deal with this issue is with great patience and kindness. The issue must be recognized, assessed and effectively intervened in.

(18) (D) Both A and C.

Usually, the onus is on the counselor when a client's privacy is violated; therefore, the counselor cannot complain about low income. The issues that arise from such a violation of privacy include difficulty in cultivating client dependence and prejudice.

(19) (A) Dementia.

Dementia is a mental disorder that causes a person to forget things quickly. It can, therefore, affect the factual comprehension of a person.

(20) (D) Any individual involved.

There are several instances when a client is not able to consent. In these cases, the client's decisions are made by a legally recognized third party who is not necessarily a parent but can be any individual involved.

(21) (B) To ensure fair and equal treatment for people regardless of their disabilities.

The Disabilities Act protects all disabled American citizens from discrimination.

(22) (C) Self-compassion.

Disabled people can only survive in this world by showing self-compassion to themselves.

(23) (D) All of the above.

It is not easy to be a disabled person when there is so much discrimination in the world. When a disabled person is mistreated, he or she may face several mental health problems, such as panic attacks, trauma, etc.

(24) (B) A few sessions.

Psychotherapy for a problem that just surfaced should ideally last at least a few sessions.

(25) (A) In a database.

A database is the most appropriate option for storing collected data. A cell phone is risky, and so is a notebook. The information can also be organized properly in a database.

Intake, Assessment and Diagnosis Answers

(26) (A) The start of therapy.

The biopsychosocial structure (BPS) is a kind of interview usually done by mental health professionals at the start of therapy. It helps counselors identify the biological, social and psychological aspects of their clients' problems.

(27) (C) Social.

The BPS is a cognitive evaluation and functioning method divided into biological, psychological and social components. Questions regarding a person's job are usually asked under the social component of the interview.

(28) (B) Subjective impressions.

The BPS is broken down into objective facts and subjective impressions. The objective facts include all the factual details provided by the client regarding a condition, and subjective impressions are the interpretations the counselor can conclude from the information provided by the client.

(29) (D) 1998.

Shea proposed his universal model for clinical interviewing in 1998.

(30) (B) Second.

The CFI is divided into three parts. The first contains a 16-question interview with the client; the second evokes the perspectives of the client's family and the third contains 12 modules.

(31) (A) Closing.

The fourth stage for Shea's universal method for clinical interviewing is closing.

(32) (C) Both A and B.

The mental status examination assesses the mental status of a client. It helps the doctor make a prognosis and differentiate between different psychiatric disorders. It contains the previous medical history of the client as well as the current details collected by the new counselor.

(33) (B) Intake.

The meeting between the client and therapist is usually referred to as intake.

(34) (C) Family therapy.

For family therapy, counselors usually refer to the system approach. They treat the family as a system where each member is dependent on the other, emotionally if not by any other means.

(35) (A) A lot of people find it difficult to open up in front of crowds.

Even if it takes more time to carry out therapy sessions in a group, as long as people are able to heal from their traumatic experiences, it is worth it. However, people often are not comfortable sharing their personal details in groups and shy away.

(36) (D) Both B and C.

When a patient dealing with trauma seeks therapy, the counselor should first inquire about the details of the event, such as in the case of the loss of a loved one or an accident. As far as a rape case is concerned, it is not advisable to talk about the details of the event with the victim unless the person feels safe and wants to open up willingly.

(37) (B) False negatives.

False negatives or missed cases rise when specificity rises. A false negative is the identification of people having the disorder as not having it. Specificity is the ability of a mechanism to target people who do not have a disorder.

(38) (A) CAGE.

Questionnaires are used to find information about clients. Recently, computerized versions of authenticated paper questionnaires are gaining popularity, such as the CAGE. Initial research regarding their popularity is also promising.

(39) (D) All of the above.

At the start of the meeting, counselors do not know much about clients. They carry out different evaluations to get to know their clients better. The BPS structure, as well as assessment and screening, is done in the initial stages. Assessment and screening are also carried out.

(40) (A) Individual evaluation.

There are three steps in a thorough substance abuse assessment: screening, problem analysis and individual evaluation.

(41) (D) All of the above.

The major drawback of self-reports is that they are inaccurate. This is because people often underreport their issues, overshare their symptoms and give diplomatic responses to fit into cultural restraints.

(42) (B) It implies that the measure evaluates the outcomes it intends to represent and provides data that is generally applicable.

Reliability implies that the measure evaluates the outcomes it intends to represent and provides data that is generally applicable.

(43) (D) None of the above.

All of the answer options are common modalities of psychiatric treatment—group therapy, family therapy and individual therapy.

(44) (C) System.

For couples therapy, cognitive and behavioral are the two techniques used. The system is the kind of therapy used to treat people seeking family therapy.

(45) (A) Posing questions empathically and nonjudgmentally.

One of the major things that people expect from a counselor when they are seeking therapy is empathy. Questions must be asked empathically and nonjudgmentally. Asking direct questions without first building a relationship and inquiring about a rape victim's experience should be avoided at all costs.

(46) (B) Can be beneficial.

People addicted to drugs are able to open more about their addiction when they are asked simple and straightforward questions.

(47) (B) Termination of therapy.

The term termination is usually used to describe the conclusion of all therapy sessions. Closing is used to describe just the ending of a session.

(48) (A) The directive approach is adopted when counselors want to manage the interview, and the nondirective approach is adopted when interviewees want to manage the interview.

Counselors usually adopt these two different kinds of approaches to deal with their clients.

(49) (D) All of the above.

There are several advantages of labor force participation for addicts recovering from mental disorders. It helps in improving self-efficacy and self-identity and offers them a sense of belonging to society in general.

(50) (D) All of the above.

Culture refers to the learned and passed-down systems of concepts and awareness, as well as rules, from one generation to the next. It also includes religion, culture, language, etc.

Areas of Clinical Focus Answers

(51) (B) No.

Aging is an inevitable process that cannot be stopped. Skin treatments and medications can delay it, but it cannot be halted.

(52) (D) Subconscious loss.

Subconscious loss is common between Parkinson's, Alzheimer's and dementia.

(53) (A) Professional caregivers.

Individuals who seek long-term guidance and support may need professional caregivers. These are trained individuals who are hired through agencies and hospitals. They are hired when family or anyone close to afflicted individuals is not available to take care of them.

(54) (B) To understand a person and be able to implement his or her decisions at a later stage.

Communication about death should not be taboo as it helps the individuals around an ill person complete the tasks the ill person desires.

(55) (B) Detachment and lack of trust.

Getting over grief is never easy for a person, and issues like detachment and lack of trust in others make it harder.

(56) (B) Depression.

The possibility of people becoming victims of depression while suffering through grief is quite high. They keep thinking about the experience and spend time alone.

(57) (A) By investing in better opportunities.

To have enough money for retirement, it's important to invest in the right places.

(58) (B) Communication.

Communication is often overlooked. Patients must know what is wrong with them, how to move forward from an illness, details about the treatment, etc.

(59) (C) Holding onto feelings.

It is quite normal for people to hold onto feelings of love, hate, etc. However, they must let go after a while as these feelings can be a threat to their mental peace.

(60) (D) Spreading hatred about the ex-spouse and blaming him or her for the separation.

Holding onto feelings of hate for the ex-spouse and shifting the blame on him or her for the separation are two of the most prominent signs of a person who is unable to let go of a relationship.

(61) (D) The child should be given the freedom to be with the other parent.

Both parents deserve equal rights to a child. And all children deserve the freedom to be themselves with each parent.

(62) (B) Emotional fulfillment.

Adopting a child means emotional and physical fulfillment and is rewarding to couples and families who are not able to have their own children.

(63) (C) By explaining how those behaviors are wrong.

Children must always be dealt with carefully. Getting angry won't stop them from practicing wrong habits. They need to be talked to kindly and patiently and assisted to understand.

(64) (D) Health.

Children must never be judged on ethnicity and religious beliefs. That is racism. They must also never be blamed for the actions of their parents. However, a thorough health check must be made before, during and after the adoption process to prevent unexpected emotional and financial expenses later.

(65) (B) Cognitive skills.

As children grow up, parents should make an effort to help them develop cognitive skills. These include the ability to process information, speak about it, think of ideas and develop them.

(66) (A) Strategies for an individual-focused approach and advocating for health-care services.

To improve a primary care provider's work, specific and detailed strategies are needed along with advocacy for the health-care services. The rest of the options won't work if there's no effective strategy in place.

(67) (A) Yes.

Legal professionals must always be consulted if parents are unable to agree on a decision for their child or during any other personal conflict. Legal professionals help in reaching an agreement that both parties approve.

(68) (C) Issues of trust and dependency arise.

Any unresolved conflict is a sign of poor communication between two partners. It always ends in trust issues in the short and long run.

(69) (B) Stay married.

Good friends will be there when a couple needs them to provide honest and sincere advice. Developing a healthy community around spouses will help them invest their time in other people and hobbies and give spouses personal space. In this way, positive friends and coworkers can prevent divorces.

(70) (C) Dividing finances, having a child, etc.

Having children and dividing finances to manage the household are the two most difficult changes in a couple's life. Having a child leads to a gap between spouses and if it's their first child, it's going to create confusion and widen an already present gap among them. The division of finances may also lead to disagreements among the couple. Therefore, honest and effective communication is needed at every stage to deal with the changes that come with having children and being in a relationship.

(71) (B) They are able to enjoy freedom.

Usually, couples get divorced when they can no longer live with each other and feel that their lives are being wasted. Divorce offers them a chance at freedom and a new life.

(72) (A) Abuse.

Abuse is the leading cause of divorce. The rest of the reasons can be dealt with through effective communication.

(73) (B) Career-oriented youth.

US youths are more focused on building a successful career and marrying late. Focusing on a career will help them gather the finances they will need to deal with the expenses that come with marriage and having kids.

(74) (D) Stress.

Stress is the main cause of a person developing angry tendencies and being abusive and violent toward a spouse and children.

(75) (C) Orgasm disorder.

During intercourse, women sometimes experience a delay in orgasm, which can be caused due to stress or other health conditions.

(76) (B) 40+.

Remarriage is most common in people above 40.

(77) (A) It strengthens the relationship and enables a fresh start.

Married couples often renew their vows and get remarried in some cases. It helps them strengthen their relationship and turn a new page.

(78) (A) Yes.

Changed eating and sleeping habits that affect a person's appearance are two signs of suicide. They indicate a person's level of sadness and inability to move on from trauma.

(79) (D) Effective coping mechanisms and counseling.

Effective coping mechanisms help an individual to deal with a situation, and counseling helps people let their feelings out, feel heard and get some good advice. This is helpful in preventing suicide.

(80) (B) So they can express their true feelings about suicide, depression, etc.

Providing a safe environment for clients ensures a healthy client-counselor relationship and enables the clients to express their sentiments about whatever they are going through.

(81) (C) Not worried, but should work on it.

If clients are able to make decisions for themselves, it means they are able to comprehend their situation and know the pros and cons of it. They are less likely to commit suicide; however, it doesn't mean that the counselor should stop working with them or take their situation lightly.

(82) (B) No.

A therapist is not expected to conduct a thorough examination of a person's mental state or capacity.

(83) (B) Ask the client if he or she intends to end his or her life and find out where the risk comes from.

A high rating on a scale of 0–9 would mean that the client is thinking of ending his or her life a lot and needs serious counseling.

(84) (B) No.

A therapist can never predict what a client might do in the future.

(85) (A) Concentrate on the risk factors associated with the client's illness.

A crisis plan is specifically designed for emergencies. These plans are designed in collaboration with the client and include the client's risk factors, stressors and protective factors.

(86) (B) Physicians.

Physicians are better positioned to work with clients because they think about the safety and well-being of the clients and can debate their thoughts and reactions with them.

(87) (A) Ethnic identity.

According to Phinney (1990a), ethnic identity plays a significant role during the identity formation stage of development. While the precision of self-definition is the primary concern for young children, during teenage years, the major concerns are the labels one chooses to identify oneself with, the extent to which one investigates one's cultural identity and the extent and essence of group identity.

(88) (D) Using status-based identity structure.

The use of a status-based identity structure is an efficient and effective way to examine the results of evolving identities.

(89) (C) Intervention.

If the situation becomes urgent, a counselor must implement a decision regarding the intervention of a third party, either a senior therapist or client's family member or friend, as decided in the crisis plan.

(90) (A) Adjustment disorder.

An adjustment disorder can be defined as a response to an upsetting event or change in a person's emotional or developmental life.

(91) (B) Children and young adults.

Although adults can sometimes become victims of adjustment disorders, children and young adults are most vulnerable.

(92) (D) Adjustment disorder.

An adjustment disorder can be defined as a response to an upsetting event or change in a person's emotional or developmental life.

(93) (A) Racial and ethnic identity.

Racial and ethnic identity can impact what is passed down to the next generation. Certain traditions, important ceremonies, religious teachings and more can be passed down through families this way.

(94) (D) Migrants.

As migrants come from a different culture and background, it is very hard for them to assimilate into the US culture. They are a minority and, thus, often face isolation and/or discrimination.

(95) (A) Yes.

According to psychological research, it is evident that adolescents who have a well-defined ethnic identity have better psychological adjustment than those who have a limited ethnic identity.

(96) (C) Mindfulness and yoga.

Healthy practices such as mindfulness and yoga can be classified as complementary mind-body therapies.

(97) (A) Under pressure or stress.

Individuals who are already going through some tension or stress are hit hardest when they have to suffer another trauma or problem in their lives.

(98) (C) Traumatic experiences.

A child goes through trauma when his or her sense of safety is invalidated.

(99) (A) Borderline personality disorder and depression.

Trauma leads to immense sadness and difficulty. Hence, it might result in borderline personality disorder and depression.

(100) (B) Their coping strategies.

Counselors must respect how clients are trying to get through a tough time, even if their coping mechanisms aren't healthy. However, they must try to change the thoughts of the clients by presenting other, healthier options.

(101) (C) Abuse and neglect.

Abuse and neglect can seriously negatively impact children's mental and physical health and sense of safety. When they grow up, they may be handicapped by the effects the abuse had on them.

(102) (A) Yes.

Individuals who go through abuse as children face difficulties in getting over it. They have to work for years to let go of their fear, anger and other heavy emotions.

(103) (B) Antidepressants.

Antidepressants and anti-anxiety medications are used in therapeutic procedures.

(104) (B) No.

According to new studies and evidence, people who choose not to handle their trauma are just as mentally healthy as those who do. Believing it's important for everyone to open up was a mistake in previous traumatic stress psychology.

Treatment Planning Answers

(105) (C) Long-term goals.

These goals are strategically set so that there is ample time to achieve them. They can include building better relationships with coworkers and starting a new hobby. They usually require a lot more character development from the client.

(106) (C) It helps the client keep track of his or her own progress.

If goals are not measurable, clients may struggle with realizing the improvement they have made over a specific period. This may have a detrimental effect on the overall therapy because the clients lose motivation. Keeping track of their progress makes clients want to continue therapy.

(107) (A) A general inability to communicate in the same language efficiently.

This is an obvious barrier as counseling requires understanding and the conveying of complex feelings and trauma. When the same language isn't shared or there is some deficit in the medium of conversation, it becomes almost impossible for the client to benefit from the therapy.

(108) (A) The transition stage.

This is known as the most challenging stage because it forces different group members with different dynamics and personalities to interact with each other and share personal information for the first time. This can lead to conflicts, emotional outbursts or divisions in the group.

(109) (B) Availability of specialized equipment and testing facilities.

A tertiary care setting is basically any large hospital facility where patients can be admitted for overnight stays. Such hospitals tend to have many facilities to treat patients in critical conditions. Tertiary care hospitals also have specialized medical staff and operation theaters.

(110) (C) Objectives – these tend to have a positive effect on the clients' motivation to achieve these goals.

According to the layout of a general treatment plan, "objectives" is the term used to describe the sub-categoric targets of major goals. These are usually made to improve client morale. Small stepping stones are a necessary part of measuring progress.

(111) (C) Providing a skilled translator who ensures confidentiality.

None of the other options is an adequate solution to this problem. Attempting to understand an unfamiliar language wastes the client and the counselor's time. Refusing the client is ethically unjust. A translator would solve the problem; however, it is of utmost importance that the translator is briefed on the importance of confidentiality.

(112) (A) The mediator must be able to pick up on unvoiced cues.

When mediators are able to pick up on unvoiced cues, they can make the therapeutic process successful as clients tend to be reserved about how they are feeling in front of each other. It is useful for mediators to infer the actual reaction of a client toward critiques or general conversation in order to address them according to their true feelings instead of the ones they present.

(113) (B) The counselor must explain to the client that the current visit will yield different results as compared to the person's previous experiences.

This is a very simple solution to a common problem. Clients tend to have access to multiple resources, and sometimes these resources prove to be unreliable or incapable of solving the client's issue. Counselors must be learned in the art of persuasion so that they are able to help clients understand that not all their counseling experiences will yield the same result.

(114) (D) The working stage.

After tensions from the transition stage of group therapy have calmed down, the group members tend to be less hostile toward each other. The environment of the working stage is much more amicable, which in turn leads to group members interacting with each other more openly. This results in acceptance.

(115) (B) Provide adequate alternate options.

It is within a counselor's basic education to protect and respect all the fundamental rights of the client. This includes aspects like religion, culture, ethnicity, race and so on. Therefore, with this in mind, the only possible solution to such a problem would be to provide an alternate option for the clients so that they do not have to forego their beliefs in order to receive treatment.

(116) (C) Abandonment is used to describe the time when a relationship between a client and counselor is ended on unsuitable terms.

This term is the alternate of "termination." Termination is the favorable route for a counselor to take when ending sessions with a client. Abandonment can cause issues for both the client and the counselor. The counselor can get a bad reputation, and the client can suffer from what could become yet another traumatic experience.

(117) (B) Debrief the secondary care physician about the client's hospital stay and change prescriptions if needed.

For the patient to fully benefit from treatment, there must be an adequate chain of communication established between all doctors. Therefore, it is necessary that the secondary care doctor be updated on the medication, events and procedures the patient has undergone during the hospital stay. This will ensure that any changes in the person's condition or prescription are followed through after the patient has been discharged.

(118) (C) Confidentiality.

Confidentiality is within the basic rights of a client. If people choose to share their personal information in order to seek treatment, it is only fair that they are assured that it will be kept private.

(119) (A) Secondary care.

General physicians usually handle primary care as the ailments of OPD are not that severe. If patients require further treatment, they are referred to a specialist who has more knowledge about their specific condition in the secondary care unit.

(120) (C) To ensure that a client and counselor are on the same page about the goals of the treatment.

This is to ensure a client and counselor start and finish on the terms they both agree on. This will cancel out any discrepancies between their perspectives on therapy.

(121) (B) Take the time to properly brief the client about every aspect of the treatment plan.

This will ensure the patient fully understands the treatment before denying it. It will also ensure that the patient has a good counseling experience.

(122) (B) To allow the client to be prepared when the time for termination arrives.

It is common for a client to develop anxiety or doubts when sessions come to an end. It is difficult for people to continue their normal lives without the assistance and advice of their counselor.

(123) (B) Patients with chronic, lifelong illnesses that refuse to heal from OPD treatment.

Such types of conditions usually require a specialist's opinion, and it is also necessary for the patient to have frequent checkups if a condition is chronic.

(124) (B) Devising an appropriate treatment plan.

The treatment plan is devised in a much later stage of the therapeutic process—usually, once all the introductions and consent procedures have been dealt with.

(125) (B) The counselor must not force the patient to make decisions based on his or her advice.

It is vital for a counselor to understand that the decision of following through is completely up to the client. If the client refuses advice, the counselor should respect that decision.

Counseling Skills and Interventions Answers

(126) (D) Both A and C.

When a counselor cannot make progress with a client, there are numerous options for resolving the problem. A consultation with other counselors in practice, including the lead counselor, will yield additional insights and ideas to help the client progress. If consultation is ineffective, another counselor may be required to provide input on a session. Usually, ending a relationship with a client is not the solution unless, after an extensive discussion with the client and lead physician, it is determined that another counselor would better fit the client's concern.

(127) (D) Both B and C.

Diversity training focuses on individual differences, whether they are demographic (age, gender, religious beliefs) or cultural. The goal of diversity training is to increase understanding of cultures and belief systems to avoid miscommunication and misunderstandings.

Cultural awareness enables clinicians to communicate effectively, both verbally and nonverbally, and to precisely perceive client facial expressions and verbal cues.

(128) (D) When the client is encouraged to apply the newly developed perspective to his or her current situation.

Individual therapy, also known as Adlerian therapy, is a method in which therapists work with clients to identify obstacles and develop effective strategies for achieving their goals.

(129) (D) All of the above.

The notion of Freud's conscious, unconscious and subconscious mind was novel and intriguing. But when you combine that with his techniques for uncovering hidden, unconscious motives, you have plenty of fodder for debate. Furthermore, his work was dependent on specific case studies, all of which affected people with "abnormal" thoughts and behaviors that were not compared to the thoughts and actions of "normal" people. Although his theories are still contentious and subject to much criticism, Freud had a significant impact on the development of psychotherapy and psychiatry, and he can be credited with much of the global growth of psychology.

(130) (D) All of the above.

Area of counseling expertise, clients' age and gender and counselor workload are all important factors that counselors should consider before they take on other clients.

(131) (D) All of the above.

The DSM's creators continue to release new editions of the manual to integrate new information, along with changes in how abnormal behaviors are viewed and changes in explanations and classifications. Scientific discovery of new disorders is continuous, and data from this research must be incorporated. Societal changes in how we think about psychological disorders also occur on a regular basis, and these changes must be reflected in the manual's text.

(132) (D) Both A and B.

Confidentiality is an important element of the therapeutic alliance because it makes clients feel safe and motivates them to share sensitive information. It aids the client's trust in the clinician rather than the other way around. At the same time, confidential information has limitations for clients who are minors, pose a risk to themselves or others or have mistreated a child, an elderly relative or a disabled person.

(133) (C) When confronted with a potential breach of confidentiality, it is incumbent upon the employee to seek advice from a colleague or supervisor.

The duty to warn is the policy to safeguard clients and others from physical, emotional or mental distress. In order to achieve those responsibilities, therapists may need to break confidentiality in order to file their concerns with those who need to know in order to avoid injury. Because breaking confidentiality is usually a tough call to make due to the therapeutic alliance with the client, clinicians are allowed to seek consultation with a colleague or a superior.

(134) (B) Disorders of the mind.

In-depth self-examination necessitates logic, good cognitive functioning and the ability to avoid hallucinations and other psychopathic events. Impulse control, personal characteristics and anxiety disorders have no effect on the client's ability to be centered on the tasks assigned by the Adlerian clinician.

(135) (A) Concentrating on the client's strengths in all parts of life.

A strengths-based assessment's primary goal is to focus on a client's strong points, accomplishments, talents and individuality. This strengthens the client/counselor relationship and gives clients hope for transformation within themselves and/or their situation. A genuine strengths-based assessment requires faith in clients and their abilities.

(136) (B) To keep people from becoming anxious.

A defense mechanism is mainly used to protect individuals from anxiety, specifically anxiety caused by unacceptable desires and impulses. Everyone has defensive capabilities, some of which are productive and mature, such as sublimation, which can transform an unpleasant, self-destructive urge into a goal to build a masterpiece. Others are detrimental to health and can deceive people, interfering with relationship-building efforts.

(137) (C) Small changes in behavior lead to increased changes, which affect the entire system.

Solution-focused therapy is a forward-thinking, goal-oriented approach to resolving human issues. The emphasis is on the client's health rather than the issue, on strengths rather than weaknesses or shortfalls and on qualifications, facilities and emotional well-being that will aid in the attainment of future goals.

(138) (B) Consult the treatment plan.

Referring back to the initial treatment plan is a great way to assess a client's advancement toward set goals. Is diagnosis on track, or has it taken on a life of its own and deviated from the initial treatment objectives? As part of the diagnostic process, a clinician may discuss these performances and objectives with the client, but he or she will first refer to the treatment regimen.

(139) (D) All of the above.

Elderly couples are apprehensive about finances, each other's physical well-being and possible memory problems. They may also be worried about being left alone when one spouse dies, requiring additional care, having to leave their home and community and remaining as self-sufficient as possible.

(140) (C) Limiting self-destructive behaviors.

Support groups address a wide range of harmful habits and problems. Mutual support for common problems, feedback data and behavioral training sessions can all be extremely beneficial.

(141) (D) Personal space.

Personal space refers to the comfortable distance that should be maintained between people. This distance will differ from one culture to the next. Americans, for example, appear to prefer twice as much distance as, say, people in the Chinese culture. The preferred personal and social distance will also vary depending on the situation.

(142) (B) Sigmund Freud.

Object-relations is a psychoanalytic theory that differs from the belief that humans are driven mainly by aggressive and sexual drives. It argues that human behavior is influenced mainly by the need for interaction with others—the need to develop relationships.

An object-relations therapist's goal is to assist a client in therapy in identifying an early visual picture that may contribute to current difficulties in one's relationships and adjusting them in ways that may strengthen the interpersonal operation.

(143) (D) All of the above.

Counselors might stop seeing clients if they are retiring from practice, leaving the agency or going through another life change that would necessitate discontinuing treatment. These decisions are not taken lightly and usually necessitate extensive planning on the part of both the clinician and the agency.

(144) (A) It focuses on exploring the relationship dynamics of the client.

The goal of systemic therapy is to understand the person in regards to others rather than in exclusion. The individual is viewed as a component of a larger unit or system, such as a couple, a family, an organization or a community.

Systemic therapy aims to identify deeply ingrained patterns in an individual's relationships, as well as with family members. The process aids in revealing how members interact and act within a framework based on their beliefs about their different responsibilities.

(145) (D) All of the above.

Conformity can be described in any of the ways listed above. When a person conforms (or changes) his or her opinions, actions or thinking in order to belong to any size group (remember, two can be a group), the individual is succumbing to "conformity."

(146) (B) Groups of reference.

This reference group includes anyone we admire, like or want to emulate. People have a tendency to believe that if they wear the same outfit, use the same beauty products or buy the same sneakers as their favorite people, they in turn will be just as popular.

(147) (A) Social informational influence.

Have you ever purchased a specific brand of something (such as a smartphone) because a friend suggested it to you? You conform not to win their approval (normative social influence) but because you believe your friend knows more than you do. That is the definition of informational social influence.

(148) (C) Consideration, emotion and action.

Changes in thinking result in changes in feeling and behavior. These transitions happen when a client and clinician form a positive treatment plan and live in the present, though the past is addressed when necessary. Cognitive therapy employs a variety of techniques and initiatives to assist people in evaluating and changing their cognitions.

(149) (D) All of the above.

Wouldn't you choose a smaller opponent if the target of your aggression was bigger, stronger and capable of causing far more harm than it is now? Sometimes governments or a larger bully are simply too much for one small group or individual to handle. The the smaller opponent is referred to as the scapegoat.

(150) (A) The family is viewed as an interconnected system, with each member playing an important role.

The family is viewed as an interconnected system. Each member plays an important role. When a family first enters therapy, many members believe that one participant is the root of all their problems. Changing ways of communicating within the family system is usually essential.

(151) (C) Encounter group.

Family therapy, encounter groups and support groups are the most common types of group therapy. Group therapy began as a cost-effective form of therapy and has since evolved into a preferred method in many cases.

(152) (C) Those who have suffered the loss of a child.

The Bereaved Families of Ontario (BFO) and the Compassionate Friends are just two of the organizations that assist those who have lost a child in their grieving process. BFO also helps children, adolescents and young adults who have lost a parent or sibling. Grieving for various family members creates different complexities for those doing the grieving.

(153) (A) People recognizing that they are not alone and getting the chance to learn from others.

Because the grieving process can be a lonely and disengaged time in one's life, having someone else around who has gone through or is going through the same emotions will help people feel less alone. It's also possible to learn from the experiences of others.

(154) (A) More exaggerated.

When a group makes an early assessment, whether it is cautious or risky, it usually becomes much more drastic after discussing it and making it final, moving toward whatever end decision they may have started with. This change toward one or more "poles" is referred to as group polarization.

(155) (C) Hearing similar remarks about one's problem/behavior from many group members.

When a team member receives similar remarks about his or her behavior or situation from many members of a group, the statement may be more persuasive than if it comes from a single psychiatrist.

(156) (C) Putting one's normal identity on hold for the time being.

Deindividuation is usually done in a group setting. A person becomes engrossed in the group action and agrees to things he or she would never usually do. Individuals become less aware of their own values and more responsive to the actions and aspirations of the group. Examples of this include joining gangs or organizations such as the KKK.

(157) (C) From the standpoint of social relationships.

The ability to identify good and evil intentions in oneself is included in the point of view of social relationships. This is evident in Kohlberg's theory's third stage (interpersonal arrangement and conformity driven). Individuals are receptive to support or opposition from others because it reflects society's conformity to the unique role.

(158) (B) Erikson.

According to Erikson, social development progresses through eight stages, each of which results in a "psychosocial crisis" that must be effectively addressed before progressing on to the next stage. In adolescence, this crisis is known as identity vs. role confusion, and it is based on the question, "Who am I?" This stage can last until the age of 20. Self-doubt is a necessary part of the process, as is playing multiple roles in the quest for identity.

(159) (C) In some cases, group members' symptoms have worsened, or new symptoms have appeared.

While group psychotherapy appears to help people, it appears to harm others. There have been reported cases of presenting symptoms worsening or new symptoms appearing. More research is required to determine the causes of the negative effects.

(160) (A) To assist patients in identifying disruptive behavior and to provide clients with a supportive structure.

Group psychotherapy brings people with similar worries together and helps them identify cognitive distortions within a supportive structure. Members of the group also alleviate emotional problems by receiving feedback, guidance and support from both the therapist and the other members.

(161) (D) Both B and C.

A clinician must be knowledgeable about induction sessions because group dynamics will significantly impact the effectiveness of the work done within its specifications.

With this in mind, a solid foundation in group counseling techniques and systems can help groups overcome obstacles.

(162) (B) Feedback and assistance.

Feedback and assistance from both the clinician and group members can help accelerate becoming aware and empowered. Members can also learn from one another vicariously. Listening to one member of the group express his or her thoughts and emotions can lead to understanding in another.

(163) (A) Eligible peers.

Peer-to-peer groups are extremely beneficial in all areas of counseling. We appear to be more open to our peers' experiences and solutions.

(164) (A) The selective manner in which people recall personal experiences.

One possible explanation for the gap between adults' current perceptions of themselves and their memories of childhood is the partial recall of our personal histories. According to neurologic studies on memory encoding, memories are stored in a different manner in children than in adults, potentially leading to a gap in how we see ourselves and our past.

(165) (B) Despair vs. ego integrity.

According to Erikson, older people go through a crisis of ego integrity vs. despair. Integrity is attained when the preceding stages are successfully completed and the reasonable adult is able to trust, is self-reliant, looks forward to new adventures and looks back with satisfaction. If the previous stages are not resolved, people may look back on life with hopelessness.

(166) (D) Psychosocial theory.

The psychosocial theoretical approach focuses on caring for others. To able to relate with and care for others is essential in all phases of development.

(167) (A) Personality.

Personality is defined as an individual's consistent and distinctive pattern of mental-interpersonal behavior. Maslow's theory of personality development includes self-actualization.

(168) (D) Our personalities change as we age.

Carl Jung theorized that people's personalities change as they age. Jungian explanatory psychology, which involves long-term psychoanalysis, is frequently thought of as a method for achieving individual growth and self-awareness.

(169) (B) A strong desire to engage in physical activity.

A strong desire to be active is not usually one of the symptoms of grief and loss. Many grieving people experience a loss of sleep and appetite, a blank feeling inside and throat stiffness. They may also experience drowsiness, an inability to act and the sensation of moving in slow motion.

(170) (A) Context.

As adults become more aware of the implications of issues surrounding the problem, perspective becomes the most important factor in problem-solving. While the problem and its remedy are important, an adult thinker is more concerned with the frame of reference (context) in which the problem exists. Children, as concrete thinkers, can only focus on the problem and, more often than not, see only one solution. Later in life, abstract reasoning develops, and adults are able to see different answers to a single problem.

(171) (D) Erikson's theory of autonomy vs. shame and doubt.

According to Erikson, Chloe has reached the stage of autonomy, shame and doubt, which may include a stormy period of willful expressions, including tantrums and stubbornness. Chloe will grow out of this stage with self-confidence, a better capacity to monitor herself and a desire to make sense of the world around her.

(172) (B) Erikson's stage of development of trust versus mistrust.

Erik Erikson's trust versus mistrust stage in the psychosocial development theory would support this approach of responding to a newborn's wails in a quick and efficient manner to build trust. If a newborn's cries are not fulfilled with parental support and care, the infant quickly learns that his or her requirements will not be met, instilling a deep sense of distrust.

(173) (D) All of the above.

An in-group is any classification in which people consider themselves to be members, whereas the out-group includes everyone else. People regard their in-group members more favorably than "all the others." In other words, they practice in-group bias and out-group negativity intellectually.

(174) (B) Observe and experiment with different behaviors.

REBT group therapy participants have the opportunity to analyze and try out habits, as well as share input and reactions. Members of the group are expected to take responsibility for helping one another as well as themselves.

(175) (A) Headaches, memory problems and breathlessness.

There are 12 culture-specific symptoms listed. Headaches, cognitive issues and difficulty breathing are three culturally bound symptoms to be aware of.

(176) (D) Yes. They are very different in terms of physical, hormonal and interpersonal makeup.

Males and females have been taught to express (or not express) emotions, illnesses and complaints in very different ways, in addition to physical, hormonal and societal inequalities. Counseling someone of the opposite gender necessitates the counselor to think and respond differently in order to achieve the same goal.

(177) (B) Inadequate positive social conventions for entering therapy.

A socioeconomic factor that may have an impact on the outcome of therapeutic counseling is a lack of social convention. If a client did not obtain a job or other counseling results, the great advantages of the counseling are negated. If there was a societal practice that did not support therapeutic counseling services, harsh feedback from loved ones could very well nullify the progress made.

(178) (C) Symbolic expression.

Symbolic representation is not one of Bandura's theories in overarching social cognitive theory. According to Bandura's psychological context, observational learning, self-efficacy and mutual dedication are all cognitive thoughts and feelings that impact human behavior and functioning. His hypothesis states that learning can occur without reinforcement simply by observing models.

(179) (C) Just carrying on as usual; others will adjust.

Understanding differences requires becoming aware of one's own societal standards and thinking patterns and adjusting one's behavior to theirs. For example, if you don't speak the language, hire a translator and apologize for not speaking the language. It is overwhelming and confusing to be unable to communicate efficiently with others and to find recognizable ways of thinking and behaving.

(180) (C) Universality.

Universality is the acknowledgment of shared thoughts and desires shared by members of a group, which validates experiences, reduces or eliminates social isolation and increases self-worth. It is not merely imitating actions, group cohesion, relating to a group (sense of validation, acceptance) or releasing emotional distress through interpersonal interaction.

Core Counseling Attributes Answers

(181) (C) Members feel free to express their ideas and sentiments.

Members can feel more comfortable sharing their ideas, sentiments and experiences without any reservations if confidentiality is maintained during the session. When beginning group counseling, the facilitator should explain the importance of confidentiality. A group counselor also needs to support all members so they can take part in the sessions.

(182) (B) Facilitators.

It is necessary to have facilitators in group counseling who can facilitate knowledge and maintain order during sessions. For groups to be effective, the group leader must assess whether they are successful. It is important to pay consistent attention to changes in members' voices and nonverbal movements or words.

(183) (C) Solving mental health and human development problems via a cognitive, behavioral or systemic approach.

Counseling is an approach to solving problems that combines mental health and human, psychological and developmental philosophies through a combination of systemic, intellectual, behavioral or interpersonal methods. In contrast to guidance, which focuses on helping people choose a suitable option for themselves, counseling helps individuals make changes and deal with life issues. Counselors offer advice and helpful ways to cope with problems that people face.

(184) (A) Practice mindfulness meditation.

To cultivate empathy, it is recommended that counselors practice mindfulness meditation. The concept of empathy is being able to understand the thoughts, events and feelings of someone without being explicit about the sentiments.

(185) (C) Respect and accept clients as they are.

Counselors should not impose their beliefs and opinions upon clients. They must accept their clients' identity and place in the world. The language counselors use must also demonstrate respect.

(186) (D) Channeling empathy.

Channeling empathy into a counseling session involves many factors, including working toward a common understanding of client sentiments, demonstrating warmth and esteem to the client and responding with similar sentiments. Exercising empathy is a critical part of being an effective counselor. Counselors who demonstrate empathy make clients feel at ease as it assures them that they are being heard.

(187) (C) They are choosing to separate the clients' behavior from who they are as people.

Understanding clients' point of view involves nonjudgmental listening. The goal is to interpret what clients are trying to say beyond the literal meaning. Nonjudgmental listening is a core component of mental health and counseling. In being nonjudgmental, counselors do not ignore the clients' feelings or behaviors. Their behavior is separated from who they are as people.

(188) (A) Listening with all your senses.

A fundamental element of listening is active listening. Listening with all of one's senses takes place when a counselor is attuned to the client. Listening actively involves using one's body, ears, eyes and heart. When a counselor uses words to show listening, this is known as verbal listening. This technique is used to show a client that the counselor is paying attention.

(189) (B) Acknowledged.

Clients feel empowered when their progress is acknowledged. As a counselor, your words should conform to your actions. Every therapist uses a different therapeutic procedure and has different techniques. It is, therefore, necessary to maintain honesty in all counseling techniques and nonverbal signals.

(190) (B) Specialty.

Therapists are normally assigned to work within diverse settings in order to provide a variety of rehabilitation and support services. Depending on individual specialty, a counselor's duties will differ based on experience and knowledge in the community in which the person works.

(191) (C) This makes it easier for therapists to stay present with the client while dealing with internal reactions.

Knowing clients' characteristics and thoughts will help therapists deal with their internal responses and stay focused on the client. This approach will promote a positive therapeutic relationship and make clients more comfortable when discussing their problems, thus preventing potential harm.

(192) (B) Sympathizing with the clients' pain and understanding client dynamics.

Therapists usually facilitate compassion in therapy by empathizing with the client's pain, learning about the client's dynamics, participating in the client's life, identifying with the client and creating a positive and healthy therapeutic relationship. To provide true compassion to their clients, counselors must constantly strive to instill feelings of empathy. It is impossible to provide effective therapy or advice to clients without knowing why they are emotional.

(193) (A) During difficult moments of life, they help clients process their emotions and manage their pain.

The purpose of professional counselors is to guide clients through the difficulties of life and guide them through grief and pain situations. Counselors owe the greatest duty of respect to their clients and are responsible for ensuring their welfare. The role of a counselor is to be effective and ethical, which includes being sensitive to ethnic diversity.

(194) (D) Empathy by clients.

One therapy assessment method is for client reports. Normally, these reports contain clients' ratings of the therapist, and the client typically labels therapist behaviors, such as nurturing and self-disclosure, as being empathic. This reflects therapist behaviors that may accompany empathy but are not necessarily part of it. It is a method of evaluating the counselor.

(195) (C) Clients are most likely to act upon it.

It is essential that a counselor always offer clients genuine counsel and suggestions since the clients are likely to act on the advice. The most calming moments of psychotherapy are moments of true mutual sincerity.

(196) (A) The counselor failed to send a valid response.

Empathetic responses by a counselor can be identified easily. A helpful response from the counselor is when the client nods or responds verbally. In the process of the therapy session, if the client becomes frustrated or sends nonverbal signals of giving up, the counselor did not provide an adequate response.

(197) (A) Meditation.

Mindfulness meditation is recommended for counselors as a way to cultivate empathy. It is the ability to understand, be aware of and be sensitive to someone else's feelings, experiences and thoughts without expressing them in an objectively explicit form.

(198) (C) Empathy.

A therapeutic connection requires empathy from the beginning, but it is an obligation during the initial stages. If clients are facing problematic subjects or are in a critical state, building an early connection is essential. It helps them open, makes them feel understood and provides a healthy and friendly environment to vent feelings.

(199) (A) In a diverse community setting.

Counselors are required to provide services in a variety of settings designed to offer support and rehabilitation to people in need. Depending on their work, their responsibilities will be determined by their experience in a specific environment and community.

(200) (D) Therapeutic values.

When therapeutic values are present, group members feel relieved, gain self-confidence and insight and feel appreciated. It is very important for group members to feel valued and gain confidence to voice their problems without any hesitation. This makes the therapy sessions useful.

Made in the USA
Coppell, TX
27 January 2023

11805090R00249